AMERICA'S LOST CHINESE

HUGO WONG

America's Lost Chinese

The Rise and Fall of a Migrant Family Dream

HURST & COMPANY, LONDON

First published in the United Kingdom in 2023 by
C. Hurst & Co. (Publishers) Ltd.,
New Wing, Somerset House, Strand, London, WC2R 1LA
© Hugo Wong, 2023
All rights reserved.

Distributed in the United States, Canada and Latin America by
Oxford University Press, 198 Madison Avenue, New York, NY 10016,
United States of America.

The right of Hugo Wong to be identified as the author of
this publication is asserted by him in accordance with the
Copyright, Designs and Patents Act, 1988.

A Cataloguing-in-Publication data record for this book
is available from the British Library.

ISBN: 9781805260561

This book is printed using paper from registered sustainable
and managed sources.

Printed and bound in Great Britain by Bell and Bain Ltd, Glasgow

www.hurstpublishers.com

*To my diasporic family with love,
to those who left, those present, and those to come.*

CONTENTS

Maps   ix
List of Illustrations   xiii
Family Tree   xvi
Foreword   xvii

Introduction   1

PART I
A CHINESE COLONY IN AMERICA

1. A Brave Son   7
2. The Only Way Out   19
3. A World Upside Down   31
4. A Vanished Dream   49
5. Silver, Silk, and Chilies   69
6. A Chinese Eldorado   77
7. Bourgeois and Mexican   95
8. The Land of the Canoes   107
9. A Reformer in Exile   127
10. An Erudite Philanthropist   139

PART II
A SHATTERED WORLD

11. The Torreón Massacre   157
12. Under the Protection of the Golden Dragon   175
13. A Butterfly of the Americas   187
14. The Great Plunder   197
15. A Confucian and American Legacy   211
16. The Roaring Thirties in Shanghai   223

17. Between East and West	239
18. Forgotten by History	251
Conclusion	265
Appendix: A Memorial from Representative Chinamen in America (1876)	273
Notes	277
Bibliography	297
Acknowledgements	305
Index	309

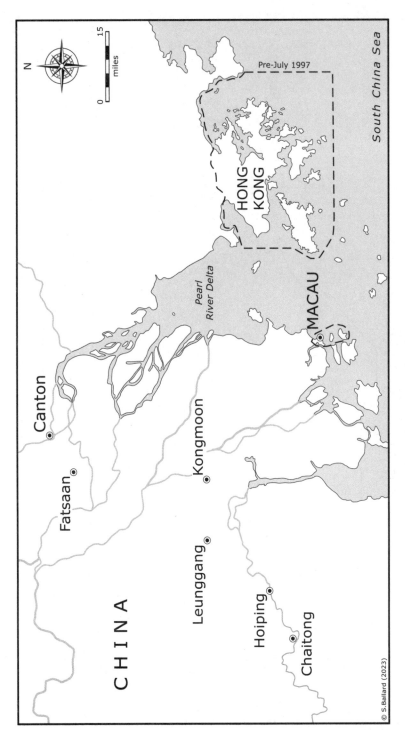

Southern Kwangtung Province

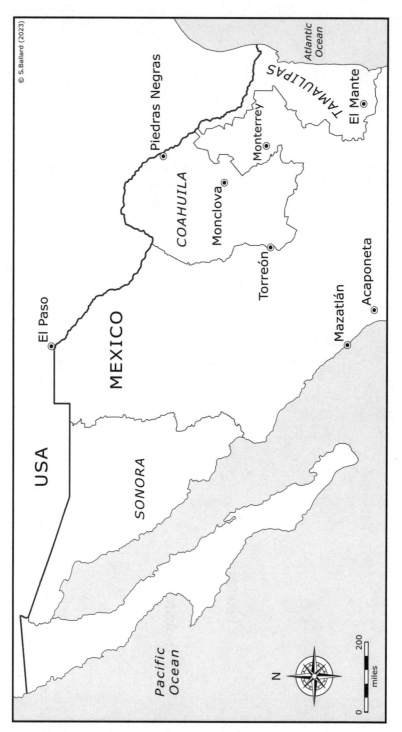

Northern Mexico

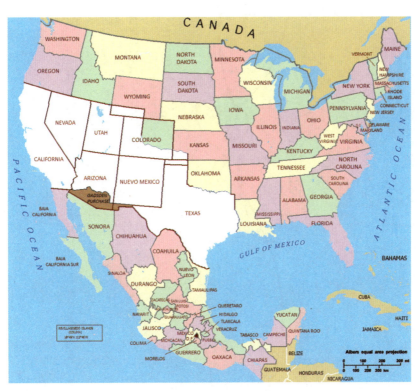
Border states (in white) expropriated by the United States in 1848
Source: United States federal government, public domain, via Wikimedia Commons.

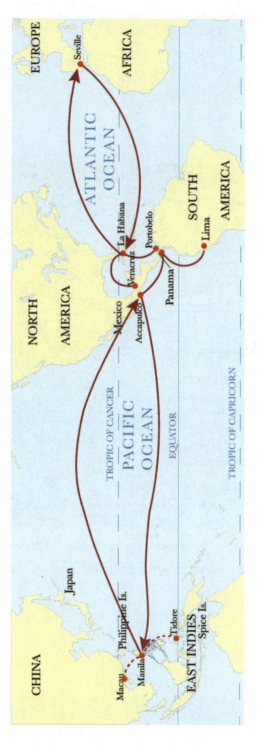

Manila–Acapulco galleon trade route

Source: Philippines Department of Foreign Affairs, public domain, via Wikimedia Commons.

LIST OF ILLUSTRATIONS

1. First photo of Hing, c. 1890, Mexico.
2. Hing's naturalization certificate, 1898, describing him as a native of the Chinese Empire.
3. Hing with his family and his three brothers, c. 1903, Mazatlán, Mexico.
4. Foon Chuck and his family, Lily in bottom left corner, c. 1905, Piedras Negras, Mexico.
5. Wong Kingfung, c. 1900, Piedras Negras, Mexico.
6. Wong Yaiwai, c. 1907, Canton, China.
7. Hing with his family during the revolution, Concha (bottom left) and Victoria (bottom right), c. 1916, Guadalajara, Mexico.
8. Meeting at Hacienda Canton, Wong Yun Wu (bottom left), Arturo Chuck (top left), General Osuna and Juan Saenz (both seated middle), c. 1919, El Mante, Mexico.
9. Foon Chuck (top left) with his brother Yun Wu (top right) and his wife, his nephew Yaiwai (bottom middle) and his son-in-law Ah Kian (bottom left), c. 1924, Hacienda Limon, El Mante, Mexico.
10. Concha, 1928, Mexico City.
11. Hing with his two younger sons, Pablo and Hector, enjoying a gilded childhood, c. 1925, Monterrey, Mexico.
12. Lily Chuck, c. 1929, Mexico City.
13. Leon family, c. 1930, Mexico City. From left to right: Pablo, Lola, Carmela (Alejandro's wife), Alejandro with baby, Jorge, Victoria, Hing, Hector, Yaiwai, Concha, Cruz, Juan, Melchor with daughter, Berenice (Melchor's wife) with baby.

LIST OF ILLUSTRATIONS

14. Leon sisters: Victoria, Concha and Lola, c. 1930, Mexico City.
15. Hing at the ancestors' village with his brother and sister-in-law, c. 1935, Hoksaan, China.
16. Hing in Western Hills, 1935, Peking, China.
17. Foon Chuck and his family, c. 1930, Piedras Negras, Mexico. Standing from left to right: Ah Kian Lee, Hortensia, Benjamin, Selina, Santiago and Ruben. Seated: Margarita, Elvira, Wing On, Foon Chuck, Cristina and Lily.
18. Yaiwai, Concha with first son, c. 1932, Shanghai, China.
19. Concha in Cheongsam on the left with mother-in-law and sister-in-law in the middle, c. 1932, Shanghai, China.
20. Caricature of Hing in Mexico City's newspaper titled *Business Entrepreneurs*, c. 1935, Mexico.
21. Hing in silk robe, c. 1935, Kwangtung province, China.
22. Leon family house in Tlalpan, 1940, Mexico City.
23. Concha with her three children and Chinese family helper, 1935, Shanghai, China.
24. Last family photograph of Yaiwai with Concha and children, 1937, Shanghai, China.
25. My mother, on SS *President Coolidge* bound for San Francisco, USA, 1938.
26. Hing and Cruz with Wong grandchildren and Felipa, 1941, Tlalpan, Mexico.
27. Foon Chuck with Concha and children, 1938, Torreón, Mexico.
28. Foon Chuck and Hing, 1938, Torreón, Mexico.
29. Leon family, 1939, Mexico City. Concha in mourning, top row, fourth from left; my mother in the bottom row, second from left.
30. Hing and Cruz with sons, 1943, Mexico City.
31. Bust of Hing, 1945, cemetery in Mexico City.
32. Chinese Classroom in Imperial China, from R. Van Bergen, *The Story of China*, 1902.

LIST OF ILLUSTRATIONS

33. Ross Alley, or "Gamblers' Alley," c. 1898, San Francisco, USA, photograph from the Arnold Genthe Collection.
34. "A picture for employers. Why *they* can live on 40 cents a day, and *they* can't." *Puck* magazine, 1878.
35. Anti-Chinese riots in Denver in October 1880. Illustrated diary of Franck Leslie. Museum of the Chinese in America, New York, USA.
36. El Dragon de Oro store, c. 1930, Mexico City.
37. The main building of Hacienda Canton, c. 1922, El Mante, Mexico.
38. Kang Youwei, c. 1905, The Library of Congress photograph.
39. The Hotel Internacional, c. 1910, Monclova, Mexico.
40. Hotel La Española, formerly Compañía Bancaria China y México, c. 1920, Torreón, Mexico, courtesy of Archivo Municipal de Torreón.
41. A cart carrying victims after the Torreón massacre, 15 May 1911, courtesy of Archivo Municipal de Torreón.
42. Yue Mae School, Hing (front, left corner) and Yun Wu (front, fourth from right), 1910, Mexico City.
43. President Álvaro Obregón with Chancellor Quang Ki-Teng at the National Palace, 19 February 1921. Retrieved from the Library of Congress, https://www.loc.gov/item/2002697251/.
44. Plutarco Elías Calles at the National Palace, 1924, Mexico City, Wikimedia.
45. Detail depicting a Chinese police officer in Diego Rivera's mural *Dream of a Sunday Afternoon in Alameda Central Park*, 1947.

GREAT GRANDPARENTS	GRANDPARENTS	PARENTS
JOE CHUCK WONG + CRISTINA VEGA DOMINGUEZ	TEN CHILDREN IN MEXICO	CHILDREN IN US AND MEXICO
FOON CHUCK WONG (1863–1950) + CHINESE WIFE (?)	ANGEL CHUCK WONG	CHILDREN IN CHINA AND MEXICO
YUN WU WONG (JOSÉ CHUCK WONG)	ONE DAUGHTER	ONE SON IN HONG KONG
+ JOVITA WOO	YAIWAI WONG	TWO SONS IN MEXICO
HING LEUNG (1866–1944) + CRUZ RIVERA NAVA	CONCEPCIÓN LEON	AUTHOR'S MOTHER
	NINE CHILDREN IN MEXICO	CHILDREN IN MEXICO
TIN PO (PANCHO) LEUNG	FOUR CHILDREN	CHILDREN IN CHINA
TWO BROTHERS IN CHINA		

WONG FAMILY

LEON FAMILY

FOREWORD

I grew up in Paris and Mexico City, between a French father and a Chinese-Mexican mother. Despite my mother's Asian features, she does not speak a word of Chinese, nor has she much knowledge of her native culture and country. For in 1938, when she was barely three years old, she had to flee the International Settlement of Shanghai ahead of the Japanese invaders, seeking refuge in Mexico. The only ties that connected her to China and her past were now buried in an old trunk containing age-yellowed photographs and family documents, many of which dated back to the nineteenth century when her Chinese ancestors left China for the United States and then Mexico. These old family stories had been long forgotten, memory being selective and no one in my family being willing to remember the massacres and humiliations of the past.

Almost a hundred years later, searching for my roots, I immersed myself in the contents of this trunk. From it, came to life the curious history of my family, which began in the Chinese province of Kwangtung (Guangdong) in the mid-nineteenth century and continued on the other side of the Pacific. Despite their distance from China, my migrant ancestors retained strong ties with their clan (that is, their extended family) and country of origin, and remembered their place in the family tree. This book traces the lives of two of these ancestors, Wong Foon Chuck (the older brother of my great-grandfather, Wong Yun Wu) and Leung Hing (my other great-grandfather, latterly known as Jorge Hing Leon). In 1875, at the tender of age of twelve, Foon Chuck fled natural disasters, famines and violence in the province of Kwangtung in the south of China to seek fortune in California. Five years later, aged fourteen, Hing followed him. This book, however, is more than a family memoir. It narrates the turbulent history of the Chinese in North America, using the lives of my two ancestors as a lens to view it

FOREWORD

with. This is history told from a personal and family perspective, made possible thanks to the untouched documents left behind by my ancestors.

In the nineteenth century, Chinese migrants arriving in the Americas experienced a culture shock and a sense of uprooting unique in their history. Foon Chuck and Hing both settled at first in San Francisco, which contained the first US Chinatown, a ghetto where Chinese culture predominated. While studying in a missionary school, Foon Chuck witnessed the anti-Chinese riot of 1877, before seeking fortune in the Wild West. Both of these early migrants were ultimately driven out of the United States by violence and by anti-Chinese exclusionary laws, some of which remained in place until 1968. In the 1880s, they began their careers as, successively, butlers, waiters, cooks, laundrymen, railway workers and street vendors, before being among the first Chinese to seek refuge and settle in Mexico. Both built large fortunes but they followed distinct paths. Foon Chuck stayed in the north of Mexico—the "Mexican Wild West"—where he built a commercial empire with the help of his multiple political and transnational connections, and became a world-famous community leader, among the first Chinese millionaires in the Americas. Hing, on the other hand, made Mexico City his home and became a dealer of Chinese art, introducing the art of China to Mexico's bourgeoisie for the first time.

The story of these two migrants is quite unique. They were involved in one of the only attempts in North American history to establish an organized Chinese colony, with huge farms, an international bank, the largest sugar refinery in the country, a school for the children of Chinese migrants, a publicly listed company, a chain of hotels, a retail network, a newspaper, and even a tramway company. Most of these enterprises served the local Mexican population as well as Chinese immigrants. Never had a group of Chinese managed to yield such economic influence over a Western territory; it would take more than a hundred years for such a phenomenon to reoccur. All this was only possible because Mexico and its government encouraged Chinese investment and migration. The colony was built under the aegis of Kang Youwei, a Chinese reformer, politician and philosopher, as part of his political movement. An advisor to the Guangxu Emperor, he was condemned to exile by Empress Dowager

FOREWORD

Cixi for his attempt to introduce reforms in China. Fearing that China would disintegrate along with the decaying Qing Dynasty and turn into a colony run by Western nations, Kang sought to unify the Chinese diaspora, leading a transnational political movement as well as becoming Foon Chuck's business partner.

Kang's Chinese colony did not survive long, sacrificed to the Mexican Revolution, which lasted for ten violent years (1910–20), killing nearly one in ten Mexicans. Over a thirty-year period, the Chinese diaspora in Mexico suffered violence unmatched in its history in the Americas, causing its almost complete extinction. The brutality began with the Torreón Massacre of 1911, one of the deadliest anti-Chinese pogroms in the Americas. During the ensuing decade further massacres followed throughout the country. In 1923 the Chinese became subject to harsh racial laws, worse than those suffered in the United States, illustrating the spread of fascist ideas in the Americas. Finally, the Chinese suffered from mass confiscations and expulsion from Mexico. These events, through which my family lost most of its fortune, are now unimaginable in a country like Mexico, and are largely forgotten.

In 1929, by their marriage, my grandparents united the two families of Foon Chuck and Hing, and took the road of exile again, but in the opposite direction from their parents. Fleeing the violence and exclusionary laws in the New World, they took refuge in Shanghai. This gave them a new culture shock, as the city was a symbol of modernity and of the future in China, a country that until then had mostly looked towards its past. After living for twenty-five years in a state of ignorance about China, and ashamed of her Chinese origins, my grandmother, one of the first women of mixed Asian and European descent in the Americas, finally found her place and could flourish in this "Paris of the East." This was the ultimate migrant city, a place of cultural fusion, where my grandparents for a few short years enjoyed a joyful existence. Ironically, they were victims of racism even there, finding themselves foreigners in their own country, illustrating the absurdity of an era that was about to be thrown into the flames of nationalism and war on all continents, forcing my family, once again, to go into exile, this time completely destitute.

This book spans a century, from 1860 to 1960, a period marked by unprecedented political and social convulsions in China, the

FOREWORD

United States and Mexico, including revolutions, civil wars, global pandemics and natural disasters. People's lives were transformed by the advent of the steam engine, making possible mass migrations over every world ocean and habitable continent. This new world geography, in which time and distance had shrunk, was a source of unprecedented exchanges between cultures, but also corresponded with the rise of nationalism, militarism and imperialism in every corner of the globe. Like many of today's migrants, Hing and Foon Chuck can be seen as straddling a fence, considered outsiders (or worse) by both their birth country and their adopted country, their allegiance always questioned by both, and their lives in the West affected by events in the Far East. For that reason, despite their many accomplishments, having lived in the margins of and between three nations, their histories had fallen into oblivion.

The main theme of this book is how migrants responded and adapted to their environment and the resulting exchanges between two different worlds, Chinese and North American. Confronted with an alien and at times hostile culture, early Chinese migrants asked themselves for the first time what it meant to be Chinese, trying to understand in what ways they were different from the populations found in the United States and Mexico. In our interconnected modern world, this theme remains relevant, forming an invisible thread throughout the narration. This discovery of new cultures was mutual, as it was also the first time that North Americans saw Chinese people. As an emerging power, China is widely discussed in the West today, but mostly at an economic and political level, much less from a human and cultural perspective. This historical testimony, of a time when returning to China was less possible for Chinese emigrants, is essentially a human narrative. It should help understand and put into perspective this early model of Chinese emigration based on family and diaspora, while highlighting cultural traits still shaping Chinese society today.

The history of Chinese–Western relations has been marred by political misunderstanding, distrust and ignorance for hundreds of years: yet there is a parallel history of a minority of individuals in both China and the West (whose lives are discussed in this book), who have gone against the current by seeking to understand each other, and proving the shared humanity between those two peoples.

FOREWORD

The historian John K. Fairbank (1907–1991), credited for building the field of Chinese studies in the United States, blamed himself and his colleagues for "one of the greatest failures in history," when they failed to anticipate and understand the 1949 Communist victory in China, setting the stage for the complete isolation of China from the West in the following three decades. He wrote: "We had no knowledge [...] and no way to gain any knowledge, of the life of ordinary Chinese people [...]. Our reporting was very superficial. We could not educate or illuminate or inform the American leadership in such a way that we could modify the outcome."[1] If Western expatriates in China—who mostly lived in ports governed by international treaties, like Shanghai—were ignorant of the realities of such a vast country, the same could be said of Chinese emigrants living in the West, where anti-Chinese immigration policies since 1880, while allowing a few students in, had made it extremely difficult for Chinese immigrants to settle and prosper, my two ancestors being notable exceptions. This inhibited the development of much pluralistic dialogue with China, paving the way for future conflicts. One purpose of this book, written at a time of heightened geopolitical tension between China and the West, is thus to provide an example of such cross-cultural dialogue in the past and to promote dialogue in the future.

The book includes a selection of vintage photographs from family albums, some from the nineteenth century. They are a living representation of the stories told and go hand-in-hand with them. The cover photograph, particularly quirky and distinctive in its embrace of cultural diversity, was taken in Mexico in 1909, and shows Hing in a Western suit, his Mexican wife in a Chinese robe and their children (some in dark uniforms, some in fluffy white gowns) with a church decor in the background, making it impossible to guess this strange family's whereabouts. My grandmother is the three-year-old girl with a ribbon looking intently at the camera in the lower-left corner. The photograph shows a joyful and confident migrant family, unaware that only a year later a violent revolution will shatter their world and bring into question their very existence in Mexico.

Many readers may recognize themselves or their loved ones in these journeys through previous centuries and across cultures and continents. While writing this book at home, I certainly felt trans-

FOREWORD

ported to other places and times. I sincerely hope that readers have the same feeling and that this book gives them a desire for distant travels. Beyond my large diasporic family, it is dedicated to all readers who, whether themselves or through their ancestors, have experienced uprooting. It is written with a sense of purpose and duty towards the memory of all the characters whose lives are mentioned. Although not a historian by profession, in my family life and my professional career I have experienced and researched Chinese and Mexican societies for over twenty years. The portraits of Foon Chuck and Hing are based principally on family documents, interviews, and the memories of relatives, as well as on the work of other historians and sinologists. I have used a degree of artistic licence in imagining their states of mind and some of the details of their early lives, while always staying true to the sources and the work of historians and contemporary social commentators. For historical accuracy, for some common Chinese names and places, instead of Mandarin, I have used the Cantonese or English transliteration in use at the start of the twentieth century. I have strived to present a balanced and lively account, putting in perspective the social and political environment which may, to some extent, explain the events described. I take full responsibility for all the opinions that are expressed in this book and apologize for any possible mistakes or omissions.

INTRODUCTION

China is a country with a centuries-long history of migrations, not only across its external borders but also between its many provinces, continuing to this day. In 2019 there were approximately eleven million people born in China but living abroad, including 2.7 million in the United States;[1] there were fifty million people with Chinese ancestry outside China,[2] the so-called Chinese diaspora, two-thirds of which live in other Asian countries; and there were a staggering 290 million internal migrant workers within China itself.[3] This means that almost one in four people in China is an internal migrant, while about one in every 130 people outside China is of Chinese descent. The distinctive role of migration in China continues to be an important source of dynamism for its society, and the study of migrations and migrants is therefore an interesting angle from which to try to understand and analyze the Chinese world.

This, however, does not mean that emigration is hoped for or well regarded within Chinese society, by either migrants themselves or the authorities. Many Chinese people remain deeply attached both to their customs and, through their spiritual beliefs, to the land of their ancestors, meaning that emigrating is often a traumatic experience, only justified by economic or political considerations. Historically, Chinese emperors preferred farmers, as they remained on their land and paid stable taxes, to merchants associated with human movement and representing a less reliable tax base. In addition, migration signified poverty and instability, with people tending to emigrate only when they were hungry. It was therefore seen as a possible sign of future rebellions against the emperor. Finally, Confucius wrote that while their parents are alive, children should not travel too far.[4] It is not surprising that one of China's most famous poems, "Thoughts on a Quiet Night" by Li Bai (701–762 CE), known by heart by many Chinese, is about yearning for one's home:

Before my bed the moonlight is bright.	床前明月光
I imagine frost on the ground.	疑是地上霜
Looking up, I gaze at the moon.	举头望明月
Bowing my head, I think of my hometown.	低头思故乡

In the eighteenth and nineteenth centuries, large population movements occurred within China, including migrations to most of its peripheral regions in the north, the southwest and the south, such as the provinces of Kwangtung and Fukien. Meanwhile, from those southern regions surrounded by mountains, emigrants tended to take the direction of the sea, mostly towards Southeast Asia and, later, as the use of steamships became widespread, towards the Americas. The largest wave of emigration from China thus began in the mid-nineteenth century, driven by a phenomenal population explosion. Between 1650 and 1851, China's population more than tripled from about 130 million to 410 million, while the population of the rest of the world only doubled. The result of a long period of peace, improved hygiene and health care, and a buoyant economy, this population explosion was not accompanied by a parallel increase in productivity or agricultural resources, as the corrupt Qing Dynasty failed to implement any reforms. The large Qing bureaucracy had not grown in line with the population either, so there were not enough civil servants to provide the most basic services, such as water management or road maintenance. Civil servants found themselves being constantly solicited by the growing population, resulting in endemic corruption, made worse by the low official salaries they received and the sale of government jobs. While the population tripled during this 200-year period, the area occupied by cultivated land only doubled, creating a problem of land scarcity. Worse, as agricultural techniques became more efficient, there was a scarcity of jobs, causing a decline in wages.

Poverty was exacerbated in China's south because there more than ninety per cent of peasants were either tenants or employed laborers, whereas in the north most farmers owned their land.[5] Only three to five per cent of the population in Kwangtung owned fifty to sixty per cent of the land.[6] For tenants, the shortage of arable land led to an increase in rents. In the overcrowded province of Kwangtung, where the population almost doubled from sixteen to twenty-eight million between 1787 and 1850,[7] the soil could barely yield enough crops to feed a third of its people.[8] Burdened by taxes and rents, many tenant farmers became heavily indebted, having no choice but to pawn or sell all their belongings—and even their children (their young daughters first), either for adoption, slavery or prostitution. During the late Qing dynasty, that practice became so widespread that various towns periodically held an open market for the purpose, child trafficking only being banned by law in 1935 but still practiced until the Communist Revolution of 1949.[9] Peasants unable to settle their debts could be arrested, beaten and jailed by local officials, and they often died in jail before their case came up for judgment. The drafting of corvée laborers for large public projects, a common form of taxation in Chinese history, created further resentment from the overburdened populace.[10] A popular folk song of the period tells of two swords weighing on a peasant's shoulders, high rents and high interest rates, and the three roads open to him: escape, prison or suicide.[11]

Such miserable conditions were often a source of rebellions, violently repressed by inept and corrupt officials. The Taiping Rebellion (1850–64) caused more than twenty million deaths, while the Red Turban Rebellion of 1854–56 caused one million deaths in the province of Kwangtung alone. The impact of seasonal floods and droughts was exacerbated by this incessant fighting, with local populations unable to maintain their infrastructure of dams and canals. A US missionary observed that public property was seldom taken care of by the local population and was often robbed for private use, a common joke being that "no one in China is so imposed on and cheated as the emperor."[12] To cope with overpopulation, land scarcity and unemployment, many families turned to exporting their male offspring to other parts of China or overseas, while maintaining their village base. For a salary, these migrants could hawk goods on poles, run small shops, manufacture handicrafts, or work on large government infrastructure projects.

Since the fifteenth century, Chinese emperors had kept the doors of the empire completely closed, both for potential emigrants and for foreigners trying to get into the country, whose influence was believed harmful. However, following the First Opium War (1839–42) the so-called unequal treaties imposed on China led to the opening of ports controlled by foreign nations, such as Canton (Guangzhou in Mandarin), Shanghai and Hong Kong. Those treaties exacerbated unemployment in Kwangtung province, with cloth merchants driven out of business by cheaper Western imports and 100,000 boatmen and port employees losing their job after the opening of treaty ports further north.[13] On the other hand, while these new ports provided Westerners access to the Chinese market, including for their opium, they also gave would-be Chinese emigrants the ships they needed to seek their fortune abroad.

As a result, between 1848 and 1888 more than two million Chinese emigrated to Southeast Asia, the Americas and Australia.[14] By the turn of the century, more than five million had already left, and by the 1920s the number of overseas Chinese stood at eight million.[15] Nearly one in fifty Chinese had emigrated, and close to one in ten in the province of Kwangtung. A common Chinese saying, which still rings true, states that "everywhere there is sea, you will find Chinese people." Of those early Chinese emigrants, more than ninety-five per cent settled in Asia, mainly in Formosa (Taiwan), Java (Indonesia) and Siam (Thailand),[16] only a small minority having sought their fortunes further afield, including 155,000 in South America and, later, 87,000 in North America.[17] If there was mass migration, it was mostly contained within Asia, as most Western countries started to constrain Chinese immigration and migrants naturally preferred closer and less costly destinations, where ethnic assimilation would prove easier. My ancestors, by choosing to emigrate to North America and not Asia, are therefore an exception, being among the very last who managed to enter the United States before it shut its doors. Undertaking such a long and perilous journey required audacity: one had to be either rich and with independent means or simply more desperate than most to make money.

PART I

A CHINESE COLONY IN AMERICA

1

A BRAVE SON

Leaving the province of Kwangtung for the United States in the 1870s, my great-great-uncle Foon Chuck and my great-grandfather Hing came from families with distinct backgrounds. Foon Chuck's family was native to Kwangtung province and had already successfully sent relatives abroad from the middle of the century. Hing's family had settled in Kwangtung more recently from provinces further north, and was venturing for the first time outside China. While the former sought to fructify its human capital, the latter, being much poorer, was simply trying to survive.

These two families, fleeing natural disasters, poverty and political instability, represent typical situations of that time. The region of Kwangtung is the southernmost coastal province in China, historically the most open to the outside world, with the port of Macau, the city of Canton, and then Hong Kong, being for centuries the main if not the only places accessible to foreigners in the Middle Kingdom. Because of its remote location, far away from China's northern capital, and due to its movements of population, the region was long plagued by various man-made calamities, including banditry, clan and feudal violence, and large-scale corruption, adding to the many floods and epidemics regularly ravaging the province. In the popular Chinese saying, "Heaven is high, and the emperor is far away,"[1] one finds a reflection of this remote province that remains true to this day. Nevertheless, Kwangtung remained one of the richest provinces in China. Cantonese merchants were known for being astute, independent and hard-working. The writer Lin Yutang (1895–1976) described southerners as "progressive and quick-tempered," in contrast with northerners, who were stereotyped as being "simple thinking and hard living," while the Chinese from the central plains, the cradle of Chinese civilization, were "inured to ease and culture and sophistication, mentally developed but physically retrograde, loving their poetry [...] and cowardly in war."[2]

Wong Foon Chuck,[3] the elder brother of my great-grandfather, was born in 1863, the second year of Emperor Tongzhi's reign, in the village of Chaitong[4] on the shores of the river Taam,[5] in the southern part of Kwangtung province. Children in the Wong clan were reminded that they shared their surname with the most revered ancient emperor, Wong Dai[6] (2697–2595 BCE), known as the Yellow Emperor. When he was born, an astrologer foretold that Foon Chuck would have an exceptional but tumultuous life, mirroring the year 1863, which marked the end of an era, corresponding to the winding down of the Taiping Rebellion and also the turn of the sexagenarian cycle of the Chinese calendar (in which the names of the years are repeated every sixty years). On the completion of his first moon, one month after his birth, relatives were invited to celebrate, bringing clothes and pigs' feet to congratulate his family, receiving in return slices of roast pork, the province's festive dish. Like all Chinese babies, Foon Chuck was first given a milk name—which is usually the name of an animal—to divert the attention of evil spirits from him. Given to him when he started school, his book-name was composed of two characters, Foon and Chuck, meaning wide and bright. This name was chosen after consultation with an astrologer and a numerologist, since one's book-name is believed to influence one's destiny.

Chaitong means "ponds all together" in Chinese, the surrounding countryside being a land blessed with water flowing from countless ponds, canals and streams, feeding the many rice fields and lush vegetation. Farmers used bamboo-made water wheels on the side of the river and chain pumps to irrigate the land. The rice was cultivated in two annual crops using ancient methods: buffalos were used for ploughing and stems were transplanted by hand, men and women wading knee-deep in the submerged fields, with a basket on one arm, putting in stems and manure at equal intervals. Before each harvest season, rice paddies turn bright green, almost fluorescent, and then golden yellow when the rice is ripe, displaying the richness of the land. While keeping its beauty, most of the natural landscape in this densely populated region has long shown signs of human transformation, with the semi-tropical forests of the past having been sacrificed to human consumption. In spring and the monsoon season that follows, this blessing of water often turns into a curse, when floods and typhoons take everything and everyone in their passage. This has happened since ancient times, China being like a giant plateau tilted from west to east, from its mighty mountains to the sea. Foon Chuck, like every young Chinese, knew the legend of emperor Yu the Great, who dug out the earth, tamed the rivers, gave the people dry land, and saved humankind from the floods.[7]

Despite the floods and famines, Chaitong was a relatively prosperous farming village, thanks in large part to its closeness to the river and to its emigrants, who were now starting to bring money back with them. The Chinese were then proud of their rivers, which were sources of fertility and food, as well as major axes of communication and exchange. The Taam river was home to many species of fish, which the villagers attracted with lights at night and then caught using cormorants. The region around Chaitong was known too for its many birds, like crows and cranes, while wild cats were still spotted in the neighboring hills. Foon Chuck's grandfather told stories of tigers scaring the villagers in the distant times when Chaitong was surrounded by forests.

In years of good harvest, the wealth was on full display during the Spring Festival, when the whole village came together, its lanes alive with daily performances by troops of local villagers dancing at the rhythm of the drums, the gongs and the firecrackers, with bright lanterns and colorful banners decorating homes. The firecrackers and the gongs served to scare the weasel spirits, the fox fairies, the little demons and the hungry ghosts, lurking and waiting in dark corners to possess the villagers in the coming year. The Spring Festival was the time when villagers cleaned their homes, bought new clothes, and honored their ancestors' tablets (slabs with dead relatives' names engraved on their faces). The tablets symbolize the ancestors' ever-present seat in the home and enclose their spirits after their death.

In China, there was no weekly day for church and rest. Farmers, and later workers, only rested and came together during the handful of yearly festivals, marking the rhythm of the seasons. For most poor Chinese in the nineteenth century, the highest and only idea of happiness was that on those rare occasions, they may have a small piece of meat to eat with their rice and vegetables.[8]

Each spring, Foon Chuck enjoyed watching the boat races on the river during the Dragon Boat Festival, also called the Children's Festival, to celebrate the spring planting of rice and the mighty Dragon King, who was thought to live in mountain caves and pools of clear water that never dried up even in the harshest droughts, and who was therefore the god of the rivers and the weather. The festival lasted three days, during which long boats of forty to fifty men, their bows ornamented with carved dragon heads, raced in pairs up and down the river, while firecrackers were fired on the shores and the gaily dressed and noisy participants paddled, waved flags, or beat drums to frighten away the river monsters.

All his life, Foon Chuck would remember his early childhood, playing with his friends and relatives in the rice fields, chasing frogs, fishing in the river and keeping crickets in woven baskets. His favorite memories were those spent with his father, riding the mighty water-buffalos and flying kites made of bamboo and rice paper in the shape of animals and dragons. The children in the village, like those in villages across China, also played knucklebones, hunt-the-tiger (hide and seek), coin throwing, and kick-the-shuttlecock (the shuttlecock was made of feathers attached by a leather string). However, once they reached the age of reason (six years old), things started to change for them: some began to work in the rice paddies, and all were taught to obey their elders, losing their freedom. Everyone in China was subject to someone else: sons to fathers, wives to husbands, fathers to clan elders, clan elders to magistrates, and magistrates to the emperor. Accordingly, obedience rather than affection was required of the Chinese child, whose life could become constrained and dull as he aged, governed by ideals of respect for superiors, dignity in front of subordinates and the suppression of emotion.[9] Foon Chuck never called his parents, uncles, or elder brother by their first names; he had to rise from his seat when they approached; he used both hands to give them things; and he could never contradict them or seek to explain himself to them—the children of wealthier households being subject to particularly strict discipline. Foon Chuck remembered how his father became stricter with him when he started attending school. His family was not wealthy but was among the better-off in the area thanks to the money sent by migrant relatives.

Fifteen miles downstream from Chaitong is the wealthy city of Hoiping,[10] an unusual city famous for being at the center of the district where Chinese emigration to the United States started in the second half of the nineteenth century. It remains today the archetypical city of emigrants. Hoiping is known for its more than 3,000 multi-story fortified towers,[11] built in the surrounding countryside with the money of emigrants. These towers were used to watch for and protect against floods and, just as importantly, against the many bandits that regularly pillaged, kidnapped and killed farmers and their families. Their characteristic stone architecture is beautiful, and often reflects Western influence. These towers, now on the UNESCO World Heritage List, serve as a tribute to these emigrants, testifying to their sacrifices abroad and the wealth they brought back with them.

Remoteness did not mean poor education either; according to one scholar, "the Kwangtung basin was one of the most academically prestigious areas of the country," with the Qing government creating special academic quotas for the province.[12] Like all his relatives, Foon Chuck went to a local school when he turned six. This was a typical village school with around ten students from different age groups studying together, each parent contributing money for the books, the school furniture, and the salary of the teacher, a lower-degree-holder of the Chinese civil service exams, also called the Imperial Examination. Teaching took place at the ancestral temple, the village's most sacred spot, a one-room building housing two altars with incense sticks burning in front of each, one with the tablets of Confucius and the other with a small statue of Wendi,[13] the god of literature. Each morning pupils knelt in front of the tablets and then bowed to their teacher and to each other in turn. Study began at dawn and continued until five in the afternoon unless the children were called to help their parents in the fields.

Foon Chuck's first textbook was the sixth-century *Thousand Character Classic*,[14] an elementary school primer consisting of a poem of 250 four-character lines, teaching moral precepts, traditional values, and about natural phenomena, often sung to be better memorized. Swinging their bodies, the boys shouted out after their teacher the characters at the top of their voices. It usually required at least a few hundred repetitions before they could read correctly. Based on memorization, a child's success in his studies depended then on hard work, strength of mind and conscientiousness rather than talent.[15] The schoolmaster beat them with a wooden ruler or a long ratan stick for every mistake: "to educate without severity shows a teacher's laziness."[16] Holding in their hands the fate of the family's heirs, the power of teachers was absolute in China. Village tutors could be recognized from far away with their stern looks, long scholars' robes, hunchback, and thick spectacles. The Wong family children were reminded that they attend school to honor their family, and exhorted to respect their teachers and friends, to be upright, charitable and of good character, to keep good relationships with their neighbors, and to improve themselves, Confucian education being then both a means to social mobility and a form of moral indoctrination.[17] The school library contained just a dozen books, which were treated with the utmost care and respect, requiring regular protection against insects and humidity.

Foon Chuck was a precocious child, well liked by his teacher.[18] He was observant and studious from an early age, and quickly learned how to read and write thousands of Chinese characters, and developed an interest in poetry and calligraphy that would accompany him all his life. He learned that skilled calligraphy was as much about the placement of each stroke as the power used to trace it, becoming the character's unique soul. Most importantly, he had the gift of communicating with adults and ingratiating himself with them.

Towards the end of the summer of 1874, when Foon Chuck had just turned eleven, excessive rain and snowfall in the mountains far off to the west caused the poorly maintained river dikes to break. For many weeks, water levels rose along the river forcing Foon Chuck's family to seek refuge with relatives living on higher ground. The village was then entirely covered in over a foot of water, like a lazy lake, reflecting the clouds, the moon, and the few remaining submerged bamboo plants. The worst was yet to come. On the night of 22 September, strong winds and rain battered the coast: a typhoon,[19] stronger than any his parents had faced before, had arrived. Even in the nearby city of Hoiping, tile roofs were blown away by the wind and hundreds of people died. The death toll in the province was devastating. According to some sources more than 100,000 died, with 7,000 casualties alone in the ports of Hong Kong and Macau—almost one in ten people.[20] When the water receded and the Wong family returned to Chaitong, they found only a few walls still standing; everything else in the village had returned to the water and the earth. Years later, Foon Chuck remained haunted by the sight of corpses floating on the river, including many drowned children. The mourning for the dead lasted several days, Foon Chuck and his brothers asking themselves what the villagers had done to deserve such wrath from the heavens. All the summer crops were lost and some of the fields were covered in sand. His parents, like previous generations, had no choice but to start again, knowing that from water and earth the blessed rice stems would soon rise again.

Fortunately, the Wong family had stored some grain in Hoiping and the crops had been abundant in recent years. Their overseas relatives were also quick to help by sending them precious silver coins to rebuild their homes. Unlike many less fortunate families, this meant that Foon Chuck and his relatives did not starve. This was a traumatic event for Foon Chuck, who all his life abroad would settle his family near large and fertile rivers, while never forgetting their destructive power. According to the *Tao Te Ching*,[21] "there is nothing more subtle and weak in the world than water; yet in attacking what is hard and strong, nothing can surpass it."[22]

The following year Foon Chuck's parents sent their twelve-year-old second son to the "Old Golden Mountain,"[23] as San Francisco is still known today in Chinese. They well knew that Foon Chuck would not find gold—as his ancestral predecessors in the emigration to the United States had been made to falsely believe in the middle of the century—but only hard work. They were worried about when the next typhoon or attack by bandits would come in Chaitong, and were unable to imagine that Foon Chuck's life in America could be harder than theirs. On the contrary, they had lofty expectations, hoping he would honor their name by becoming a wealthy merchant. For two decades already, the Wong family had been forced by floods and poverty to emigrate abroad, focusing on trade and diversifying themselves away from an agriculture that could no longer adequately feed them. Foon Chuck's parents worried of course, like all parents, fearing that the Fan-Kwei[24] (foreign devils) might harm their precious son, or worse, that the gods might take him away.

Foon Chuck was unafraid, many of his relatives having undertaken the two-month-long trip before him; he knew he was worth at least as much as them. He dreamed of bringing honor to his ancestors.[25] An essential feature of Chinese civilization, the titles and honors a person earns by his own merits throughout his life are not inherited by his descendants, but rather by his ancestors. For the Chinese, there is no worse stigma than being called unfilial.[26] Parricide was considered on a par with crimes of lèse-majesté, and was punished by the harshest sentence—*lingchi*, or slow slicing. Since ancient times, the life of an elderly parent had been considered more important than those of a wife or a child, countless ancient tales giving examples of such sacrifices. Foon Chuck was taught at school that "filial piety is the root of all virtues, the source of all teachings, and the twin virtue of loyalty."[27] The Chinese character for filial piety (孝), Xiào, is made of two symbols: the one at the top meaning old/group, resting on another meaning child/son, at the bottom. Filial piety had always been linked to the state and the maintenance of social order, a father being to his family what the emperor was to the state, the same social system governing both the family and the empire. The Chinese looked to their sovereign as they would to a father, with the utmost loyalty but also expecting him to treat his subjects with kindness and fairness. Since the ties of blood alone were binding, this system could have perverse effects. The courts, for example, often put aside the rights of individuals, punishing entire families for the crime of a relative, while the robbery or even murder of a distant stranger was seen as a lesser crime than acts of violence within one's own clan.

Emigrating from China did not mean exiting one's family: male heirs living far away still inherited upon the death of their father. Those living far away retained the moral obligation to contribute a share of their earnings to their clan, and more in times of natural disasters, as well as the assurance that their participation in the inheritance would not be diminished by time or distance,[28] the notions of filial duty and inheritance being ingrained in the Chinese concept of family. The huge migratory phenomenon therefore did not undermine the pillars of Chinese civilization, built since ancient times around traditions, family values and ancestor worship. In contrast to the West, eighty-five per cent of the Chinese population share the hundred most common surnames.[29] The surname Wong (or Huang in Mandarin), for example, was the seventh most common Chinese surname and was shared by forty-two million people in China in 2010 (a quarter being in Kwangtung province) and more than seventy million worldwide, being the most widespread Chinese surname in the United States.[30] Chinese civilization is like a collection of family lineages dating back thousands of years. A British diplomat in China recalled a century ago with some exaggeration that "the commonest Chinaman can trace his descent back by memory from two hundred to five hundred years, or even more by referring to his genealogy back at home."[31]

With sometimes all the inhabitants of a village sharing the same surname, Chinese rural societies in the nineteenth century were organized according to the different clans, which collectively owned their land, ancestral halls, and often schools, and had a strong degree of solidarity. With their ancestors having occupied their land for hundreds of years before them, the natural heads of the clans held almost unlimited power in their district, sometimes making it difficult for even the imperial magistrates to discharge their duties.[32] This was exacerbated by the practice of magistrates working in provinces where they were not native and only for a limited number of years, being forbidden to marry local girls or to own land there—rules which continue to this day in communist China to avoid corruption. Clan elders often acted as judges in local disputes, since villagers distrusted lawyers, who were seen as outsiders trying to tell them that right is wrong and wrong is right.[33]

This form of society was prevalent throughout China, but more so in the southeastern provinces like Kwangtung and Fukien than in the north, due to the communitarian organization required in rice cultivation and because the northern capital was further away. This way of organizing society was later replicated in the Chinese diaspora: clans constituted transnational networks of mutual aid for migrants. This is why migrants from the same province tended to regroup and monopolize migration in particular regions of the world, such as the Cantonese in North America, the Fukianese in Malaysia, the Hakkas in Borneo and, a century later, the people of Wenzhou in France and Italy. During my own career in China, I met several people with my last name who, for this reason alone, helped me and played important roles in my life. All this meant that departing migrants were expected to return one day to their ancestral land. Overseas Chinese communities, associations and guilds were considered integral parts and important extensions of their family clans back home.

Foon Chuck's parents felt sad to see their second son leave but were consoled by the thought that his two brothers would remain in Chaitong for the time being. In San Francisco he was to study at a school run by Westerners and be received by one of his uncles, who was to ensure that he continued learning Chinese. His parents were relieved that he was to pursue his education in America, although they were surprised to learn that the foreign devils even had schools, and wondered what their son would study if not the Confucian classics.

Like all educated Chinese, Foon Chuck had been learning these classics by heart, despite not yet understanding their full meaning,[34] since all writing was until the start of the twentieth century in classical Chinese, very different from spoken Chinese. Only after a few years of rote learning would teachers reveal to students the meaning of the characters they had memorized. Chinese people could often read a character or sentence without knowing its meaning. Since ancient times, the Chinese spoken and written languages had operated in different spheres. The vast majority of Chinese people were only competent in spoken Chinese and so were excluded from the knowledge found in books, as well as from political, religious and administrative power. In few cultures has an independent written language played such an essential role in social, political and religious life, enabling the federation of such a large empire despite its countless different dialects: the characters of Chinese have the same meaning throughout China but are pronounced differently in every region. Before leaving for America, in his six years of schooling Foon Chuck had already memorized the *Classic of Filial Piety*, the *Analects of Confucius*, and started reading some of the other books of the Confucian education. His studies were not only about memorizing;

his teacher also described events and people to illustrate the correct behavior of a gentleman as prescribed by Confucian education. This education had for centuries had a political and governmental function, shaping China's civilization and maintaining the empire's cohesion. The common belief was that in ancient times men had been better, wiser and more honest.[35] Students were taught that memorizing a book could and should alter the way a person behaves in his everyday life: readings and actions should be in accord.[36] Foon Chuck would always remember the texts he learned at school, his early Confucian education having a definitive impact on his later life.

In China, plagues, famines and other kinds of natural disaster had been thought for centuries to precede changes in the mandate of heaven. For the emperor, or Son of Heaven, was deemed responsible for such disasters due to his neglect of his duty. In 1875, the Cantonese were therefore not surprised to learn of the death of Emperor Tongzhi. People wondered, however, who would now rule, since Zaitian, now the Guangxu Emperor, was only four years old. But nobody seemed particularly anxious, since as observed by a missionary, the Chinese were taught not to worry about or meddle in the running of the state, leaving those concerns to magistrates paid for that task.

* * *

The costs of Foon Chuck's trans-Pacific trip and education in the United States will be significant, but the family are relieved to have one mouth less to feed, anticipating that investing in such an ingenious child will one day pay off, as they have seen happen before with other relatives abroad. Before his departure, Foon Chuck kowtows in front of his family's altar, on which are placed the precious ancestors' tablets, burning incense to solicit their blessings. He fears their spirits will not accompany him to America nor protect him so far away, and he promises them that he will be back one day. He wonders what America will feel like, a land which people say is without ancestral ghosts. He, like his contemporaries, believes that a man has three spirits, of which after death one resides in his tablets, the other in his tomb, and the third in the heavens, the latter reappearing later in a new state of existence. Wealthy Chinese therefore make sure that their graves occupy the most splendid sites, with the best views and Fengshui,[37] according to the art of the Master of Wind and Water, or Chinese geomancy. In general, the more educated a person, the greater his belief in and fear of Fengshui.[38] More care was taken over the Fengshui of one's grave than one's home.

Foon Chuck makes a two-day trip by sampan boat directly from Chaitong to the English port of Hong Kong, or the "Fragrant Harbor" in Chinese. Since his trip is on water, he sees little of the British colony and its white masters, other than their tiny white houses in the distance perched on what is today Victoria Peak. He is intrigued by the ships' noisy steam engines, as he has never been so close to one in his life before, thinking that those machines are surely behind the foreign devils' power. Their stench combined with the smell of rotten fish makes him feel nauseous, and he wonders how this harbor can be called fragrant by the locals. The steamships make a strong contrast with the many boats along the river near his village, which are towed or poled manually, or powered with a stern wheel, worked by twenty or thirty distressed men in treadmill fashion, who, despite the strain on their naked bodies, tread on against wind and tide for less money than the coal would cost were the work done by steam.[39] This cheap and abundant labor is one explanation for China's lack of interest in Western technology in the nineteenth century, and the absence of an industrial revolution there.

When he boards his ship, Foon Chuck is given a bucket that he will keep for the duration of the crossing; it is filled once a day for him to drink and wash. The rows of wooden bunks below deck are so crammed that there are barely seventeen inches between them. Realizing that he is one of the youngest among his more than 400 fellow passengers, Foon Chuck feels a sense of solidarity with them, presumably all fleeing the previous year's murderous typhoon and the resulting famines, making now this uncomfortable and perilous journey together. Yet he also feels privileged, since the others are mostly illiterate and, having incurred significant debts to pay for their transportation, will have to work as laborers when they arrive. In contrast, his family supports him for his expenses and education, and he already has close relatives in the United States to welcome him. As his ship leaves the Chinese coast, Foon Chuck finds comfort in the old adage, "Reading ten thousand books is not worth traveling ten thousand leagues."[40]

2

THE ONLY WAY OUT

My great-grandfather Leung Hing[1] was born in 1866, the fifth year of Emperor Tongzhi's reign, in the village of Leunggang[2] in Hoksaan County (meaning "the hill of the cranes")[3] in the province of Kwangtung. His surname originates from Mount Leung in Shaanxi province, which was given as a reward by Emperor Xuan Wang (reigned 827–782 BCE) to the family's founders for defeating the western barbarian tribes. Hing's parents were joyous, since Hing was not only their first son but was also born in the year of the tiger, a good omen. To ward off malignant influences from his future, they traveled to a nearby temple to pray to the God of longevity and placed around Hing's neck a string of amulets given to them by the local monks. At birth, he was called Little Tiger by his parents and later Goh Goh,[4] meaning elder brother. He was given in his teens the character Hing as his first name, meaning "occasion to celebrate."

Leunggang is in a region of small hills and lies fifteen miles west of the city of Kongmoon,[5] another important emigrants' city, and forty miles northeast of Chaitong, the Wong family's village. Both Leunggang and Chaitong belong to the region of Sze Yap,[6] meaning "Four Districts." Despite being near the provincial capital of Canton, the inhabitants of this region speak the Sze Yap dialect, which is very distinct from Cantonese. Hoksaan county does not possess the elaborate and ancient stone architecture of Hoiping or even the larger houses of Chaitong. Leunggang was then a small and impoverished agricultural hamlet perched on a hill, far from any river and still further from the coast, housing a couple of dozen families. A cluster of trees on one side and a small pond on the other guarded the village against evil winds, since spirits were known to be unable to make turns. The Chinese believed then that the best water came from mountain springs, followed by rivers; the worst was stagnant water from wells or ponds.

A typical Leunggang house was a mere hut with one room, a half-burnt clay-pot on the side and earthen floors. As with most Chinese houses, the room faced south, to receive the healthy sunshine all year round; this room was hallway, kitchen, shrine and bedchamber all in one. Hing remembered playing there with the family's dog and later with his brothers. On days of worship, the scrolls of Heaven and Earth or of the appropriate god were hung on the wall opposite the door and during Spring Festival, the ancestors' tablets were placed on the dinner table. All peasants in China, even the poorest, lived together in small fortified hamlets to protect each other against bandits and rebellions, living in constant fear of being attacked by outsiders. The village walls were often made of dense and spiky bamboo, there not being enough stones to build them. Bamboo was widely used in southern China to build houses, as water pipes, and to make boats, ropes, hats and paper; this is still the case today. It is revered by poets and painters as a symbol of virtue, its deep roots denoting resoluteness, its hollow interior modesty, its straight stems honor, and its movement in the wind flexibility.

The Leung and Wong families differed in many ways. The Leungs had only settled in the province of Kwangtung five generations earlier, having fled famines further north. When they settled in Hoksaan in the eighteenth century, all the good flat land in the plains and near the rivers was already taken. Bloody conflicts then took place throughout the province between natives and the northern newcomers. This feudal and often ethnic violence between rival clans continued to plague the province until the beginning of the twentieth century, causing thousands of deaths every year. It was not unusual for those feuds to survive over many generations, requiring the erection of fortified walls around villages. Ironically, if clans were a source of protection, they were very often also a source of violence and disunity, caused by fights over inheritance between branches of the same families, due in part to the prevalent polygamy.

Hing was the eldest of four brothers, and his family did not own land. Unlike the Wong family, they were tenant farmers, and had

THE ONLY WAY OUT

never sent relatives abroad. With poor harvests for several years in a row, they had fallen behind on their debt. Before each Spring Festival, Hing felt shame seeing his father forced to beg his creditors to give him until the next harvest season, the new year being the time in China to settle one's debt. Everything in their home had already been sold to the pawnbrokers of Kongmoon. Nevertheless, shame and pride being powerful feelings, his father still hosted relatives and friends during Spring Festival, even if the family was left with nothing to eat afterwards. This sacrifice was necessary to show that they still had good standing and to bring them luck in the new year. During those festival days, villagers avoided talking about death or unpleasant subjects, which would bring misfortune, and instead gave flattering remarks and good wishes to each other. Hing promised himself that one day he too would invite relatives and friends to eat at his home, gaining their respect for him and his family. This habit of frugality and self-sacrifice in order to be generous with family and friends was common among Chinese farmers, and would later be replicated by migrants in the Americas.

Hing and his family survived one day to the next, facing imminent eviction. The only reason Hing's father had not yet been sent to prison was because he had four sons, now his only fortune, serving as an unspoken guarantee for his debt. He had already received threats that he would have to sell one of them, since they were healthy and unusually tall. This would not have been uncommon at the time, but Hing's father always refused, preferring the whole family to deprive themselves but stay together, and having nothing more precious than his sons, whose descendants would carry the Leung surname. He believed that as trees are raised for shade, "children are reared for old age,"[7] and was scared that they could be stolen from him by creditors, bandits or the many corrupt officials often conniving with them.

In Hoksaan, like in most of Kwangtung province, women labored bare-legged together with their male relatives in the rice fields. In the rainy season, they worked under immense rain-hats made of bamboo leaves, while in the winter they and their babies were covered in layers of clothes, since in the south home fires were used only for cooking, not heating. Since women were useful to their families outside the home, the practice of foot-binding had already disappeared in the province long ago, except in the wealthier families. But foot-binding was still widely followed in the rest of China during the nineteenth century, especially in the north, with more than forty per cent of Chinese women having their feet bound. A girl's beauty, and even character, was judged by the size of her feet rather than by her face, since "a plain face is given by the heavens, but poorly bound feet are a sign of laziness."[8] Perversely, although the Manchus, in control of China since the seventeenth century, had banned the practice and Manchu women did not bind their feet, it became more common. The Han Chinese majority saw it as an act of defiance against their hated Manchu rulers, showing that "our men have surrendered but not our women."[9]

Hing's mother was hard-working and thrifty, making the little food the family had stretch over weeks, and so gaining the respect of her husband and children. Hing was fond of his mother and sisters, yet during meals he and his brothers still helped themselves right after their father, while his female relatives had to survive with whatever was left on the table after the males of the family had eaten. Hing later remembered how men and women in his village often did things separately, like not sitting and eating together or not praying in the temple at the same time. People said that men and women are equal to each other, and are both equal to the highest people in the land, only twice in their lives: when they get married and when they die—times when they could wear the silk clothes of the nobility.[10] In ancient tradition, one of the reasons given for the separation between the sexes was to allow fathers and sons to develop more intimacy and thereby create a more harmonious society. This tradition was more strictly adhered to in affluent households. Since girls would customarily leave the family when they married, joining their husband's family, they were seen as less valuable than boys. According to an ancient saying, "Eight Lohan [saintly] daughters are not equal to a boy with a limp," and fathers who were asked how many children they had would usually exclude their girls in their reply.[11] In later life, love for one's mother took precedence over love for one's wife, so that Chinese women received greater consideration only with age, and mainly from their male children.

Many rural Chinese women—especially in northern China—were malnourished, took too little exercise, and indeed rarely left their homes. They were often continuously pregnant and caring for

THE ONLY WAY OUT

young children, while anemia, rickets and lung diseases were common. Women often died years earlier than their husbands. Women's legal rights were also lacking. Confucian principles dictated that there were seven reasons a man could divorce his wife: for example, her becoming ill, not bearing children, disrespecting her in-laws, speaking too much, and causing arguments were all considered sufficient reasons for divorce, although a man could not divorce his wife if she had nowhere else to go.

The daily diet of Hing's family consisted of wild yam or rice with boiled greens, accompanied occasionally by a bean curd paste. They rarely ate meat at festivals, and Hing remembered feeling hungry all day and having to settle for wearing shorts, since his family lacked enough fabric to make him long pants. Unlike Foon Chuck, Hing never attended elementary school, and was only able to recognize a few dozen characters. There were no public schools, which made studying a luxury beyond the reach of most people. Illiteracy rates were over ninety per cent. As far as he could remember, Hing had always worked, in his first years by gathering roots and weeds for fuel, and later in the fields, from dawn to dusk and under sun and rain.

Yet Hing felt fortunate just to have a family, as the roads around his village and nearby towns were full of vagrants and beggars, abandoned by all, often crippled, covered in vermin, disfigured, and malnourished. Although some beggars were poor peasants with families like his, others were alone and hopeless. When hunger did not kill them, bandits or soldiers did. In the late Qing dynasty, beggary and peasantry became inseparable: many poor peasants begged during the slack season and returning to their village for the harvest.[12] In his early years, Hing was terrified by the sight of them, almost as much as by the hordes of bandits who had already come twice to loot his village. The last time that they came, Hing remembered, they kidnapped one of his cousins since there was nothing else to steal. Hing feared that he or his brothers could be next. From a young age, Hing knew that his family was his most precious—indeed his only real—possession, and felt ready to sacrifice himself for them, as they did daily for him.

* * *

Unable to earn a decent living in the village, the Leung family ventures outside. Hing is regularly sent away from his village between planting seasons to nearby towns like Fatsaan,[13] located fifty miles away, where he works for a pittance in porcelain workshops for several weeks. More important than his meagre salary is giving his parents one mouth less to feed. To enter the city, Hing passes by Fatsaan's imposing gate and walls, next to the grand temple dedicated to the city's god, or the "master of the city wall and moat,"[14] to whom the citizens pray for protection in times of famine or war. Hing wishes that his tiny village of Hoksaan could have such mighty protectors, as surely the bandits would not dare attack them.

Entering Fatsaan, Hing's senses are overwhelmed by new smells, sounds and sights. He marvels at the tea houses, where hundreds of guests are hitting the tables with small pieces of bamboo, playing Mahjong; at the large money changers, where sums he cannot even imagine are transacted daily; and at the food and medicine markets, with animals from earth and sea he had not known existed. Hing has never seen such a concentration of humanity, especially near the central market and the Yamen[15] (the magistrates' headquarters), where public executions and tortures occur daily and where every side street is occupied by countless vendors and hawkers of all sorts. He sometimes joins the crowds congregating around ballad singers and storytellers telling tales of Kung Fu, ghosts and romance, who perform daily from noon to midnight in the public streets and squares. One day, aged ten, Hing has the biggest fright in his life when he sees for the first time a missionary walking on the streets, making him run away before the foreign devil can catch him.

* * *

Four years later, in 1880, the villagers of Hoksaan found out that agents were hiring laborers to work in the United States, with the cost of their passage to be deducted from their future wages. Many had already left the village. Both saddened and hopeful, Hing's father decided to enroll his eldest son for that long and perilous journey. Hing—being healthy, of tall stature and strong build, and looking older than his fourteen years—was readily accepted. To his father's relief, Hing would guarantee his debt in this way, helping to carry the enormous burden that had been hanging over the family for so long. Thus, like Foon Chuck five years before him, Hing set off to the port of Hong Kong to board his steamship to the United States. His three younger brothers stayed with his parents for now, hoping that they would soon join him.

Hing, like most emigrants, bought his travel ticket on credit. The ship's captain would be reimbursed upon arrival at his destination by friends, relatives or employers of the emigrant, who would have to work to repay this debt.[16] Sometimes, entire Chinese villages sponsored the emigration of their members, with a relative traveling with the group to ensure that all loans were settled. During the nineteenth century, this movement of people became an organized international trade involving brokers and emigration agencies in ports around the world. The system became subject to countless abuses, with many emigrants finding themselves bonded to unscrupulous extortioners and traffickers, often associated with the infamous trade in so-called "coolies," or indentured laborers.

As emigration numbers increased, ships became increasingly overloaded, disgorging on their arrival sick, starving or dead passengers. Hing bought his ticket on credit, and so had to work unsalaried, or as an indentured laborer, until he paid off his debt. He did not, however, suffer from the kinds of abuses that coolies faced. Coolies were frequently illegally coerced and forced to work in inhumane conditions by employers, with little or no chance of paying off their debts. In the Americas, the trade in Chinese coolies was mainly centered on Cuba and Peru, where coolies replaced former slaves to work on sugar plantations and in mines. Conducted mainly from Macau and involving an estimated quarter-of-a-million Chinese bound for Latin America, the trade in Chinese coolies flourished from 1847 until it was abolished in 1870, driven by public outcry and pressure from the British and Chinese governments. Thereafter, in the United States and Mexico, although many migrants were directly hired to build railroads or work in plantations or mines, they were free to repay their debt and later move on to other activities in their host country, as Hing would later do. All the same, many experienced the harsh treatment suffered by coolies decades earlier.

* * *

Hing bows to his parents one last time and waves goodbye to his brothers before taking to the road with other young people of his district. Their mothers are heartbroken, worried that they will lose their sons forever. Without them, they fear that their husbands may one day abandon them, leaving no one to take care of them in their old age—the sad fate of many migrants' mothers. Hing's mother places around his neck a protective charm given to her by a monk to guard him against evil spirits. Like the other superstitious villagers, she is terrified of the United States, believing that Westerners have evil eyes, bewitching all the places they pass. A Western missionary in China observed that most religious worshippers at the time were women.[17] In return, Hing vows to his mother that he will be back one day to take care of her.

After a short journey by sampan boat, Hing for the first time in his life gazes at the immense South China Sea and feels the salty breeze on his face, making him suddenly realize the length of the journey ahead. Hing is surprised by the hundreds of boats in Hong Kong harbor, each filled with poor fishermen and their families, like a floating village on the sea, women with babies tied to their back pulling heavy fishing nets. Hing is amazed that people can live on water. The boat people are among the lowest ranks of Chinese society (a status they have until the twentieth century). Seafarers in the Middle Kingdom lead some of the harshest lives, with their homes being at the mercy each year of the mighty typhoons.

Hing has never ventured so far outside his village, but he is not afraid, feeling reassured to be with so many Sze Yap compatriots. Upon boarding the United States-bound ship, a large label is placed around his neck, indicating his name, his village, and the place he will work for at least three years to reimburse his ticket and all the intermediaries who have organized his trip, as well as part of his family's historic debt. His ticket cost almost $50 and he owes almost as much in commission to the recruiting agent and in visa fees—more than $3,000 in today's money. Although only fourteen, Hing understands that his family's fate now rests on his frail shoulders: if he does not repay their debt, the collectors will take his brothers away and harm his parents. For centuries, these have been the responsibilities of an eldest son in China. At the same time, Hing's new obligations to his future employer also give him a sense of peace. In his village in China, he was constantly worried about his family's future or about being kidnapped by bandits, but he is now under the care and protection of his employer, and his fate has been decided for him for at least the coming years.

* * *

Already far from family and home, Hing realized that he must now rely only on himself. An imperial decree had prohibited emigration since the fifteenth century. By leaving their country, emigrants thus became outlaws, punishable by death by beheading, the dynastic authorities perceiving them as traitors, deserters, rebels and conspirators who had rejected their filial duties. In the decades before my ancestors' departures things had started to change, and the emigration ban was only vaguely enforced as the Qing Dynasty understood that emigration functioned as a safety valve for its densely populated provinces. In addition, returning emigrants brought back valuable foreign currency remittances, badly needed by the bankrupt dynasty. In 1859, emigration was finally recognized, at least in the province of Kwangtung, where a new proclamation by the local governor acknowledged that people were "free to leave China provided they emigrate of their own free will," while the following year a treaty between Britain and China further canceled any restrictions on emigration.

However, it would take time for full liberalization to occur and hence emigrants like Foon Chuck and Hing were left without diplomatic protection, remaining vulnerable to abuse in their port of departure, on their ships, and abroad. At the time, the main concern of the Chinese authorities, who did not want to admit that their citizens were leaving to find a better life, was to tackle their mistreatment abroad, especially the indentured laborers. Not until 1893, thirteen years after Hing's departure, did an imperial edict officially revoke the ban on emigration, also allowing expatriates to return home freely. In 1895, following the recommendations of the reformer Kang Youwei, the Qing Dynasty even began to encourage overseas Chinese to invest their savings back in China, providing finance to develop its nascent industry.[18] This is exactly what the Communist regime would also do a hundred years later at the start of the reform era in the 1980s, in the Special Economic Zone of Shenzhen, just one hundred miles from Hoiping, across the border from Hong Kong. If the Cantonese were the first migrants to leave China, they were also the first to come back, showing their pioneering and entrepreneurial spirit. Hong Kong's wealth today is a tribute to their success. Around 1910, just before its fall, the Qing Dynasty radically changed its position and began to encourage its people to leave, finally recognizing the many benefits of emigration to the country.

In the late nineteenth century, Chinese emigration to the United States was considered a temporary absence. Hing and Foon Chuck expected to return after ten or twenty years of work, or after having made enough money to "return to their home village in silk robes"[19] and be honored by their relatives for the rest of their lives. The reality was different and, like them, many migrants never returned. Only a minority got rich in America; most toiled for decades, earning just enough to survive and send a little money to their families back home. Many successful emigrants preferred to stay abroad rather than return home, in order to amass even greater wealth or because they were worried about being kidnapped and robbed upon their return. Less successful emigrants either lacked the means to return or, out of shame, dared not come back, often hiding their poverty from their families at home, thus reproducing the fable of the American Dream,[20] the myth of return becoming for them a form of self-deception. Of those who did return, some lost their savings on their journey, by gambling their money away or by becoming victims of pirates.[21] It is estimated that between a quarter and a half of the first Chinese immigrants to the United States returned to China after a few years.[22] As a result of their return, the US populace viewed the Chinese in a negative light, as sojourners, transitory people unwilling to assimilate.

In the mid-nineteenth century, thirty years before Foon Chuck and Hing arrived in the Americas and at a time when workers were scarce, the California Gold Rush (1848–55), and the subsequent construction of the Central Pacific Railroad (1865–69), were magnets attracting Chinese immigrants to the United States. Chinese migrants were often seen as providing cheaper, more disciplined, organized and reliable labor than migrants of many other nationalities. This explains why ninety per cent of the workers who built the Central Pacific Railroad were Chinese.[23] The sociologist Mary Coolidge, in her study on immigration, wrote: "In the first few years, the Chinaman was welcome, praised, and considered almost indispensable, for in those days race antipathy was subordinated to industrial necessity."[24] Mark Twain commented that "[The Chinese] are quiet, peaceable, tractable, free from drunkenness. A disorderly Chinaman does not exist, and a lazy one is rare. So long as a Chinaman has strength to use his hands, he needs no support from anybody [...] he always finds something to do."[25]

By the time of the 1880 census, when Hing arrived in the United States, nearly 300,000 Chinese immigrants had entered in the previous decades and 105,000 were now present in the country, constituting 0.2 per cent of the US population.[26] Three-quarters of them were concentrated in the state of California, representing about eight per cent of California's population. Most of these Chinese immigrants were from the districts south of the city of Canton.

These levels of immigration were facilitated by the Treaty of Burlingame of 1868 between the United States and China, which encouraged trade and established a cordial immigration policy. This treaty was progressive for the time, stating that both countries "cordially recognize the right of man to change his home and allegiance and the mutual advantage of free migration."[27] Anson Burlingame (1820–70) was a US abolitionist, congressman and diplomat in Peking, who became an envoy of the Chinese court to the Western powers. In his obituary, Mark Twain wrote of him that "he had outgrown the narrow citizenship of a state and become a citizen of the world; and his charity was large enough and his great heart warm enough to feel for all its races and to labour for them."[28] The treaty that Burlingame helped negotiate aimed to ensure that the Chinese remained free and voluntary migrants rather than coolies subject to coercion and exploitation. This suited US lawmakers, who were primarily concerned about wage competition from Chinese migrants driving down the salaries and conditions of US workers.

When Foon Chuck and Hing arrived in the United States, the conquest of the west was still unfinished. California, which embodied the American Dream, had only been annexed to the United

States in 1848, following its war with Mexico. From 1850 to 1870, the new US state's population increased from 93,000 to 600,000 settlers,[29] all eager to enrich themselves quickly and who, for the most part, would see their hopes shattered. California's population of pioneers and migrants was, of course, not limited to the Chinese. In 1880, foreigners already made up thirty-eight per cent of California's population, mostly coming from Europe, despite the costs of travel from Europe to California being between three and five times higher than from China.[30] Nevertheless, unlike European immigrants, the Chinese could not become naturalized US citizens due to racist laws, making them perpetual aliens in their new land. Upon arrival in the United States, immigrants faced difficult living conditions, with life expectancy in the country in 1850 being only thirty-nine years, not much higher than the life expectancy of thirty-five in a city like Peking at the time.[31] Chinese immigrants did some of the most difficult jobs, and earned significantly less than white Americans. But those salaries still represented many times what they could earn in China, and the money they sent back home enabled their families to live well. This was the reason why Foon Chuck and Hing were now on their way to the United States.

3

A WORLD UPSIDE DOWN

The year is 1875 and after six weeks of travel Foon Chuck is relieved to finally see the bay of San Francisco, its gentle succession of green hills reminding him of Hong Kong and making him feel like he is still in China. When he disembarks, he meets his uncle and bows to him, thanking him profusely for sending money to Chaitong after the typhoon a year earlier and now inviting him to the United States. Foon Chuck has only skin on his bones and is barely able to stand; his uncle must help him walk. But he is not worried and is enthusiastic to finally start his new life in the Golden Mountain. He marvels at the well-laid slabs paving the wide avenues, the broad pedestrian sidewalks, the public squares and parks, the pipes carrying running water into people's homes—and, when night falls, the thousand gas lights coming from everywhere, as if the sun has not entirely disappeared.

* * *

Foon Chuck was warmly welcomed and immediately felt at home in the missionary school of the Chinatown Presbyterian Church run by Reverend Augustus W. Loomis (1816–91). Founded in 1853 to welcome the first Chinese migrants in America, it was the oldest Asian Christian church in North America and the first Chinese Protestant church outside China. His uncle had placed him there to learn English, knowing this would allow him to find better-paid jobs later, few Chinese being fluent in the language.

Since an 1860 law, San Francisco public schools had not admitted Chinese children, even while many Chinese parents paid the same taxes as the state's other residents. The few young Chinese in San Francisco who had the privilege of not having to seek employment were therefore forced to study in missionary schools, which also gave adult classes in the evenings and on Sundays. Classes were often overcrowded. The missionaries quickly realized that to read the gospels, the Chinese would first have to learn English.[1] In 1885, only ten years after Foon Chuck's arrival, under pressure from a Chinese couple, the San Francisco Board of Education opened a public school that was reserved for the Chinese. Not until 1947 were non-segregated public schools established in the city, which was nevertheless one of the most cosmopolitan in the United States.

Reverend Loomis had decided to become a minister at the age of sixteen, graduating from Princeton Seminary twelve years later. He then moved to China as a missionary, settling in Ningpo in the province of Chekiang (Ningbo and Zhejiang in Mandarin), where he opened a school and quickly learned the local dialect. In 1850, for health reasons, he returned to the United States. After running a school for Creek Indian Nation children, he was asked in 1859, aged forty-three, to lead the first Chinese Presbyterian Church in San Francisco, a position he would occupy until his death in 1891. He was among those US Protestants who believed that the United States had a special duty, and even a manifest destiny, to help convert Chinese immigrants and who therefore did missionary work in their own country. Although he refused to get involved in politics, Reverend Loomis testified in front of the US Congress in 1876 that the Chinese did not pose a threat to US institutions, for which he received much opprobrium.[2]

In 1870 Loomis founded his school for Chinese immigrants, located at the corner of Jackson Street and Dupont Street (now Grant Avenue) in the heart of San Francisco's Chinatown. Originally named the Globe Hotel School, being located in the four-story Globe Hotel, it was later renamed the Loomis Memorial Presbyterian Mission School.[3] Demonstrating great dedication to the task, Reverend Loomis learned the Sze Yap dialect in order to attend to the needs of his community, and in 1872 published one of the first practical bilingual Chinese and English language study books, including lively dialogues and letters, useful to children, businessmen and missionaries alike. In 1877 a fellow missionary wrote that Reverend Loomis, by his uniform gentlemanly conduct and recognized scholarly ability, commanded the esteem and respect of all who knew him. Though quiet and unostentatious, he was widely and favorably known among the [San Francisco] Chinese population as their friend and counselor. He had been faithful and persistent in visiting the Chinese in their shops and factories, and sometimes found a favorable opportunity to converse with workmen.[4]

* * *

Foon Chuck is initially surprised to see boys and girls in the same classroom, as well as the indiscipline and unruliness of the students. Some behave as if they know more than the teachers and want to replace them, something unimaginable in China. In truth, his new instructors, in their patience, good humor and relaxed teaching style, are most unlike his teacher in China, who demanded that students always sit upright, keep their feet together, speak and walk slowly, and respect their textbooks.[5] Yet his missionary school is known for high academic achievement, holding annual public examinations to showcase its students' academic progress, and even sending a student to the Imperial College in Peking in 1872. Initially a school for girls, it will come to have seventy-one students by the end of the century, including thirteen girls, three-quarters of whom are members of the church's Sunday school, a small number compared to Chinatown's population of 30,000 people, emphasizing that it is still a childless society.

Foon Chuck is studious, quickly learning to read and write in English, a language he finds easy compared to Chinese. He is touched and surprised by the kindness shown to him by Reverend Loomis and the other missionaries, despite their very different ancestry. This raises questions for Foon Chuck. Could it be that all those who follow Jesus Christ are like this? But how then to explain why so many "foreign devils" mock and beat his compatriots in China and the Americas?

Religious instruction is woven into the curriculum. Foon Chuck is surprised by his first bible classes, where texts are read and commented on by the group. Although these classes in some ways resemble the moral Confucian lessons taught in his village school, children in China are asked simply to revere and fear temple deities, without much explanation of the beliefs lying behind this reverence.

Foon Chuck sees that Reverend Loomis and the other missionaries are satisfied with his dedication and progress. He has never felt as proud as when he has his first discussion in English with Reverend Loomis. He is conscious of the privilege of learning first-hand about the strange thoughts and habits of the mysterious foreigners. Reverend Loomis treats him like an adult, showing the same curiosity about China as Foon Chuck feels about the United States. The boy enjoys telling his teacher about the life of his family in Chaitong. He admires Reverend Loomis' efforts to master the Sze Yap dialect, something which gains Reverend Loomis the respect of his students, making their learning mutual.

When he returns to his uncle's house in Chinatown on the weekends, Foon Chuck feels the difference between the kindness inside the school and the brutality and venality of the outside world. However, his uncle sternly reminds him that he is there to become a successful merchant and to honor his ancestors. He is certainly not to become an ordinary missionary, for he belongs to the Wong clan and not to a foreign god. In 1864 Mark Twain opined about Chinese utilitarianism, writing that: "[their] ingenuity is beyond calculation [...] they appreciate good and bad but only in reference to business, to finance, to trade, etc. Whatever is successful is good; whatever fails is bad."[6] In his later life, Foon Chuck will strive to prove himself a successful merchant, like his uncle had hoped for, but one, unlike in Twain's description, who also follows the moral principles of his early Confucian and now Christian teachers.

* * *

Foon Chuck developed a special bond with Reverend Loomis as he was one of the only students who had arrived directly from China in his teens rather than being born in the United States; he therefore reminded the reverend of his early missionary years in China. Not having any children himself, the reverend developed a fatherly affection for his students, especially those who were far away from their parents like Foon Chuck. One year after his arrival, Reverend Loomis proposed that Foon Chuck become a butler in his house at 1550 Jones Street.[7] After consulting with his uncle, Foon Chuck gratefully accepted the offer. He was thrilled to serve the family of such a generous person while continuing his studies, taking the opportunity to learn more about the customs of these mysterious foreigners, and finally start sending money to his family. Chinese butlers enjoyed an excellent reputation throughout San Francisco for their cleanliness and talent as cooks. Most of the large mansions in the city employed one, and this was the only profession where the Chinese could earn as much as white Americans—up to $50 a month,[8] or $1,500 in today's money. It is unclear whether or not Reverend Loomis paid Foon Chuck so much, but whatever he did not earn in cash he received in affection and education. In exchange, Foon Chuck sometimes helped cook Cantonese dishes for his adoptive family, reminding them of their missionary days in China.

Back at his uncle's house on Sundays, Foon Chuck was relieved to eat Chinese food again, finding the meals at his school and Reverend Loomis' home bland. He would never have imagined that one day he would miss a simple bowl of rice so much. People say Chinese consciousness is defined by food, family and perseverance, in that exact order. In China, rice was the main dish, not a mere accompaniment to other dishes; instead the other dishes were supposed to complement the rice. Foon Chuck found it hard to get used to his new country's diet: consuming beef and milk (especially accompanying Chinese tea) would have been unthinkable in China, where oxen and cows were only used as a man's helpful companion for ploughing his fields. Killing cows for their meat had even been prohibited by law in past dynasties. In truth, however, Cantonese people were known throughout China for eating a wide variety of animals, or, as the saying goes, "everything that crawls is food for the people."[9]

It was not just the food that surprised Foon Chuck about Western meals. Dinners in Reverend Loomis' house seemed to be less about eating than about chatting, drinking and showing off silver utensils and porcelain plates—strangely called "china." Back in China, a dish is placed in the middle of the table and shared, each person picking from it one mouthful at a time. Separating a large portion for oneself as in the United States would be frowned upon. Chinese meals are usually eaten in silence, sharing dishes in turn, instead of over a good conversation like in the West. Foon Chuck also found uncivilized the use of knives and forks instead of chopsticks; in China the absence of both knives and plates at the dinner table meant that animal bones, chopped beforehand into small pieces, were chewed with relish before being spit out onto the table or floor.

In China, knives are strictly restricted to the kitchen, since Buddhist tradition dictates that to cut animal flesh is sinful, which is why Chinese food always comes in small pieces and butchers were considered outcasts, unable to enter the service of the state. Foon Chuck recalled that during the days preceding the Spring Festival in Chaitong, knives were forbidden even in the kitchen, to avoid bringing bad luck onto the family in the new year.

San Francisco's Chinatown counted more than 130 Chinese grocery stores, and Foon Chuck enjoyed seeing the food on display there, with ducks hanging from hooks, carts loaded with offal salvaged from the slaughterhouse, hundred years' eggs,[10] swallows' nests, shark fins, dried and fermented seafoods and vegetables, and so many other pungent Chinese ingredients never eaten by Westerners. Chinatown looked like a giant kitchen, full of smells and noises, quite a contrast with Reverend Loomis' neighborhood. In ancient Chinese writings, foreigners arriving in the city of Canton were first supposed to "change their bowels"[11] to get used to their new lives in the Middle Kingdom.[12] Foon Chuck could certainly relate to this idea, and he hoped that Reverend Loomis' family too could "change their bowels" and enjoy Chinese food with him.

Foon Chuck was surprised by the politeness in the United States: please and thank you were used constantly, even with subordinates or strangers, unlike the harsh treatment of servants he witnessed back in China. This was quite a contrast with the image of white barbarians with which he had arrived, an image of "foreign devils," ignorant of all Chinese rules of propriety and ceremony. He was annoyed, though, by Mrs Loomis' request to have her wooden floors mopped and her beds made daily: the dirt floors at his home in Chaitong did not require such care, and beds had no linen to be bothered with. And he was surprised by the habit of keeping doors and windows closed: the Chinese were anxious to always keep a draught in their houses, so that the spirits who occupied the air could leave.[13]

Foon Chuck was intrigued above all by women in the United States. He could not understand the idea that they should make themselves attractive to men before being able to form a family. In China, where every respectable woman was betrothed from a young age by her parents, this would have been considered degrading. Even after years in San Francisco, Foon Chuck was still shocked whenever he saw men and women walking arm in arm on the streets, something that would be considered disgraceful back home. He found it hard to conceive that women were almost equal in their positions to men, and he wondered what would happen if Chinese women were so free and educated.

What Foon Chuck liked most about the Western way of life was the Sunday rest, which he thought to surely be the sign of an advanced and wealthy civilization. After church, he was allowed to return to the home of his uncle, who unfortunately did not always follow this particular Western tradition, forcing his nephew to study Chinese and help him with his work.

Foon Chuck enjoyed discussing business with his uncle, a subject he thought even more important than those he studied in the missionary school. But what he liked most was to practice calligraphy and to read in Chinese with him, something he could not do with Reverend Loomis. He would continue to study and revere those precious Chinese ideograms all his life; they remained for him an essential link with his native country and culture. To be literate in the Confucian classics, a Chinese scholar must master more than 5,000 characters—a lifelong endeavor. At the turn of the century, San Francisco's Chinatown counted at least six Chinese daily newspapers,[14] and Foon Chuck enjoyed reading the Chinese news with his uncle and cousins, a habit he kept all his life. Newspapers were rented, resold, loaned and passed from one migrant to the other until they became unreadable shreds of paper. They were often read aloud to groups of illiterate workers, constituting for them an important connection with their homeland. There is an ancient Chinese tradition of collecting old written papers, either calligraphed or printed, incinerating them and throwing their ashes into the sea, instead of mixing them with vulgar household waste.[15] Like in many Chinese cities, this tradition was followed in San Francisco's Chinatown, whose streets were dotted with wooden boxes in which to deposit old papers, highlighting the reverence for literacy and education, as well as the desire to maintain ancient customs, among the Chinese residents, even so far away from home.[16]

Chinese immigrants faced negative stereotypes in the United States. Their leaders were described as despotic; Cantonese merchants were portrayed as cunning and dishonest; and the Chinese generally were described as immoral, polygamous, pagan, misogynistic, inveterate gamblers and enemies of progress, killing their baby girls and binding their feet. Of course, female infanticide was a crime in China, but it was still practiced across the country, to the extent that there were complaints by magistrates that "girls are becoming so scarce and expensive, that the common people cannot afford to marry, and public morals are endangered."[17] Western missionaries in China used to leave woven baskets next to rivers with signs instructing parents to deposit unwanted babies there. On footbinding, the prominent Chinese reformer Kang Youwei, who campaigned against the practice, observed:

> All countries have international relations so that if one makes the slightest mistake, the others ridicule him and look down on him. Ours is certainly not in a period of isolation. Now China is narrow and crowded, sick with opium and with its streets full of beggars. Foreigners make fun of us for these things and blame us for being barbarians. But there is nothing that makes us the object of ridicule as much as foot binding.[18]

> [Westerners are] strong and vigorous because their mothers do not bind their feet and therefore have strong offspring.[19]

In this context, much of the US populace believed that Chinese migrants could never assimilate into the United States—and, in particular, into white society. In the nineteenth century, those negative views were not limited to ordinary people but were also spread by leading Western intellectuals, including Ralph W. Emerson, Horace Greeley and John Stuart Mill.[20] In truth, Westerners were held in equal contempt on the other side of the Pacific in the Chinese literature of the time.[21]

Chinese in the United States were not allowed to marry white women, attend white public schools, testify against whites in court, or buy land. They were, furthermore, afraid to buy real estate in a country where they could not become citizens or enjoy the full protection of the law. They were discriminated against and banned from working in mining, and this was later extended to other trades.

Except for a dozen northeastern states, most of the Union maintained strict laws against interracial marriage dating back to before the Civil War. Interracial marriage therefore remained a marginal phenomenon during the nineteenth and early twentieth centuries in the United States. These anti-miscegenation laws were not repealed in California until 1948, and continued to be enforced in most southern states until 1968, including in Texas and Florida. Until the early 1960s, more than ninety per cent of the US population were against mixed marriages.[22] In 1926, Wu Jingchao, a sociologist who studied at Qinghua University and the University of Chicago, identified mixed marriage as an essential feature of overseas Chinese communities around the world, from Mexico to Peru and Malacca to Hawaii. He presented the absence of mixed marriages in the continental United States, Canada and Australia as an aberration, only explainable by white racial prejudice.[23]

Being the main port where they disembarked, San Francisco's Chinatown was the de facto capital of the Chinese in the United States, the place where they felt most at home. Many Chinese immigrants settled there and never saw much else of the country. Between 1860 and 1870, San Francisco's Chinese population grew from 3,000 to 12,000, becoming ten per cent of the city's population. This constituted almost one in five Chinese people in California. The figure increased to close to 30,000 in the following decade.[24]

As Arnold Genthe's old photographs show, Chinatown, before the great fire of 1905, was a place almost entirely devoid of US culture. Many Chinese had their heads shaved, keeping only their pigtails, a custom imposed by the Manchus as a symbol of submission and initially abhorred in China, but which quickly turned into an accepted tradition. In the United States, pigtails even became a badge of Chinese identity and an indication that the migrants wanted to return home one day. In early-twentieth-century China, Western-educated Han Chinese started cutting their pigtails as an act of defiance and a symbol of modernity. The act was decried as immoral by conservatives and they were labelled "fake foreign devils."[25] In contrast, some migrants to the United States wore their traditional dress—robes for men and trousers for women—giving white Americans further apparent proof that the Chinese did everything the wrong way around.[26] A visiting Chinese diplomat noted in his diary that Chinatown looked surprisingly like the city of Canton and that less than one per cent of its people wore Western clothes.[27] The buildings, too, were specific to Chinatown, being Western in their structure but decorated with Chinese signs and lanterns, and hosting pawnshops, curio stores, opium dens, gambling houses, temples, fortune tellers, boarding houses, herbalists, houses of ill repute and theaters playing shows day and night. Migrants were fond of street performances, of the kind they remembered from their villages in China, and they kept actors and acrobats in high demand.

The truth was that many Chinese planned to return home and for this reason rarely adopted the ways of the United States. A journalist wrote of Chinatown that, "I never saw a foreign population so utterly, and one might say unalterably, isolated from all the native community around him as he and his fellows here seem to be."[28] Sacramento Street, the main street in the heart of San Francisco's Chinatown, was called by the immigrants "The street of the men of Tang."[29] During the Tang Dynasty (618–907 CE), the region of Kwangtung was incorporated into the Chinese empire and since then southerners have called themselves "men of Tang." The Tang Dynasty was recognized as the most brilliant in China's history, and so this became a way for the migrants to celebrate their origins in the face of racism and abuses.[30] Every Chinatown in the world, from Paris to London, is still today called "the street of the men of Tang" by overseas Chinese, just like the old Sacramento Street.

San Francisco's immigrants had precarious living conditions. Most had no room of their own, with two or three men working and then sleeping in shifts, on shared makeshift bunks in their workplace—often an underground and windowless cellar, later concealed behind a false door or hatch, to hide illegal immigrants. There were almost twenty-seven Chinese men for every Chinese woman in the United States, making it almost impossible for Chinese migrants to start families. This absence of family life and households resulted in many Chinese migrants succumbing to the vices of opium, gambling and prostitution, and was one of the main reasons why they could not assimilate, unlike other migrant groups.

Chinatown was not, however, a society of bachelors. In 1890, half of the Chinese in the United States were married, but ninety per cent of them to spouses who lived in China and who they rarely or never saw. In traditional Chinese culture, even women with unbound feet rarely left the house and they traveled even less. It was therefore not only prohibitively expensive but simply culturally unthinkable for most migrants to bring their Chinese spouses to the United States. In 1870, seven out of ten Chinese women in San Francisco were prostitutes,[31] most of them having been kidnapped in China or sold by their families and trafficked to the United States. They soon exceeded 2,000 women, working in appalling and unsanitary conditions, close to slavery, many dying of exhaustion and venereal diseases, abandoned by all. With so few Chinese women in California, they often earned a fortune for their employers—money the women themselves never saw—with their Chinese and white customers willing to pay weeks' worth of wages to spend a short time with them. Very few of them were allowed to buy their freedom and settle outside Chinatown, but there were exceptions, like the intrepid Polly Bemis, who married a white settler, later gaining standing in her community in the state of Idaho.[32]

As early as 1875, the Page Act controlled the immigration of Asian women "for immoral purposes," meaning that would-be female Chinese immigrants had to demonstrate their morality before being allowed into the United States. Reverend Loomis organized a shelter for Chinese prostitutes at his church, strongly advocating their cause with the US public. He argued that they could still "return to virtue" by marrying Chinese men who were, after all, desperate for wives and who did not see them as "fallen women" but instead as virtuous daughters who had dutifully obeyed their families' wishes.

Male Chinese immigrants to the United States who could not build a family there were not necessarily left without heirs. It was common practice to adopt (sometimes by buying) boys and young men, who would carry one's name forward. These adopted sons either stayed in the ancestral village in China to continue the family lineage there, or later joined their fathers in the New World. The Chinese were criticized for their lack of family values, but the main reason they were in the United States was to escape starvation and to meet the needs of their families in China, for whom they were sacrificing themselves. As a Chinese saying puts it, "a bitter life is better than a comfortable death."[33] Chinese migrants' alienation from US society can hence be contrasted with their strong community ties and transnational family bonds, which were often invisible to outsiders.[34]

The difference between Chinese migrants in the United States, living in poverty, and the upper-class white migrants in British Hong Kong, living lives of privilege, could not be greater. But both were largely male migrants far away from their homes, and products of a shared and turbulent history. Like a distorting mirror, they share striking similarities in the way they led their solitary lives across the globe. A British missionary in South China wrote of his compatriots in Hong Kong that they lived "a life without families, adhering to their English Club system," had a "low state of morality," and "a national drinking habit," living near "the gambling dens of Macao and Kowloon."[35] A reverend wrote of the English in Kwangtung that "hardly a foreigner devotes an hour to learn the language of the Chinese, the effect [being] to keep the two parties totally separated from each other in all those offices of kindness, sympathy, regard, and friendship."[36] In truth, until the Opium War, the Imperial government had banned the teaching of Chinese to foreigners, fearing their influence. This was an era full of absurdities and ironies, one in which modern transport had allowed mass migrations in every direction and on every continent, spreading a similar sense of alienation across the globe.

* * *

In 1880, five years after Foon Chuck, Hing arrives in San Francisco. He and his fellow passengers are received by compatriots from their respective districts near Canton. As they leave the docks of the Pacific Mail Steamship Company, Hing is surprised and reassured by the large number of Chinese around him speaking his village dialect, and he feels as if he has not entirely left China. All the same, San Francisco is utterly different from Chinese cities: Hing is puzzled by the absence of protective walls, and wonders whether there are no bandits in the United States. He stares at the first Westerners he sees, finding it hard to imagine how men can walk in such strange and tight trousers, wondering how far they can bend their knees or how they manage to stand back up if they fall. The Chinese are used to squatting for many of their daily activities, including to eat, work, prepare their food, rest and go to the toilet, and their loose robes are well suited for this. Since they were not used to squatting in this way, the first foreigners in the Middle Kingdom were believed to have only one long bone in their legs and hence to be unable to fully bend their knees. Some of the Americans are red-haired and green-eyed, with faces covered in hair, making discordant sounds when they speak: truly a look and a language of devils, Hing thinks. The sound of English makes an odd combination with the clickety-clack of the Americans' leather shoes, which look even more uncomfortable than their clothes. Like Foon Chuck, what Hing finds most intriguing are the foreign women in their wide robes sweeping the ground, which he finds so inappropriate and indecent compared to the trousers Chinese women wear. He notices how fast they walk with their large feet, often looking determined and commanding.

Hing is told that he is too young and frail to work in mining or the railroad. He is brought to a laundry and introduced to its owner Ah Fong, to whom he will be an apprentice for three years. He wishes he could earn more money, but his body is still too fragile and weak for hard labor. Laundries are one of the few trades still open to the Chinese, laundry work being considered degrading and tedious but essential given that in the frontier state of California women, who might otherwise do the laundry at home, still make up less than eight per cent of the population. Laundries are well suited for the Chinese, not requiring much capital, know-how or use of the English language. At the end of the nineteenth century, twenty per cent of the Chinese in California work in laundries, compared to eleven per cent as cooks, ten per cent as merchants, and ten per cent in mines. Soon, laundries open in most cities throughout the United States, becoming the main occupation of the Chinese in these places.

Ah Fong comes from the same district in China as Hing and is a member of the Sze Yap Company, an organization that represents all immigrants from the four districts southwest of Canton, including Hoksaan and Chaitong, and which controls most of San Francisco's laundries (most are also members of the laundrymen's guild). Despite the distance, Hing still feels his close connection with China, because of his debt, his membership of the Sze Yap

Company, and this vast network of fellow countrymen supporting each other. Observing that Hing is a dedicated worker, Ah Fong does not treat him badly, but makes him work more than fourteen hours daily, almost without rest days. Hing spends his first two years lifting heavy bags of laundry, sorting, marking, and placing the clothes into large vats, where they are heated and washed throughout the day. The clothes have often been worn continuously for months, their dirt and unbearable stench reminding him of the beggars near his village. Before deducting expenses, his salary barely exceeds $10 a month (about $300 in today's money) which is used entirely to repay his debt. Despite the risk of aggression by the city's many young thugs, known to unleash their dogs on the Chinese, Hing is often asked to deliver clean laundry to nearby addresses in Chinatown and beyond, carrying it in large bundles on his shoulders hanging on a pole, as in China. These walks outside the laundry terrify him but also give him rare moments of freedom, each being an adventure and affording him an opportunity to observe the strange Westerners. He wonders what is more dangerous, venturing outside of Chinatown and facing the white devils or outside of his village in China and risking being robbed by bandits.

Ah Fong explains to Hing that there are more than 2,000 laundries in San Francisco[37] with 5,000 Chinese compatriots working in them, which he has a hard time imagining. What a strange place this is, he thinks, as there is not a single laundry in the whole of China, where washing is the work of housewives and servants. The laundry functions almost twenty-four hours a day with another apprentice working while Hing sleeps in the back of the shop. As one of his sons later recalled, Hing kept dreadful memories of the steamy and dusty air saturated with coal particles constantly congesting his lungs, as well as of the water leaking through the ceiling, drop by drop, not letting him sleep even when he was exhausted after a long and hard day. In his third year, he finally has the responsibility of holding the heavy irons, weighing eight pounds, which are heated over coal stoves, quickly immersed in water, and applied onto the clothes. At first Hing fears getting burned, but Ah Fong is a good teacher, and Hing is soon able to iron the clothes by himself. What he fears most, though, is not burning himself but scorching the customers' precious shirts, as any damage will be deducted from his meager pay, lengthening his servitude even further.

* * *

Lacking family units, defenseless, without religious communities, and unable to speak English, many migrants had no choice but to turn to Chinese secret societies or triads to find work or simply a sense of belonging. Triads acted like mafias and were frequently involved in illegal activities, including drug-dealing, illegal gambling and prostitution, fighting each other for control of these lucrative trades, and often exploiting the very migrants they were supposed to protect. Hing, Ah Fong and their fellow workers sadly realized that some of their own compatriots had turned into their worst oppressors, gaining from their work and prolonging their servitude. To avoid aggression, Ah Fong had to pay the triads hefty protection fees, while Hing was asked to contribute a small share of his wages. The triads, built along clan lines from back in China, fought for influence and power, displaying disunity and narrowness of mind and reproducing violence from their home provinces in China.

This, plus the fact that the Chinese spent their salaries in Chinatown or sent them directly back home, did not endear them to the locals, causing further alienation. The Chinese thereby came to be regarded by many as lacking moral values, as prone to infighting, and as naturally servile, with the men willing to work in quasi-slavery and the women willing to prostitute themselves. Chinese men were further depicted as effeminate since they did women's work like cleaning and cooking,[38] often lacked facial hair, still wore their robes and pigtails, and mostly lived celibate lives. Beyond harsh living conditions, the migrant experience in the United States was therefore marked by alienation, profound solitude, and lack of a spiritual life. During his visit to San Francisco in 1903, Liang Qichao (1873–1929), the well-known exiled politician and disciple of Kang Youwei, himself from a farmer-scholar family from the Sze Yap region, deplored that his overseas compatriots were merely clan members and not citizens of a nation, with a "slave mentality,"[39] unable to organize politically, lacking ideals and not yet ready to live in a democracy.[40] He added that "The Chinese people can only be governed autocratically [...]. They cannot enjoy freedom."[41] This opinion, coming from a Chinese intellectual, sounds harsh and cruel today, given the difficult and solitary lives of his compatriots. However, Liang Qichao, who was a fervent Chinese nationalist, later praised Chinese emigrants for being "humble and diligent, initiators of civilization, of an expansive and vigorous race, and a contrast to whites, who are arrogant and dislike hard work,"[42] a line which served his political agenda.

San Francisco's Chinatown was governed by the Six Chinese Companies,[43] a benevolent organization founded in the 1850s, which must be distinguished from the triads. These six companies were run by the richest and most educated merchants from the six different regions around Canton, where eighty per cent of the Chinese migrants came from. Foon Chuck's uncle played an important role in the Sze Yap Company, the first and largest of the six companies, to which Hing and Ah Fong belonged. Upon disembarking, new migrants were encouraged to register and pay their annual dues to become members, often not having a choice if they wanted to keep their employment. In principle, the companies were volunteer organizations that helped Chinese migrants come to the United States and return to China, provided a social safety net by caring for sick and hungry migrants, provided them with loans and protection, found them jobs, helped with legal problems, enabled them to send money to their families in China, protected them from racist abuses, opened schools and temples, and tried to deter prostitution, encouraging migrants to lead a moral life. They also arranged for the return to China of corpses for burials.

Even migrants who could not afford a journey back home during their lifetime usually made sure that they saved the two dollars necessary for their corpses to be buried in China, being unable to imagine a more dreadful condition than for their spirit to roam in a strange land, homeless, uncared for and unfed.[44] They believed that their only path to the spirit world was through the soil in China and they feared otherwise that their physical graves, often segregated in American cemeteries, would be vandalized. The return of the bones of Chinese immigrants' corpses began in 1855, initiating thousands of transpacific journeys to repatriate bones over the next hundred years. Americans were often outraged by the Chinese practice of exhuming dead bodies to extract the bones to be sent to China, and they tried to legislate against it. By 1913, 10,000 coffins were being sent annually from the United States to China, and this continued until the Communist Revolution of 1949, when coffins piled up on the San Francisco docks, unable to make the journey anymore.[45]

The Six Chinese Companies also had a darker side, having some of the attributes of the triads. They profiteered from migrants, kept tabs on their debts, and would not let them return to China before these were repaid. Perversely, while the Chinese were denied fundamental legal rights by the United States, the Six Chinese Companies were criticized for establishing their own tribunals and rendering justice to their members, sometimes violently. This meant that they bypassed the US civil courts, leading them to be accused of lawlessness. A visiting Englishman wrote that, "[The Chinese] is law-abiding against the whites, but within Chinatown every kind of lawless outrage goes hardly checked."[46] The Six Chinese Companies were also represented by white American lawyers, who assisted them in their dealings with the US government. Before the first Chinese consul was appointed in San Francisco in the 1880s, they constituted the de facto representative of the Chinese government in the city. Although there were benevolent institutions in China—like asylums, hospices and hospitals—the Six Chinese Companies, a private and volunteer organization, ironically in many ways offered more social services for the diaspora abroad than the government of the bankrupt, corrupt and decadent Qing Dynasty did in China itself.

* * *

On a hot summer day in 1877, having just turned fourteen, Foon Chuck witnesses San Francisco's Chinese population start to panic as a mob of thousands of angry protesters attempt to throw them out of the city. He has never before seen an anti-Chinese riot. Reverend Loomis warns the students to stay indoors but also reassures them that they are safe inside the school, as a place dedicated to God. Foon Chuck's home province of Kwangtung is well known for being a place of endemic violence between rival clans, but he had never himself been one of the targets of the violence. The experience drives home to him that not all Americans are like the missionaries. For two days, the violence continues unabated on the streets outside Chinatown, and on the third, the crowd is finally dispersed by the US Navy.

Foon Chuck was later to learn from his uncle that the protesters killed four Chinese and set fire to twenty-five Chinese laundries. Since the Six Chinese Companies had asked for the protection of the municipality, Chinatown escaped the vandalism, guarded by the army, the police, and a brigade of 5,000 citizen volunteers, fearful of the workers' party taking power in the city. The government was bound to protect the Chinese under the Burlingame Treaty, and so it later paid compensation to the victims, proof that the United States was still ruled by law. Foon Chuck feels grateful to Reverend Loomis and the many Americans defending his compatriots, but wonders with horror what would have happened without them, fearing that things will become increasingly difficult for the Chinese in the United States in the years to come.

4

A VANISHED DREAM

As the United States' economic boom ended in the 1870s and 1880s, the economic depression, coupled with a steady stream of new migrants from Central Europe, worsened US attitudes towards foreigners and the Chinese in particular. With the completion of the Pacific Central Railroad in 1869, 10,000 Chinese became unemployed overnight, and so started to compete with white Americans for manufacturing jobs. By 1870, the Chinese constituted one in twelve people in California, and one in four workers.[1] In 1875, when Foon Chuck arrived in San Francisco, the economic crisis and the resulting stock market crash helped push California's unemployment rate to nearly thirty per cent,[2] causing misery for many Americans.

Despite the crisis and repeated warnings from the Six Chinese Companies not to keep coming, in 1870–75 more than 80,000 Chinese immigrants arrived in the United States,[3] encouraged by the new steamships making the crossing more affordable. Due to famines in China, the flow of Chinese migrants to the United States reached its peak in the 1870s.

Warning of the "yellow peril," the *New York Times* described "the risk of California becoming a huge Chinese colony," adding that, "If there were to be a floodtide of Chinese population—a population befouled with all the social vices, with no knowledge or appreciation of free institutions, or constitutional liberty [...]—we should be prepared to bid farewell to republicanism and democracy."[4] California senator John F. Miller warned that if forced to compete with the thrifty Chinese, whom he compared to machines, white men and their families would be reduced like them to "misery, want, self-denial, ignorance and dumb slavery,"[5] Labor leader Denis

Kearney who brandished the slogan "the Chinese must go," also allegedly stated: "There is no means left to clear the Chinamen but to swing them into eternity by their own queues, for there is no rope long enough in all America wherewith to strangle four hundred millions of Chinamen."[6] In the 1870s, the United States turned its back not only on Chinese migrants but on the whole of China, the value of its trade with China having fallen from nine million dollars in 1864 to only one million dollars in 1865, as most US companies doing business in the Middle Kingdom had already closed their doors.[7]

In 1876, the Six Chinese Companies wrote a short but passionate plea to President Ulysses Grant, defending the Chinese contribution to the United States and responding to the various criticisms made against them (see Appendix). The Chinese also had protectors, including railway barons, industrialists, merchants, missionaries and simply honest people dismayed by their unfair treatment. Not all politicians were against them: some in Washington D.C. preferred to keep friendly commercial relationships with China and opposed the xenophobic politicians on the west coast. But in the face of a crisis-stricken economy and mostly hostile public opinion, they could not prevent the adoption of a series of anti-Chinese laws. In 1879, the California state constitution forbade municipal companies from recruiting Chinese workers, and even allowed cities to segregate them into certain neighborhoods. In 1880, the year of Hing's arrival, the Treaty of Burlingame was amended, now limiting the number of Chinese immigrants allowed into the country. Finally, in May 1882, Congress passed the infamous Chinese Exclusion Act, the first legislation of its kind, which prohibited all Chinese immigration to the United States, initially for a period of ten years, with exceptions for teachers, students, tourists and certain merchants. There was a specific ban on Chinese women. According to the Chinese-American activist and journalist Helen Zia, this legislation inhibited Asian American political development for decades.[8] In addition to racial discrimination, the legislation discriminated according to social class and sex, distinguishing between what were considered good and bad migrants. For the first time in US history, an illegal residency status was clearly defined, turning the country into a "gatekeeping nation," as described by historian Erika Lee.[9]

As a result, the flow of Chinese migrants was reduced from tens of thousands a year to just a few hundred. In 1888, the right of return to the United States for Chinese already settled in the country was canceled, leaving thousands of Chinese stranded outside of the country. This was the same year that the Statue of Liberty was unveiled in New York City's harbor with the following words on its pedestal:

> "Keep, ancient lands, your storied pomp!" cries she
> With silent lips. "Give me your tired, your poor,
> Your huddled masses yearning to breathe free,
> The wretched refuse of your teeming shore.
> Send these, the homeless, tempest-tost to me,
> I lift my lamp beside the golden door!"[10]

But in 1885, outraged that the Chinese immigrants had been asked to contribute funds for the building of the statue, a Chinese American activist wrote in *The Sun* (New York City):

> Whether this statute against the Chinese or the statue of Liberty will be the more lasting monuments to tell future ages of the liberty and greatness of this country, will be known only to future generations. Liberty, we Chinese do love and adore thee; but let not those who deny thee to us, make of thee a graven image and invite us to bow down to it.[11]

* * *

During these troubled years, Foon Chuck remains relatively protected inside Reverend Loomis' home and school. But in 1878, after three years of study, he decides to leave school when a cousin finds him a job as a waiter at the Jackson Hotel on California Street.[12] Aged fifteen, he wants to gain practical work experience while continuing to improve his English. He enjoys his new job, where he meets new people every day, and he is astonished by American society. Of course, the United States has huge social inequality and rampant racial discrimination, but in comparison to China it seems to him to be a much more equal and open society. His clients are willing to chat freely with him, a simple migrant waiter, about their lives and occupations. He doubts that this could ever happen in China, where foreigners are seen as barbarians and servants treated as inferiors, taught since a young age to accept their low status as fate, with little chance of advancement. Foon Chuck wonders whether this spirit of equality is a result of the Westerners' religion. In any case, it is a spirit certainly bound to cause chaos and revolution in China if applied there.

Hotel guests are surprised to see and hear a Chinese boy express himself in such good English and with such self-confidence and good manners, as well as having a Western-style haircut. Most of the other Chinese they meet in the docks or along the railway have pigtails and are unable to utter a single English word. Many Chinese do not dare speak or even practice English, fearing that Westerners will make fun of them. Of course, this alienates them further from US society. On the contrary, feeling himself to be in a privileged position, Foon Chuck enjoys conversing with his clients, trying to prove them wrong in their prejudices against his people. He becomes more optimistic about his future in this country. He is curious to learn about the careers of the guests in the hotel and the guests enjoy telling him about their jobs, tipping him generously. He sees this job as another learning opportunity—one that cannot be found in books. He tries to learn from everything he does, thinking of the Chinese proverb, "if three of us walk along, one of my companions will be my teacher."[13]

Despite this early professional success, after consulting with Reverend Loomis, his uncle wisely decides that his generous tips are not a good enough reason to stop studying and that he should return to his missionary school and the service of Reverend Loomis for another three years until his maturity.[14] Both agree that it would be a waste of his intellectual abilities if he abandoned school so early.

Now fluent in English, Foon Chuck can enjoy the school's broad and enlightened curriculum, including history, philosophy, physiology, government and astronomy, subjects he could have never studied in China.[15] He also enjoys arithmetic, finding that he can count faster with his abacus than any of his teachers. The most popular of all classes in the school is geography, which has an American-Chinese teacher, and which will undoubtedly influence the young Foon Chuck in his future transnational career.

* * *

Foon Chuck was grateful to Reverend Loomis' family for recognizing and developing his intellect, and he felt a special emotional bond with them. They believed that Jesus had given him a gift for learning, which should not be wasted, and Foon Chuck would not contradict them on this point. Seeing Foon Chuck well versed in US culture and having mastered the English language, Reverend Loomis felt vindicated in his missionary work. In addition to Christian values, he had sought to share with Foon Chuck what he took to be the specifically US ideals of self-reliance, indomitable energy, progress and science, hoping that when Foon Chuck returned to China he would spread these values there. Six years earlier, the first group of Chinese students to attend American schools on Chinese imperial scholarships did not share Foon Chuck's fortune. Their scholarships were cancelled, as their Imperial sponsor "felt alarmed at the rapid rate [at which] the students were becoming imbued with the spirit of their environment—they were developing into more like go-ahead Americans in their ways than the humble and sedate subjects of the emperor ... The students would soon fast turn into foreign devils unless sent home at once."[16]

At first, Foon Chuck was not sure what to think of Jesus and of Christianity, which was completely foreign to him. He enjoyed hearing biblical stories, but he could not understand why Jesus had not taken steps to ensure that his message was heard in China earlier. He also found it hard to comprehend the concept of original sin and that Jesus died for his father on the cross, a contradiction with the Chinese concept of ancestor lineage and worship. From a young age, he had been taught that to earn the respect of his family he had to honor his ancestors and be compassionate, which was not in contradiction with Jesus' teachings. He could not help feeling moved by Reverend Loomis' doctrine of Christian love, and was in awe that this family had welcomed him, a foreigner, amongst them. Perhaps, he thought, Christianity was the reason why Westerners were so prosperous, fostering trust between people of different backgrounds, allowing economic exchange and the development of society. But, as before, Foon Chuck did not dwell on these spiritual questions for long. His main concern was to prove to his family back in China that they were right to trust him.

In 1881, aged eighteen, it was time for Foon Chuck to leave his American foster family. He thanked them and they promised to pray that he would stay on a righteous path all his life. Aware of the privilege of having been introduced to Western culture and spirituality under their care, he felt optimistic that he could get on among Westerners and do business with them. He now understood how they thought, having already lived a third of his life in the United States. He did not yet feel entirely Christian or ready to renounce his Chinese beliefs, but he certainly felt touched and even transformed by the principles, love and exemplary life of his adoptive family.

Of course, Foon Chuck's case was an exception. By the end of the century, despite proselytizing efforts, only 1,931 out of 120,000 Chinese migrants had joined the Protestant Church in the United States,[17] and most who joined were among the poorest immigrants. Reverend Loomis' Presbyterian church counted less than 130 members. It did attract many curious Chinese to its Sunday services, which became a spectacle for passing Western tourists, but, faced with increasing amounts of hostility in a xenophobic US society, few of these attendees felt compelled to become regular church members.

In a tragic irony, US politicians used the lack of Chinese Christian conversions as evidence that the Chinese immigrants would never assimilate into society, and on this basis they pressed on with their exclusionary laws. Nevertheless, over his thirty-two years in San Francisco, Reverend Loomis never abandoned his fight to provide a spiritual haven for Chinese migrants, arguing passionately that his proselytizing work could not be reduced to numbers of conversions alone and would be proven right on judgement day. As he put it, "All [God] makes us responsible for is [...] faithful preaching, whether men will hear or [...] forbear."[18] Reverend Loomis' unwavering faith was a rare beacon of hope in the midst of the racial and physical violence pervasive in US society at the time. He would prove to be an exemplary model for Foon Chuck all his life. The 1904 Encyclopedia of Missions wrote posthumously of Reverend Loomis that "his whole [academic] work has been of the highest value. He was a man of great intellectual attainments," while one of his friends gave a more personal eulogy:

> Nature gave him a strong, brave, and manly soul. Divine grace and truth had quickened, purified and enlightened his conscience [...]. With him the one supreme thing was duty. He was not ambitious,

A VANISHED DREAM

had no aspirations beyond doing his work [...]. His religion before the world consisted in the faithful performance of duty.[19]

Having finished his schooling, Foon Chuck at first returned to his ancestral village in China for five months to visit his family. On the ship to China, thinking that he had finally left behind the hundred gambling dens of Chinatown, he despaired when he saw many of his returning companions spend the days gambling their savings, so hard-earned during their stay in America. These savings they kept jealously in narrow wooden boxes of eighteen inches, which they also used as pillows, all being distrustful of each other and yet willing to lose their money to fate. Foon Chuck read the Bible and other stories to his fellow passengers to distract them, but also, following Reverend Loomis' example, to transform them, hoping that one day his companions would lose their habits of gambling and smoking. Back in Chaitong, Foon Chuck told his relatives about the differences but also the similarities between Chinese people and Westerners, as well as the commercial opportunities offered by the United States, which he now felt ready to exploit so that he could finally bring honor to his clan. During his stay, Foon Chuck's parents arranged for him to get married.[20] But the young couple did not spend much time together as, after only five months in China, Foon Chuck was already on his way back to America. Marrying migrants before their departure, or in this case on a return trip home, was a normal practice, which created stronger ties between the migrant and his ancestral village, and provided ageing parents with relatives to take care of them. Moreover, until the Communist Revolution of 1949, it remained legal in China to have several wives, explaining why migrants in the Americas were accused of bigamy.

Accompanied by several relatives, Foon Chuck returned to San Francisco in 1882, the year of the Chinese Exclusion Act. His ship was seized by immigration authorities, and, according to one of his grandchildren, he had to be smuggled into the country. The Exclusion Act had suddenly closed the doors on the Chinese, and Foon Chuck wondered with dread whether he would be able to stay and work, now that he had already spent six years and made lasting friendships in the country.

While the Exclusion Act was now in effect, it would take several decades before a proper immigration enforcement service became fully functional. This explains why, emboldened by the act, many US citizens decided to take immigration matters into their own hands. Anti-Chinese riots took place in fifty-five cities besides San Francisco in the western United States.[21] The scattered violence of the 1870s was becoming a systematic purge of the Chinese in an epidemic of mass roundups, expulsions, arson and murder.[22] A Chinese migrant who worked as a servant and later became a pastor wrote that:

> The Chinese were in a pitiable condition in those days. We were simply terrified; we kept indoors after dark for fear of being shot in the back. Children spit upon us as we passed by and called us rats. However, there was one consolation: the people who employed us never turned against us, and we went on quietly with our work until the public frenzy subsided.[23]

In 1885, the worst atrocity occurred in the mining town of Rock Springs, Wyoming, where 500 Chinese, hired first in 1875 to replace striking workers, were now refusing to join white miners in a strike for increased wages. In the ensuing riots, twenty-eight Chinese workers were killed (eleven of them burned alive in their cabins), fifteen others wounded, and the rest thrown out of the city,[24] without a single conviction for the rioters. Chinese workers were driven away from their homes and cities, and warned never to return, otherwise they would be shot or hanged. In that same year, in Tacoma, Washington, between 800 and 900 Chinese were expelled by a mob of 500 armed men with the police standing by and the mayor reportedly participating in the evictions.[25] One of those responsible, Judge Wickersham, still remembered several years later: "We did a great and good work [...]. If given equal chance, the Chinese would outdo us and gain possession of the Pacific Coast, we cannot compete with them, not because of their baser qualities, but because of their better."[26] At the time, the Chinese represented less than one per cent of the state of Washington's population. In 1886 alone, following evictions and violence, 20,000 victims fled the small towns and countryside of California to take refuge in San Francisco's Chinatown, a real ghetto but somewhere they knew they would be safe. The Chinese were time and again criticized for breaking strikes and so being against the workers and on the side of the exploiters.

A VANISHED DREAM

Of course, this treatment of the Chinese, like the treatment of several other groups in US society, undermined the US self-image of a melting pot nation. The Scottish author Robert Louis Stevenson was horrified by the contempt in which white Americans held the Chinese, whose forbearance in the face of the cruelest insults he could only admire,[27] while Mark Twain wrote in 1895:

> I was never disposed to make fun of the Chinaman; I always looked upon him as a pathetic object; a poor, hardworking, industrious, friendless heathen, far from home, amongst a strange people, who treated him none too well. He has a hard life, and is always busy and always sober, therefore I never could see anything to make fun of in the Chinaman. No, he is not wanted in America. The feeling is that he ought to go, but America is a place for all people, it seems.[28]

In 1882, Foon Chuck's uncle offered him the chance to use his language skills to start a business in San Francisco. Although flattered and thankful to his uncle for his help all these years, he refused. San Francisco was simply too crowded and badly affected by the economic crisis. Foon Chuck missed his village, and longed for a pastoral life, away from a crowded city where his countrymen were addicted to opium, prostitution and gambling, vices he had repeatedly promised Reverend Loomis and his uncle he would stay away from. This refusal of the offer of an elder demonstrated his independence of mind and self-confidence. He had heard that there were better business opportunities in Texas, along the border with Mexico, where the railroad had just been completed and everything else remained to be built. He therefore took the opposite direction to many of his compatriots, who were fleeing the violence across the Pacific coast to take refuge in Chinatown. He was not afraid to venture out alone, having a hunch that his fate would be decided on the virgin and bordering territories of the southern United States, and thinking of the Chinese adage, "the teachers open the doors, but you enter by yourself."[29]

Thus, in 1882, Foon Chuck borrowed money from a cousin, jumped into a stagecoach, and after a journey of twenty days arrived in El Paso, Texas, a typical boomtown on the Mexican border. At the connecting point for the South Pacific, Texas Pacific, and Topeka Santa Fe railroads, its population grew from less than 500 people in the 1870s to more than 10,000 in 1890. The city became wild and violent, with prostitution and gambling reigning supreme; it was named the "Six Shooter Capital" because of its anarchy.

Foon Chuck was dismayed to find that he had moved away from the vices of San Francisco's Chinatown only to find an even more godless and lawless place. He did not know what to make of the Wild West, his education in a missionary school not having prepared him for such a violent life. While Kwangtung province was corrupt and dangerous, it still belonged to the Chinese empire, and so did not have the same level of lawlessness as El Paso, which both scared him and gave him a strange sense of freedom. Every day, he witnessed fights of all kinds; it was hard to figure out who was on the right and who the wrong side of the law, inasmuch as the law had any force. Some Americans mocked him for his short stature, Western dress and bookish looks, and were taken aback when he answered them in refined English. He noted with sadness that racism was not limited to places with large Chinese populations like San Francisco, as he had hoped, but was present everywhere, being a distinctive feature of the whole United States. He now realized how essential his education in San Francisco would be, not only for his future business success but simply for his survival in the Americas. Later in life, he would make sure that his children never forget the importance of speaking different languages and of a good education.

Although the first transcontinental railroad had been completed in 1869, the Southern Pacific Company continued to build the train line between Los Angeles and San Antonio in Texas. This employed Chinese workers, and so Foon Chuck was not the only Chinese person in El Paso. Using his language skills, he got himself hired by the railway company as a cook.[30] This was a demanding job—he was responsible for the daily food of one hundred people—even if it was not as hard as the jobs of many other workers. Of course, this was not the first time Foon Chuck had cooked, having already used his culinary skills while working for Reverend Loomis.

Like most natives of Kwangtung, he had learned to prepare Chinese food from a young age and he would enjoy cooking for his whole life. Chinese immigrants were accustomed to preparing their meals with their own ingredients, many imported from China, including rice, fermented tofu paste, salted vegetables, and all kinds of dried food such as mushrooms, fruits, and seafood, since they could not stand the meat-rich local diet. A well-known Chinese idiom states that "eating cabbage and tofu brings peace to the body."[31] In Chinese culture, good nutrition is known to affect both body and mind, with only proper nourishment ensuring mental alertness, and flavors serving to promote the circulation of the Qi, or vital force. The boundaries between food as medicine and food as nutrition are often blurred to this day.[32] The Chinese dislike drinking cold water, thinking it will make them sick, and the habit of drinking only boiled and hot water, as well as their more balanced diet, made the Chinese railroad workers more resistant to diseases than other workers. Unsanitary living conditions back home in China had also made them more adaptable and resilient in the face of harsh environments, as they proved during the epic construction of the Central Pacific Railway through the Rocky Mountains.

Chinese workers, whether in mining or railway construction, were usually supervised by a bilingual foreman.[33] The foreman was responsible for organizing and managing the tasks of his fellow workers, keeping their accounts, and representing them in negotiations with their employer. Cooks, with their organizational skills, were well-positioned to be foremen and often held that position.[34] Cooks have often played important roles in Chinese history, which of course involves a long tradition of gastronomy. Just as they blend flavors to create harmonies, so they have been compared to leaders who create harmonious societies. Foon Chuck, then, was ideally placed to occupy this function, not only because he was fluent in English and Cantonese, but also because he knew how to write them, a skill that was rare and that won him the respect of his compatriots, which was crucial for a foreman to have. Literate people in China were assumed to be well educated, and so were approached for advice on all sorts of matters.[35] Many migrants, despite their long hours of work, strove all their lives to learn more Chinese characters, hoping that this knowledge might prove useful to them one day, when they would finally return to the land of their ancestors. Illustrating the primordial and transformative nature of that knowledge, the Chinese word for civilization or culture (文化) is made of the two characters meaning "writing" and "transformation." Beyond his culinary contribution, Foon Chuck tried to improve the lives of the workers under his supervision, advising them to cut their pigtails, adopt local customs, save money, and lead moral and spiritual lives. Moreover, in negotiations and arguments with their white bosses, he knew when and how to play the card of his Christian education in order to overcome the cultural distance between them. Foon Chuck loved his job, and considered it worthy and noble, seeing for the first time his purpose in life and why God had sent him to the United States, so far away from his ancestors. In just six months as a cook, he earned enough to repay his cousin and send some money to his parents.

In addition to his work as a cook and foreman, he sought investment opportunities for his family. He felt that El Paso was already too developed for his purposes, and in conversations with several businessmen he was advised to move east along the Mexican border, further from civilization and closer to the US frontier territories. He resigned from his position and, via a ten-day journey by stagecoach, he arrived in Del Rio, more than 400 miles southeast of El Paso. A few days later, he befriended a local businessman named Richard Lombard, who was both intrigued and impressed by such an ambitious young Chinese man. As a committed Christian, Lombard was particularly impressed that Foon Chuck knew about the teachings of Jesus. He encouraged him to preach the gospel to his compatriots, advising him to move further south along the border to another railroad town called Eagle Pass, where he offered to take him. Eagle Pass was another typical US–Mexico border town but with a population of only 3,000 (who were mostly Mexicans) and not yet booming like El Paso. There, Foon Chuck found another job as cook, this time for someone his autobiography names only as Mr Monroe, a Los Angeles businessman whose main interest was a restaurant serving workers building the Mexican train line between Piedras Negras (the Mexican town across the border) and Sabinas, a hundred miles to the south.[36] Foon Chuck enjoyed his work here even more than in El Paso; Monroe treated him as a true partner and this new town was less violent and wild. More importantly, it seemed to Foon Chuck that he may have finally found a place in the United States where he was not subject to racial abuse. The restaurant was so profitable that Monroe decided to open a new branch in town, which he entrusted to Foon Chuck. That same year, Foon Chuck became a founding member of the First Presbyterian Church of Eagle Pass, giving him a loving community and spiritual comfort, and reminding him of his missionary school.

He had arrived at the Mexican border at an opportune time. Mexico's economy had been buoyant since 1881, when the government awarded nine concessions to railway companies, mainly from the United States, to build more than 4,000 miles of railway track, a pharaonic project unprecedented in Mexico's history. This, along with the Chinese Exclusion Act and the economic crisis in the United States, led Foon Chuck, now twenty-one, to learn Spanish, his fourth language after the Sze Yap dialect, Cantonese and English. He then abandoned an earlier plan to move north to San Antonio. He enjoyed conversing with the Mexicans, and, as with English, was convinced that learning this new language would prove to be an important advantage, especially since so few Chinese and Americans spoke it fluently. Mexico, still less developed than the United States, seemed like a place full of possibilities. With the new railway lines, Foon Chuck imagined that in twenty years the Mexican side of the border would be as developed as the US side, and that to get rich he just needed to find the right investments, so that the simple passing of time would make him wealthy.

In 1884 Foon Chuck finally found the investment opportunity he had been looking for. Deploying capital from his San Francisco family, he bought the Central Hotel in Eagle Pass for $700, or $21,000 in today's money. Even though the laws on land purchases by foreigners were less strict in Texas than California, this was still a bold act for a young Chinese who had never invested in his life. His earlier experiences in hospitality in San Francisco, El Paso and most recently in Eagle Pass itself gave him confidence that he could make a success of this investment.

He asked his family to send relatives to manage the property, and two of his cousins joined him from San Francisco a few weeks later. He found the job of hotelier too long and tedious, preferring to delegate it to others so that he could focus his efforts instead on new business opportunities. His San Francisco relatives did not know where to put Eagle Pass on a map but, despite his relative inexperience, they entrusted Foon Chuck with the money, knowing him to be sincere and thoughtful. They were not disappointed: the following year, he sold the hotel to an American family for $1,200, realizing a handsome profit.[37]

He immediately reinvested the capital and started selling Chinese products along the railway line on the Mexican side. He built himself a house near the hotel, which ended up being too large, so he partially converted it into a Chinese curio store. In less than two years, he had gone from being a cook to a restaurant manager, a hotel investor, and now a merchant, showing a keen eye for opportunities in whichever shape they came. A joke told of how Chinese travelers were always slower than those from other nationalities because they stopped all the time, not to admire the landscape, but to look for business ventures. With his aspirations set on Mexico, the Eagle Pass border became his base, and later that of his family for many years to come. He was attracted by its cosmopolitan nature, a border town that seemed to be both of the US and of Mexico, like him at the crossroads of different cultures.

* * *

Meanwhile, in San Francisco, after four years of hard work, Hing has finally settled his debts and part of those of his parents. Work conditions in his laundry continue to be hard, and he suffers from swollen feet, a chronic cough and hand injuries due to the heavy irons he wields all day. But he is better able to endure the work now: his muscles have grown and, most importantly, he finally sees the color of the money he earns.

Unlike Foon Chuck, Hing has no missionary friends, and so his sense of exclusion from US society is more acute. While not understanding the words, he and his companions have learned to recognize racist limericks on the streets, such as: "Ching Chong Chinaman sitting on a rail, along came a white man and snipped off his tail."[38] One day, while he is making a delivery outside Chinatown, young thugs follow him, screaming insults, calling him "Chink," and throwing rubbish at him. Burdened by heavy laundry bags, Hing is terrified, knowing he cannot escape. He is used to insults during his deliveries, but this time the thugs go further, pulling him by his pigtail, throwing him to the ground, and covering his laundry with mud. Hing is not seriously injured, but he has never felt so humiliated and vulnerable in his life. He feels he will never be welcome in this strange continent. He wishes he could defend himself, but he knows that to provoke the thugs would just make things worse, exposing him to greater danger. He has nowhere else to go and no other choice but to endure the torments. Back in China, some people are not only angry but starving, and willing to commit even greater crimes to survive. He takes fortitude from thinking about his family in Kwangtung and invoking the spirit of his ancestors. Hing at this time exemplifies the saying of Laozi: "Being deeply loved by someone gives you strength, while loving someone dearly gives you courage."[39]

* * *

Hing's laundry faced several difficulties by 1884. Ah Fong explained that the foreign devils were trying to close all the laundries in San Francisco and thus drive the Chinese out of the city. First came the rule that all laundries in wooden buildings had to have a license, then came new taxes, and now they were prohibited from carrying laundry bags on poles and their working hours were limited. In 1875 the city had even passed a law ordering that any Chinese person who was arrested must have his pigtail cut off, a great indignity. Some of these laws were successfully challenged in the courts by the San Francisco laundrymen's guild. Ah Fong was bitter about rules that made no sense, and, like the entire population of Chinatown, lived in fear of the next riot or attack.

Having taken a liking to Hing, Ah Fong offered to partner with him and move together to the eastern United States, which was more welcoming to the Chinese than California. In addition, the journey east had become cheaper thanks to the new railway that their compatriots had just completed. But Hing had heard of increasing numbers of violent acts against the Chinese throughout the United States, especially since the Exclusion Act. In 1885, he was advised by friends from Hoksaan to move abroad, and in particular to Mexico, where he could earn more money by working in the booming railway construction sector. All he had to do was to register his interest with the Sze Yap Company in San Francisco, and the railway company would take care of the rest. Hing had never considered Mexico as a possible place of work, but the higher wages, Mexico's milder climate, and the atmosphere of fear in San Francisco convinced him to take that step. Thus, as he turned twenty, Hing bid farewell to Ah Fong and, like Foon Chuck before him, was soon on his way to Mexico. Unlike Foon Chuck, though, Hing was reticent: he was afraid to venture so far away from Chinatown and his people. But he was not alone: he traveled to Mexico with other Chinese workers, all employed on the railway, who would be like his family for the next few years.

In 1883, the year after the passing of the Chinese Exclusion Act, the diplomat Xue Fucheng (1838–94), then the Chinese ambassador to Europe, summarized in his diary his aspirations for China's emigration policies:

> We should sign emigration treaties with Brazil and Mexico for Chinese laborers and establish consulates there for their protection. In these, we must clearly demand fair treatment for our people, even after their work is completed, so that they do not suffer the humiliation of ill-treatment and deportation, which the American authorities have recently imposed on them. Under the protection of our consulates, our people will not be threatened by the natives and will be able to buy land, build houses and raise families there. After several generations, their descendants may even invest in China on account of their heritage. In all likelihood, we will be building a new China outside of China so that our people can prosper in the coming years. This initiative will strengthen our nation, feed our people, reduce our national deficit. It is therefore essential to implement such a policy as soon as possible.[40]

These long-term aspirations were held by many Chinese intellectuals at the time, who often saw emigration as a miracle cure to solve many of China's domestic problems. In 1888, Zhang Yinhuan, China's ambassador to the United States, appalled by and powerless to stop the bad treatment of his compatriots, considered the installation of Chinese migrants in Mexico and Brazil, soliciting the signing of conventions with those two countries. Two years earlier, while visiting San Francisco and meeting the Six Chinese Companies, he was shocked by the immorality of the local Chinese mafias, who were fighting one another and oppressing the migrants. He advised his countrymen to "carry out the practice of people from the same community, respecting each other, to let the other race know that the Chinese look for each other, to avoid being taken advantage of [by other communities]."[41]

A VANISHED DREAM

Zhang Yinhuan was born in Nanhai, like the reformist thinker Kang Youwei. In 1898, now back in Peking, Zhang would be one of the few Qing dynasty civil servants to support Kang's reform movement (see Chapter Nine).[42] The fact that a disproportionate number of progressive Chinese diplomats originated from Kwangtung province is not a coincidence: this was the Chinese province that was most open to the outside world. Two years later, Zhang was assassinated by Chinese conservatives during the Boxer Rebellion,[43] an anti-foreign insurrection in northern China widely covered in the Western press for its massacre of missionaries and Christians, including more than 30,000 Chinese converts, and an event which only increased the alienation of Chinese communities in the United States. This violent anti-colonial uprising and the resulting occupation, looting and atrocities by the Western powers demonstrate how widespread racism and xenophobia were on both sides of the Pacific at the start of the new century.

In 1882, almost 40,000 Chinese immigrants entered the United States; in 1887 only ten did. Due to xenophobic laws and violence, the Chinese population in the United States fell from 106,000 in 1890 to 61,000 in 1920.[44] This was despite the Chinese fighting back in the courts and the streets, with strikes and protests, and many using fictitious birth or immigration documents to get around the laws. Those who remained in the country felt more isolated than ever. The spontaneous violence prevalent at the end of the nineteenth century was progressively stamped out in the twentieth, but was replaced by stricter enforcement from a better staffed US immigration department. All the same, while in 1870 only one per cent of Chinese immigrants to the United States had US citizenship, by 1900 ten per cent did. In 1902, President Theodore Roosevelt, known for his anti-Chinese sentiment, made the Chinese Exclusion Act permanent. In 1903, a Chinese military attaché was violently assaulted and humiliated in San Francisco by two policemen. Released the next day, he committed suicide, unable to stand the indignity he had suffered. His funeral was the largest ever held in Chinatown.[45] In 1905, three high-society Chinese tourists from Shanghai with valid documents were humiliated by immigration officers and denied entry in Boston, creating outrage among both Chinese and US elites. A prominent Chinese

American journalist, Ng Poon Chew, founder of the first Chinese newspaper in America, *Chung Sai Yat Po*, and who later became Foon Chuck's friend, wrote that the Exclusion Law had been "carried out with such vigor that it had almost become an extermination law."[46]

In 1905, the deterioration in the treatment of Chinese immigrants in the United States had implications on the other side of the Pacific, prompting protests and a widespread boycott of US products in most major Chinese cities, at the instigation of Kang Youwei.[47] *The Times of London* reported, "The Chinese have awakened to a consciousness of nationality. Outrages on Cantonese who have emigrated to the Pacific Coast are no longer resented only by the people of Kwangtung. They make all Chinese indignant."[48] A student passing the Imperial Examination in northern China in the previous year remembered being asked to write an essay about the US ban on Chinese immigration.[49] This is suggestive of the growing influence of the diaspora in Chinese public opinion. In a 1906 letter to President Roosevelt, the outraged Kang Youwei, having himself faced difficulties entering the United States, wrote: "The future historian will marvel why the enlightened American, who permits the free dumping of the riff-raff and the off-scouring of Europe, who welcomes the assisted emigration of European paupers and criminals, should single out the Chinese for exclusion."[50] Following those events, while keeping the Exclusion Act in place, Roosevelt made an order that the exempt Chinese classes be treated more cordially and in accordance with the law.

Kang tried to enlist the support of industrialists like John D. Rockefeller and Andrew Carnegie, frustrated that a progressive country like the United States had such bigoted laws. He failed to understand that the anti-Chinese laws were in place not to please the elites he appealed to, but because the United States was a democracy and those laws were popular with the vast majority of the electorate. The Exclusion Act was not abolished until 1942, when China became a war ally of the United States, but restrictions remained in place until the Immigration and Nationality Act of 1965, which prohibited discrimination based on race, sex, nationality, place of birth or residence, and after which immigration from China began again. Almost a century after Foon Chuck and Hing

A VANISHED DREAM

emigrated, members of their families from Hong Kong would be part of that second wave of Chinese migrants to settle—this time successfully—in the United States.

5

SILVER, SILK AND CHILIES

Foon Chuck and Hing were among the first Chinese migrants to enter Mexico, and they had little idea what they would find on the other side of the border. At first, Mexicans were surprised to meet Chinese people; many were unaware of China and confused the migrants with Native Americans or mestizos (people of mixed Indian-European ancestry), trying to speak Indian languages or Spanish with them. This made Foon Chuck and Hing feel like they had entered another world. In fact, China–Mexico relations had a rich and multi-faceted history of nearly 300 years, though few at the time were aware of this, and Foon Chuck and Hing had several things in common with the local inhabitants of their new country.

To begin with, Mexico and China share the same latitude and therefore have various foods in common, both having great world cuisines. Second, 10,000 years ago, the first inhabitants of the American continents, the native Americans, migrated from Asia through the Bering Strait. Therefore, their two people share a common though distant ancestry. Third, on Christopher Columbus' first voyage to the Americas, when he landed off the coast of Mexico, he was looking for and believed he had arrived somewhere near China. In the decades following 1492, until the 1564–65 voyage of Miguel López de Legazpi from Mexico to the Philippines, Spain continued persistently its voyages of exploration to finally arrive in China from the east. Fourth, while in 1880 trade and cultural exchanges between China and Mexico were almost non-existent, in the seventeenth century, when the Chinese and Spanish empires were the two greatest powers on earth, transpacific exchange between the two empires became fundamental for their respective economies and for world trade. This trading relationship continued for some 250 years. During this period, China and Mexico, which then belonged to Spain, were indebted to each other both economically and culturally. As will be explained, Foon Chuck and Hing's own migration two centuries later was partly the result of this history.

Some former Iberian colonies like Mexico differ from the colonies of other European powers by being largely mestizo. Since the beginning of its conquest, religious and political imperatives meant that the Spaniards did not forbid marriages between settlers and natives, and sometimes even encouraged them. As soon as the conquistadores set foot in Mexico, their leader Hernán Cortés fashioned alliances with local tribes by marrying some of his lieutenants with Indian princesses, and many more marriages and extramarital relationships followed. Before the conquest, Mexico was the third most populated territory in the world, but interactions with the conquistadores decimated the Indian population, which went from about twenty-five million to about one million—a ninety-six per cent fatality rate—mostly due to diseases brought by the Spaniards. The Christian colonists tried to make sense of this annihilation of the native Americans: a Spanish Franciscan missionary, Jeronimo de Mendieta, stated that "God is punishing the Spaniards for their harsh labor practices by depriving them of native workers."[1] Further north, an English colonist wrote in 1633 that, "In sweeping the natives, God intends to make room for us here, thereby clearing our title to this place."[2] Whatever God's reasons, by 1650 mestizos already accounted for twenty per cent of the population of Mexico, the second largest ethnicity in the colony;[3] they were shunned by both Indians and Spaniards, the latter debating whether they deserved to be ranked as "people of reason." By 1910, more than half of Mexico's population was mestizo and only around thirty per cent were Indian, a proportion which would continue to decrease. This stands in stark contrast to other colonial empires in North America, Asia and Africa, where very little racial mixing occurred between European settlers and local populations. Carlos Fuentes, the Mexican writer, suggested that this was simply due to racism.[4] Unlike in a predominantly white California, Foon Chuck and Hing could not ignore the fact that not only was their new host country racially mixed, but the natives had common origins with them, which both surprised and somehow reassured them.

SILVER, SILK AND CHILIES

After the seven maritime expeditions of Admiral Zheng He in the early fifteenth century, which brought him into the Indian Ocean and as far as the Persian Gulf, the Ming dynasty turned inwards, prohibiting not only all immigration and emigration but all maritime trade in Southeast Asia, a prohibition called the "Sea Ban."[5] Fearing that free contact with foreigners would lead to plots against the dynasty, the imperial court preferred to concentrate its resources fighting the Mongols; the coastal region of China looked like a dangerous border, bubbling with piracy, smuggling and disorder. Its fears were such that in some areas, the government even banned living settlements within fifteen miles of the coast. In 1567, however, provincial officials in the southern coastal regions, who were more concerned with economic objectives, succeeded in overturning the Sea Ban. From 1644, the new Qing dynasty, ruled by the Manchus, briefly banned maritime trade again, but this ban was permanently lifted in 1727. A nomadic tribe from the northern steppes between Korea and Russia, the Manchus continued to view the coast with suspicion during their reign, the official ban on emigration hence remaining in place until the end of the nineteenth century (see Chapter Two).

Between 1565 and 1815, with the end of the Sea Ban, maritime trade across the Pacific between China and Mexico flourished. The so-called Manila Galleon Trade was centered on the port of Manila in the Philippines, where Chinese merchants came to sell their products. The galleon ships used by the Spaniards were ten times larger than those used by Columbus a century earlier on his voyage to America. Huge quantities of merchandise were involved, and the trade contributed to the beginning of globalization, having a large global economic and cultural impact, spreading across Asia, the Americas and Europe. In the words of one historian, "No other regular navigation has been so trying and dangerous as this, for in its 250 years the sea claimed dozens of ships and thousands of men and many millions in treasure."[6] The eastward passage was especially arduous, taking an average of seven months, while the westward voyage with favourable winds and currents lasted only three. At the height of its power in 1700, the Spanish Empire was so vast that it was called "the empire on which the sun never sets;" the Philippines, seized in 1571, was so remote from Spain that it was administered from Mexico, then called the Viceroyalty of New Spain. At that time, the Spanish Empire had a land area twice as large as the Chinese Empire, but with only half its population.

The Manila Galleon Trade flourished for both political and economic reasons. The ancient Silk Road—the more direct and traditional trade route from Europe to Asia, via the Indian Ocean or the Levant—had become less secure with the rise of the Ottoman Empire. In addition, when the king of Spain became the king of Portugal in 1581, with the two countries forming the Iberian Union, the previous Portuguese trade monopoly over the Indian Ocean trade routes was temporarily broken, allowing for a better integration of the Americas into the overall trading system of the Spanish Empire. In terms of economics, while Europe had nothing to offer to China, which had less interest in European products than Europe had in Chinese ones, the Middle Kingdom had developed a voracious appetite for American silver, which it had used as its monetary standard since the fifteenth century. The Chinese had one of the most elaborate taxation systems in the world, requiring all taxes to be paid in silver, including from small farmers. China was not producing enough silver to make this sustainable, and this at last stimulated the first trade outside the Middle Kingdom. Since Peru and Mexico were mining most of the world's silver and all coins were minted in New Spain, trade between Mexico and China was the natural outcome. Up to a third of the metal produced in the Americas was shipped to China from Acapulco, a lucrative trade for the Spaniards, the price of silver to gold being initially almost twice as high in China as in Spain.[7]

The Spanish silver coin minted in Mexico, the Real de a Ocho, became the first world currency, being widely used in Europe, China and the United States, where it was legal tender until the US Coinage Act of 1857. Many currencies around the world, from the US dollar to the Chinese yuan, were based on it; the well-known dollar symbol "$" originated in Spanish America, perhaps inspired by the Pillars of Hercules that were engraved on Spanish coins. In the nineteenth century, Mexican dollars were still widely used throughout the Asian rimland, including Kwangtung province. Although these coins were disfigured by chop marks—stamped Chinese characters[8]—Foon Chuck and Hing knew that the silver coins back home originated from Mexico, predisposing them favorably towards their new country.

SILVER, SILK AND CHILIES

The Manila Galleon Trade was conducted in Manila because the Ming empire would not allow foreigners on its soil. Silver, precious stones, metals and various agricultural products from the Americas, as well as manufactured items from Spain, arrived first at Manila, and were then distributed to the Chinese ports of Macau and Fukien. First brought a few decades earlier by the Portuguese trade via the Indian Ocean, from this time Mexican and South American plants spread in China, transforming the country's eating and agricultural habits, and thus becoming a basis of its diet and culinary tradition. These included corn, potatoes, sweet potatoes, peanuts, tomatoes and chilies. The historian Alfred Crosby writes:

> No larger group of the human races in the old world was quicker to adopt American food plants than the Chinese. While men who had stormed Tenochtitlan with Cortez still lived, peanuts were swelling in the sandy lawns near Shanghai, maize was turning fields green in South China, and the sweet potato was on its way to become the poor man's staple in Fukien.[9]

Several famous Chinese regional cuisines, which make extensive use of chili peppers, such as that of Szechuan province in the southwest, would probably be different today without the American trade. Nowadays, chilies remain indispensable to many Chinese dishes, and in dialect are called sea peppers,[10] giving an idea of their foreign origin. Some of these New World crops, such as potatoes or maize, can be grown on marginal arable land and more intensively than indigenous crops, and they played a key role in the increase of Chinese agricultural production and thereby in the growth of China's population. This same population growth became, centuries later, one of the reasons for Chinese emigration to the Americas. In any case, it was not surprising that Foon Chuck and Hing now found in Mexican cuisine far more similarities with their own culinary tradition than when they lived in the United States.

Curiously resembling global trade in the early twenty-first century, during the Manila Galleon Trade, Europe and the Americas exchanged money for Chinese manufactured goods. The Galleon Trade promoted China's manufacturing sector and helped sustain its population growth, but also created major imbalances in its economy. With the massive influx of foreign money, trade became the primary means of enrichment, undermining the Confucian ideals of agriculture and scholarship that had prevailed in previous centuries. The consequent rise of the gentry-merchant class caused the fragmentation of the traditional Chinese elite.[11] Fluctuations in the value of silver also resulted in a more volatile Chinese economy, sometimes being a source of inflation, and encouraging corruption from officials, as well as migratory movements and large differences between rich and poor. Such imbalances caused a moral decay in society and various movements of revolt. The often conservative and protectionist attitude of Chinese economists and leaders today may be partly due to this history of monetary dependence in previous centuries.

In the other direction, from China and the rest of Asia, silk, precious stones, ivory, porcelain and spices arrived at the port of Acapulco, on the Pacific coast of Mexico. The German explorer Alexander von Humboldt said when visiting Acapulco in 1803 that the city was "the most renowned trade fair in the world."[12] It was therefore Mexico City, long before London or Amsterdam, that became the first globalized city, the first city in which Asia, Europe and the Americas met. The cultural influence of the Manila Galleon Trade spread through the Hispanic world. For example, the use of fans among women in Andalusia can be traced to the Galleon Trade, with the ports of Cadiz and Seville being amongst its main beneficiaries. Considerable fortunes were built on the trade, as Mexico City's beautiful colonial architecture bears witness. In 1625, an English priest commented on the city:

> Both men and women are excessive in their apparel, using more silks than stuffs and cloth. Precious stones and pearls further much this vain ostentation. A hat-band and rose made of diamonds in a gentleman's hat is common, and a hat-band of pearls is ordinary in a tradesman.

He noted the city's wide streets and thousands of coaches, some of which exceeded the cost of the best of the court of Madrid and elsewhere in Europe, since in Mexico "they spare no silver, nor gold, nor precious stones, nor cloth of gold, nor the best silks of China to enrich them."[13]

However, the Galleon Trade did not lay the foundation of a stronger, multifaceted Mexican economy, since the Spanish Crown did not allow the creation of local industries and a local economy that might compete with its own.[14] Besides, the Mexican nouveau riche were not held in high esteem by the Spaniards in Madrid: Miguel Cervantes wrote of the New World as "the refuge of all the desperadoes of Spain, the church of rebels and sanctuary of murderers, those former ruffians after gaining wealth in the colonies, settle down in Spain cloaked in new-found respectability."[15]

The attitudes of the Spaniards towards Chinese merchants were even worse. Resenting the success of the merchants, who refused to convert to Christianity, the Spaniards overtaxed them and forced them to live segregated in a ghetto outside of Manila, an echo of their treatment of the Jews back in Spain. In 1603, outnumbered and fearing a Chinese rebellion and invasion, the Spanish colonists massacred more than 20,000 Chinese in Manila with the help of Filipino and Japanese forces. Soon afterwards, trade resumed as if nothing had happened, and more massacres of Chinese followed throughout the seventeenth and eighteenth centuries. Years later, Foon Chuck and Hing strolled through the elegant streets of Mexico City, oblivious to this history and not suspecting that most of the colonial buildings they saw were erected largely from profits generated by the Spaniards' trade with China in previous centuries. Their own businesses were just a new form of an exchange between East and West which had begun centuries before them.

In 1535, the Mexican Mint became the first ever corporation on the American continent, almost a century before the first corporations in the United States. Belonging to the conquistador Hernán Cortés, it minted all the silver from Mexico and Peru. Its magnificent colonial building still stands today in the heart of Mexico City, built over the foundations of the Black House, a black-painted room without windows, part of the palace of the Aztec emperor Moctezuma, where he meditated on his clairvoyants' predictions. The original building has been transformed into the National Museum of Cultures, the only museum of its kind in Latin America, with exhibitions on China, Europe and the Middle East, an apt testimonial to the building's history. In 1803, Alexander von Humboldt visited the mint and remarked that "all the silver produced by the European mines in one year would not last fifteen days in the Mexican mint [...]. The workshop is the largest and richest in the world and in one year can mint three times as much as the sixteen mints in the whole of France."[16]

During the Manila Galleon Trade, several Spanish captains took their Asian servants back with them to Mexico. In this way, 40,000 to 60,000 Asians, mainly Filipinos and Chinese, settled in Mexico during the trading period, called "Indian Chinese" by the local population, a sign of their distant shared ancestry. They became barbers, salesmen, dancers, scribes, tailors, shoemakers, goldsmiths and shipbuilders, testifying to the diversity of talents they contributed to their new country. Next to the Zócalo, Mexico City's main square, there was a large Oriental market, selling all sorts of Asian goods. A well-documented incident occurred in the 1630s when Mexico City barbers staged a protest against their Chinese competitors, who undercut their prices. For 200 years, until the start of the twentieth century, Mexico and the Philippines were called Big Luzon[17] and Small Luzon respectively by the Chinese, Luzon being the main island of the Philippines archipelago, demonstrating the economic and cultural ties between those two distant places. Of course, Foon Chuck and Hing were unaware of this history and of the Chinese immigrants to Mexico who preceded them.

The Manila Galleon Trade slowed in the eighteenth century, ending in 1815, during Mexico's war of independence from Spain, when it became associated with colonial exploitation. Various factors contributed to its decline. First, the advent of steamships and the better control of the African and Indian seas by the European powers made it safer for European traders to take the direct sea route to Asia via the Indian Ocean. In 1715, Spain lost its monopoly over the Atlantic trade to Britain, which began trading directly with China, bypassing the Americas. Finally, in the industrial revolution, Europe began to manufacture its own textiles and porcelain, reducing the demand for Chinese products other than tea. At the same time, in the eighteenth century the global process of demonetization reduced the price of silver. All these factors put an end to a period of unprecedented trans-Pacific trade, which is unlikely ever to be repeated on such a scale. But it would take only thirty years after the last Manila galleons crossed the Pacific for the terms of trade to change radically and new ships to make the same crossing, this time with cargoes even more valuable than before—loaded with migrants instead of porcelain and silk.

6

A CHINESE ELDORADO

In the late nineteenth century, while the United States had a relatively strong government and a well-defined national project, Mexico was still politically divided and had only a nascent bureaucracy. After a long war, Mexico gained its independence from Spain in 1821. The following fifty years were marked by conflict between liberals and conservatives as well as by wars against two invading powers, the United States and France. By 1876, a decade before Foon Chuck and Hing crossed the Texan border, Mexico was an exhausted country, hardly having enjoyed a period of peace since the start of the century. It was also fractured, with its political and economic power divided between three distinct groups: the *caudillos* (local political leaders), the *hacendados* (the often brutal and quasi-feudal absentee landowners) and the Church. Many parts of the country were still under the control of Indian tribes, who were often in conflict with the government, which was trying to dislodge them.

From 1876 to 1911, Mexico fell under the dictatorship of General Porfirio Díaz, a conservative and paternalistic figure who encouraged economic expansion and favored landowners, private capitalists and the Church. A mestizo of humble origins, President Díaz firmly believed in positivism, the theory promoted by French philosopher Auguste Comte among others, who saw science as the basis of progress. "Order and Progress" was Díaz's dictum, one which Brazil adopted as its national motto a few years later.

The 1883 Virgin Land Colonization Act encouraged investors to exploit all the land in the country that was left fallow, affecting a third of the country's territory, a phenomenon unprecedented in Mexico's history. From 1877 to 1893, more than twenty-five million hectares of land transfers occurred; much of the land was taken from Indians in the northern states. In 1895 twenty per cent of Mexicans possessed land; by 1910 only two per cent did, with seven million Mexican *peones* (low-skilled agricultural laborers) living and working in haciendas owned by an elite of only 834 families and land companies, for wages of only one fifteenth of those of a worker in the United States, little better off than a serf or slave.[1] This situation, involving a lack of land ownership by peasants, echoed the unstable social situation in southern China, which Foon Chuck and Hing had just left.

If Díaz's government produced economic expansion, as Mexico became Latin America's fastest growing economy during his regime, it also created resentment among the disadvantaged classes, such as the poor farmers, the new proletariat, and the Indians, dispossessed of their land or struggling to adapt to modernization. Many Indians demanded autonomy and communal ownership of their land, stating that "God gave all Yaqui [Indians] the river, not a piece to each man."[2] Díaz summarized his own views perfectly when he wrote that "we should not feel safe until we see every Indian with his goad in hand, walking behind a team of oxen and ploughing the fields."[3]

Díaz was widely admired in the Western world. Tolstoy called him "the political genius of the era;" Andrew Carnegie, "the Moses and Joshua of his people who guided them for the first time along the road of civilization;" and Theodore Roosevelt, "the Greatest statesman now living;"[4] while a US journalist wrote of him that "[he] has transformed the warlike, ignorant, superstitious and impoverished Mexican masses, after centuries of cruel oppression by the greedy Spaniards, into a strong, progressive, pacifist and prosperous nation that honors its debts."[5] But those views of foreigners could not hide the reality that during his rule Mexico became an even more fractured, unequal and unjust country. Díaz created an urban police of gendarmes, modelled on the French gendarmerie, and expanded the rural police force, the Rurales, who often recruited from amnestied bandits, in order to protect the interests of the large farmers. He sent federal troops around the country to maintain order and keep the poor under tight control. Those who were barefoot and wore the rough white pants of the Indians were kept out of Mexico City by the police, so as not to spoil the modern image of the capital for foreigners and wealthy Mexicans.[6]

This did not stop the poor from migrating to Mexico City, living in vast shanty towns among piles of garbage and countless cantinas, suffering from malnutrition and alcoholism, so that in 1910 the city had higher mortality rates than Madras and Cairo.[7] One in two babies in the country died before the age of one.[8] There was no progress for the impoverished, who feared the police as much as the affluent classes respected them. In 1895, close to ninety per cent of the Mexican population was considered poor.[9] This portion of the population was largely illiterate, and subsisted day-to-day with barely enough of the staple foods (corn, chilies, tomato, pumpkin and beans) to survive. More than half of the working population was made up of poor rural workers, with another twenty per cent being artisans and industrial workers,[10] whose workdays lasted more than sixteen hours. Of course, this would provide an almost limitless number of soldiers for the violent revolutionary cause a decade later. In 1911, Díaz's regime was overturned by a bloody popular revolution led by Francisco Madero. But when Foon Chuck and Hing arrived in the 1880s, they could not foresee that Mexico would become a dangerous, violent and politically unstable place for Chinese immigrants, even more so than the more liberal United States that they had just left.

Mexico was a country rich in natural resources and potential; but many in the country believed that its population had not been able to exploit this potential because it was deficient both in quantity and quality, the local Indians having a natural inability to become good citizens. In a 1901 speech, Díaz's brilliant treasury minister, José Yves Limantour, did not hide his contempt: "The weak, the unprepared, those who lack the necessary tools to triumph in the evolutionary process, must perish and leave the field to the strongest."[11] Díaz wanted to modernize Mexico by attracting foreign capital, promoting European immigration, and building extensive transportation networks. Under his regime, a large part of Mexican industry and infrastructure thus came under foreign, and particularly US, control. By 1910, 75,000 Americans were living in Mexico (who, for most, would leave during and after the Mexican Revolution), the US owning a quarter of Mexican territory and Mexico representing half of its total investments abroad, William Randolph Hearst famously saying: "I really don't see what is to prevent us from owning all of Mexico and running it to suit ourselves."[12] But, while he managed to attract US and European capital and entrepreneurs, Díaz failed to bring in the white workers he hoped for, with few willing to settle outside the cities and accept the modest way of life of the local workers.[13] To fill this void, his government turned to the Chinese, highlighting their efficiency rather than their origin,[14] even calling the Chinese "engines of blood." In the early twentieth century, therefore, Mexico became one of the top destinations for the Chinese in the Americas, the 1882 Exclusion Act in the United States coinciding with the Mexican government's efforts to go in the opposite direction and attract Chinese laborers for its booming economy. In contrast to its northern neighbor, Mexico under Díaz considered any restriction of free passage for migrants to be a violation of their fundamental human rights, as enshrined in the 1857 Mexican constitution.

At the same time, although mestizo himself, Díaz was openly condescending towards the American Indians, and he saw Chinese workers as a tool to improve the racial balance of the Mexican labor force, making it whiter and more mestizo. This was considered less ideal than European migration but was still felt to be progress towards his vision of a white Mexico—a true phenomenon of state racism.[15] A social commentator in 1908 criticized the regime for fostering "the opinion in our country [...] that we are people who know less, are less able, can do less and are worth less than the other nations of the earth."[16] All the same, the Chinese were not encouraged to settle, gain Mexican citizenship, or marry Mexican women; they were viewed instead as temporary workers. Even though everyone was equal under the constitution, another belief at the time was that only people with reason, meaning educated whites, were worthy of the powers conferred by citizenship.

* * *

In 1885, Hing is surprised at how easily he crosses the Mexican border, feeling thankful that the Mexicans need him for the construction of their railroad, in such contrast with the situation in the United States. For the next few years, he works in a team of Chinese laborers on the railroad extension in northern Mexico, spending his days hammering rails under the blazing sun. They work side by side with Mexican workers, but at first the two groups keep mostly to themselves.

Hing has never seen a desert before. He dislikes the arid landscape, so different from the semi-tropical humidity of his native province. He was not fond of the weather in San Francisco, especially in winter, but finds the summer months in his new country unbearable. His new construction job is harder work than his laundry job; he has never been so exhausted in his life and his body aches. The work is not especially dangerous, although he witnesses several accidents as their Chinese foreman pushes them in their advance through the desert at an increasingly frantic pace. For his sacrifice, he earns up to $40 a month ($1,200 in today's money), much more than in San Francisco. He sets aside more than half of this to send to his parents. But he wonders how long he will be able to keep up such hard work. Unlike with Ah Fong, he feels that his new and faceless American employer has little concern for his well-being. He and his companions often protest to their foreman about the lack of proper food and the mistreatments they suffer. They are outraged by the prices they have to pay for their daily necessities in their employers' store, feeling even more powerless and isolated than in San Francisco. Their only connection to China remains the Six Chinese Companies, who keep a benevolent yet distant and highly interested eye over their welfare, sending news to their relatives and remitting their earnings back home, from which they deduct a hefty commission for their role.

* * *

As Hing and Foon Chuck worked on the extension of Mexico's rail infrastructure, China too made its first attempts to build a modern railroad in various parts of the country. The initial experiments were hard to implement and mostly failed. Chinese villagers were concerned that the passing railroad would disturb the Fengshui of their village and the balance between heaven and earth. The Chinese government viewed the railroads with equal suspicion, as a way for foreign nations to extend their power in China, quite a contrast with Mexico, whose entire railroad infrastructure was built precisely to improve its ties with its northern neighbor. One of the early lines, from Shanghai to Woosung, opened in 1876 but was dismantled shortly afterwards and its station converted into a temple, after an oblivious farmer was killed walking on its tracks. In 1885, one US company even sent a 1,000-foot miniature model of a working railway to Empress Dowager Cixi, who, although amused, was not convinced to adopt the foreign devils' modern form of transportation.[17] A century earlier, Emperor Qianlong had already informed the English king George III: "We possess all things. I set no value on objects strange or ingenious and have no use for your country's manufactures. Our ways bear no resemblance to yours."[18] Cixi would radically change her views towards the end of her reign, almost two decades later.

Diverted from the United States by its Chinese Exclusion Act, more than 60,000 Chinese immigrated to Mexico from the late nineteenth to the early twentieth centuries, seventy per cent of them arriving through the United States.[19] Like Hing, many were hired as indentured laborers directly by Mexican and foreign companies and worked in appalling conditions,[20] especially in agriculture and railroad construction, like the coolies three decades earlier. An advertisement in Hong Kong read as follows: "Chinese colony for Mexico. All will receive a lot of money there. Will make $500 the first year and $1,000 the following. Will have soon more money than the Mandarins. Much rice and vegetables cheap. Good ship with no diseases. Lots of space."[21]

According to Mexican government statistics, while the official Chinese population in Mexico consisted of only 1,023 people in 1895, it rose to 13,000 in 1910 and peaked at 24,000 in 1926, still representing a modest 0.2 per cent of the country's population and around twenty per cent of all its foreign immigrants[22]—the second-largest group behind the Spaniards, who accounted for forty per cent of immigrants to Mexico.[23] In the states of Yucatán and Sonora, these early Chinese workers participated in the colonization of virgin Mexican territories through agriculture and railroad construction. They served Western colonists, often putting themselves in conflict with the local Indians. Some of these Chinese immigrants, however, also established novel relationships with those Amerindians who were unwilling to assimilate, selling them goods and forming mixed couples. Chinese migrants continued to enter Mexico at pace until 1928, even after the violence of the 1910–20 revolution, because the Chinese still saw parts of Mexico as attractive and as a bridge to the United States. Moreover, in contrast to the United States, Mexico was only just beginning to exert control over its borders, with an understaffed, underpaid, and easily corruptible immigration service. As a result, many Chinese likely entered Mexico illegally, so that the Mexican government's official statistics likely underestimate the actual numbers. In 1908, the Mexican legation in China estimated that 60,000 Chinese had already entered Mexico,[24] but only 13,000 were residing in the country according to official figures. If these figures are broadly correct then up to 45,000 Chinese had either left North America or were living illegally in Mexico or the US.

In 1886, Hing had just turned twenty and at five feet ten was the tallest in his team. The Leung family came from northern China and had always been a head taller than most Cantonese, a source of pride for them. He had not only grown taller but also stronger, and he felt that people no longer tried to intimidate him, as they had when he first arrived in San Francisco six years earlier. Hing would remember those years of hard labor for the rest of his life. Later, all his sons inherited their father's tall stature and sturdy physique, several of them becoming athletes: Hing would encourage them to practice sports so that no one would dare bully them. At first, Hing did not observe in Mexico the same racism towards the Chinese that he experienced in the United States, but, as in the north, he did witness contempt shown to the Native Americans in the country.

Every Saturday night, after receiving their pay, Mexican workers went to the nearest village to have a drink at local cantinas, known in Mexico as places where customers often leave by being carried out feet first. Drunken Mexican workers sometimes attacked Chinese workers. One of Hing's children recalled that, being the tallest, Hing was often called in for help by his compatriots. As in the United States, Hing noticed how docile and timid his fellow Chinese were in the face of the bullying and aggression they suffered. He ventured that the reason could be that the Chinese did not know the local language and so were unable to speak back. At the turn of the century, an American missionary in China observed that,

> The Chinese dislike fighting, although they do not readily yield. Their dislike is not from fear of pain, but because they do not like to be considered rude. They are able to bear more pain than we are [...]. When a Chinese really does lose his temper, he uses very bad language, but he does not come to blows. If the insult or injustice is so great as to provoke murder, he does not kill the other man, but himself, because in doing so the other man is looked upon as a murderer, since he was the cause of the deed. They often kill themselves by swallowing poison, after first hiring men to carry their bodies to the door of their enemy.[25]

Hing was aware that the foreign devils called him and his compatriots cowards, yet he knew that, although his people were more temperate and not as demonstrative as the Mexicans and Americans, they displayed their courage in different ways from them. A character trait common to many Chinese migrants, considered a virtue in China, was their forbearance, being able to stand life's sufferings without complaining or showing any stress or sadness, which were both seen as signs of a weak character. Resentment and negative feelings were then kept repressed within, sometimes until the migrant's death. A familiar Chinese expression, conveying that state of mind and used to this day to describe a harsh life, is to "eat bitterness,"[26] which was the lot of most migrants in those days.

Hing's compatriots generally did not drink, but some had pipes and were addicted to the betting game of Fan Tan, which helped distract them from their miseries, and which had been banned by California legislators a couple of years earlier. During their rare moments of freedom, aside from washing and mending their clothes, they smoked opium or gambled, both of which Hing avoided at all costs, knowing they would make him lose the little money he had managed to save. Hing knew well the deleterious effect of gambling on his people, thinking of the saying that "at the gambling table, there are no fathers and sons." If Hing, like most Chinese, believed in fate and destiny, he did not trust luck, relying all his life only on himself and his hard work. He preferred to spend his free time learning Spanish with the Mexican workers, some of whom became his friends.

On Saturday nights spent around the fire, Hing enjoyed chatting under the stars, finding strange the feeling of solidarity and fraternity. In China, he had wanted to put as much distance as possible between himself and anyone who was not from his clan or village, always being on his guard not to be robbed, beaten or kidnapped, as he saw happen to so many of his relatives. In his overcrowded province people were everywhere, every field was full of laborers, hills were cultivated to their very crests, and pedestrians filled the roads, cities and canal sides. In Mexico, by contrast, he found himself in empty country full of virgin land. In 1885, the population of his new country was almost forty times lower than China's, its population density almost ten times less (and almost twenty times less than the overcrowded province of Kwangtung). Nonetheless, he and his Chinese compatriots remembered with nostalgia their lives and families back home, their kinship being now their only link to their homeland. They also discussed their plans for when they would have set aside sufficient money or had had enough of the railroad. Some thought about working in mines, others wanted to open their own laundries and asked Hing for advice, while many dreamed of becoming merchants.

In 1888, after three years of exhausting work and with his first savings in hand, Hing was advised by other workers to try his luck in the trade of goods along the newly opened Mexican railway lines. At the age of twenty-two, he contacted a San Francisco trading company (via the Sze Yap Company) to obtain goods that he could easily receive by rail. To get him started, they offered him credit, which he added to his few savings, purchasing his first stock of merchandise. Through their family-based credit system, the San Francisco merchants knew Hing's family address in Hoksaan, and would hold his family accountable for any missing repayments. In addition, those same merchants were well acquainted with Hing, knowing he had already worked seriously for eight years in San Francisco and Mexico. This was another important feature of the Chinese diaspora, where each person's credit was known to everyone else, as within a large family. Each member of the clan abroad strove all his life to keep a pristine reputation within it, as if he had never left his ancestral village.

One sign of their mercantile mindset was that, no product in any Chinese market had a fixed price, everything being always a haggle between buyers and sellers, each carrying their own scale, if not two, to avoid being cheated by the other side. In the eighteenth century, having met Chinese travelers in the French court and read the tales of Western missionaries in China, the philosopher Montesquieu suggested that, due to their climate and land, the Chinese could only survive through hard labor and industry, which gave them a great greediness, not tempered by laws, with the result that in China deception was not only widespread but permissible.[27] The common Chinese opinion, still true today, was that anyone deceived in a business transaction was alone responsible for his loss, for not having shown sufficient caution. Ironically, the Chinese held identical views about Westerners. An imperial advisor in the nineteenth century opined: "The whole country of England relies for its livelihood on the trade of its crowd of merchants. Superiors and inferiors compete against each other. There is none who does not look only for profits. If that country has some undertaking afoot, they turn around first to listen to the command of the merchants."[28] In any case, Hing found the Mexican markets and stores infinitely less animated and noisy than those in his home province of Kwangtung or even in California, and was surprised at first to find Mexicans so apparently dispassionate about business.

Now that Hing had learned some Spanish, he felt confident in convincing Mexicans to buy his products. Since he did not have enough capital to set up a physical store, he bought himself a suit and became a street vendor, like those in China, going door to door between wealthy Mexicans' homes. He also decided to cut his pigtail, knowing that he must look as Mexican as possible and that his parents would understand when he returns to China without it. This made his head feel light and free, and he himself felt different; he could not have imagined that this act would be so liberating. He soon realized that Mexicans were curious about anything Chinese, finding he could earn higher margins by selling Asian handicrafts, which Mexicans had never seen and did not know the real value of.

Over the next ten years, Hing transported his business throughout Mexico, traveling from city to city with a large chest full of goods. Having never spoken to a Chinese person before, his customers were surprised to see this tall and distinguished Chinese vendor knock at their door and speak their language. They felt flattered that Hing had learned Spanish and was dressed like them. Most of Hing's clients were educated people, and they marveled at the delicacy of the Chinese goods he sold, which represented what they imagined of ancient China more than did the poor Chinese workers they sometimes came across on the roads. Hing knew how to flatter them, suggesting to them how valuable and rare his products were. Another benefit of selling Chinese handicrafts was the limited value they had to the many bandits roaming Mexican roads, who were even more ignorant than his clients about the value of his merchandise.

As his business grew, instead of selling door to door, Hing sometimes displayed his goods in a large city hotel. Selling Chinese art to Mexicans made him joyful and proud of his culture, as he himself discovered its refinement through the objects he sold. He enjoyed his interactions with his Mexican clients, seeing himself as bridging two different worlds. Ironically, it was only by moving away from his Chinese compatriots that Hing became fully conscious of his differences to the locals and felt for the first time what it meant to be Chinese. Like Foon Chuck before him, he had found his calling, and he could not believe that he was now earning in a single day more than he could earn in a month of hard work in China. He found the north of Mexico too flat and dry, and so tried over the years to move towards the plains of central Mexico or the coast, which had a milder climate, more hills, and lush vegetation, reminding him of his native region. The north had also become too crowded with Chinese competitors, and he found that the wealthy Mexicans in the large cities of central Mexico were more educated and more interested in buying his products.

Hing's experiences were typical of that era. In the late nineteenth century, Mexican railroads, mines and large farms developed an organized system of recruitment of contracted Chinese laborers, in collaboration with the Mexican government and the Six Chinese Companies of San Francisco. Initially recruited to Mexico to serve as contract workers, many later became merchants, small traders, grocers, tailors, laundrymen and restaurant owners. Long before Mexicans learned to appreciate Chinese cuisine, migrants began to open the ubiquitous "Cafés Chinos" where bread and snacks were served, which continued to offer their services in several Mexican cities all through the twentieth century.

Although this was not in the Díaz government's plan, more and more Chinese in the north avoided manual jobs in mining and the railway to focus exclusively on local trade and small businesses, providing daily services to an expanding domestic market, serving not Chinese but Mexican customers. The transition to small businesses was relatively easy, requiring little start-up capital—usually $600 to $800—often lent by San Francisco merchants. With a real demand for previously unavailable services, the Chinese quickly found a loyal clientele. Importantly, these small businesses were all transnational, buying their products from Chinese wholesalers located across the border, who traveled regularly to Mexico to supply their clients. Another advantage was that many merchants belonged to Chinese fraternal societies, buying their products in bulk at near wholesale prices, more cheaply than any of their Mexican competitors. By 1930, nearly forty per cent of Mexico's Chinese had become traders; twenty per cent were farmers, less than ten per cent worked in industry, and only one per cent in mining, quite a contrast with the situation of their compatriots in the United States.[29] With neither capital nor contacts abroad, most poor Mexicans were unable to elevate themselves from their peasant roles in the large haciendas; the Chinese, on the other hand, formed a new petty bourgeois class, mostly in the northern Mexican states, like Sonora.[30]

The cultures of the early settlers in the United States and Mexico stood in stark contrast. The Anglo-Saxon and Eastern European settlers in the United States brought a mercantile culture, whereas the early Spanish settlers in Mexico retained an agrarian mindset. This cultural difference between north and south across the border is still visible today. It meant that Chinese merchants, as well as newly arrived European businessmen, found limited competition in Mexico. The Chinese were the first to introduce the practice of itinerant trade, door to door and village to village, which had been unknown in Mexico but widespread in China for centuries. They sold vegetables, rice and other foodstuffs, not only quickly penetrating the market but also gaining a certain notoriety among Mexicans. They introduced new sales techniques, such as giving away free products to build customers' loyalty, and were also willing to carry large inventories. Like the hated employee stores of large haciendas, Chinese stores also provided credit to customers, thus creating a relationship of dominance and dependence. While they prospered, they quickly made friends with some of their clients but also enemies among the most disadvantaged Mexicans who did not understand their rapid success. At the beginning of the twentieth century, twenty years after my ancestors' arrival, Chinese stores had become ubiquitous in most northern Mexican states. Two decades later, around 1920, the Chinese had developed a virtual monopoly in small businesses and groceries in the north of Mexico, something that could never have happened in the United States on such a large scale.

In 1893, aged twenty-seven, after having successfully worked for five years as a merchant, Hing decided to travel back to China. He brought money, which his parents used to build a new house. There are no available public records, but according to family rumors, like Foon Chuck earlier, Hing may also have married at this time.

After thirteen years abroad, Hing was delighted to finally be home and to see his parents and brothers again, whom he would soon bring to Mexico with him. Lured by the prospects of growing his business, after a stay of only six months Hing returned to Mexico, where he arrived in 1894 via San Francisco and the Mexican port of Mazatlán. Ah Fong being long gone, Hing felt both apprehensive and curious about visiting San Francisco's Chinatown, where he had landed fourteen years earlier. Surely, he thought, no one would dare to bully him now that he was grown-up and wealthy. But he was only allowed to transfer ships in the United States, not disembark.

He harbored mixed feelings about his earlier experience in the New World: it had been a time of hard work and exclusion, yet a necessary step for him towards becoming the successful man he was now. Just as had happened ten years earlier, he did not encounter any problems entering Mexico. His first photograph was for his passport, taken around that time, and beneath which his daughter wrote in her family album, "my dear father when he was young and handsome."

In 1898, an important and happy event took place in Hing's life. Thirteen years after he had first arrived in Mexico, he received his naturalization certificate, signed by President Díaz himself. He was among the first thirty or so Chinese to receive naturalization, most of them merchants like him.[31] This happened after the adoption of the Alienage and Naturalization Law of 1886; the Chinese would account for more than half of Mexican naturalizations over the following decades. Still, unlike in the United States, naturalization remained rare among the foreigners in Mexico. Only a few dozen Chinese were naturalized each year until 1910, when the number rose to seventy. Unless they became wealthy, like Foon Chuck and Hing, the Chinese tended not to be welcomed in this way in Mexico.

Hing adopted the Mexican name of Jorge Hing Leon, Mexicanizing his surname from Leung to Leon. This widespread surname is also the name of a Mexican state; it means lion in Spanish, which Hing imagined was the Western equivalent of the tiger, his animal symbol in the Chinese calendar. He took the name Jorge because the letter J in Spanish is pronounced like his first name, Hing, in Cantonese. Years later, though, his grandchildren would call him by his Chinese name, being for them Abuelo Hing (Grandfather Hing). At the same time, Hing let his mustache grow, which gave him a more masculine look and the air of a bourgeois merchant. By contrast, in his home province in China, before reaching old age any facial hair would have then been considered bad taste, with the many barbers in Canton busy shaving expertly every single hair off their customers' faces, including their eyelids.[32] For Hing, as with his pigtail earlier, it was as though his gradual transformation into a Mexican must be accompanied by a corresponding physical change. The thirteen years that he had lived in Mexico so far had been years of loneliness and vagrancy—not only being far away from his Chinese family, but never having a home to himself. Paradoxically, in contrast with San Francisco, it was this very isolation that pushed him to get closer to the Mexicans, to become friends with them, and now to become one of them. Into his thirties, with his Mexican citizenship and savings in hand, Hing finally felt ready to start his own family.

A year later, in 1899, more than thirty years after the Treaty of Burlingame between the United States and China, and eighteen years after a similar treaty between Brazil and China, a Treaty of Friendship and Commerce was signed between China and Mexico, allowing the free movement of goods and people between the two countries, which accelerated Chinese immigration. This was the first time that Mexico and China established official diplomatic relations, previous discussions having been held through US diplomats. Matías Romero, the Mexican diplomat behind the treaty, believed the Chinese would adapt well because their country enjoyed the same climate as Mexico, and the Chinese shared ancestry with the local Indians. Against the backdrop of this treaty, dissatisfied with and in defiance of the colonial powers, the Qing government in China refused the new gold standard and the US silver dollar, continuing instead to index its reserves to Mexico's old silver peso, the Real de a Ocho, as it had done for centuries. The treaty also mentioned the sale of precious metals to China, as metals accounted then for eighty per cent of Mexican exports. Already in 1884, the first steamships began to make the direct journey from Hong Kong to the Mexican port of Acapulco, less than one hundred years after the end of the Manila Galleon Trade and less than fifty years after the inauguration of the Hong Kong-San Francisco route further north. Until 1900, Mexico's Atlantic ports, such as Tampico, still accounted for most of the Chinese migrants arriving by sea, who mostly came via Cuba, many to be smuggled into the United States. After the signing of the treaty and the Mexican government granting shipping concessions to Chinese and Japanese companies at the start of the century, the ports on the Pacific coast became the main entry points for the migrants, including Mazatlán and Acapulco.

With only seven per cent of Chinese Mexicans being women in 1926, a distinctive feature of Chinese migrants in Mexico was the relatively high rate of mixed marriages.[33] It is estimated that between a tenth and a fifth of Chinese migrants in Mexico (with higher numbers among those who became merchants) ended up living with or marrying Mexican women,[34] compared with a much smaller minority in the United States. Frequent interaction between Chinese business owners and their female clients and employees created opportunities for romance and marriage.

Most Mexican women marrying a Chinese immigrant came from the middle or lower classes, and were of Indian or mestizo background: the white elite tended to refuse to marry anyone of color. These mixed unions were often mocked or disapproved of by Mexican society, being seen as marriages of convenience with polygamous Chinese men. This feeling was particularly strong among the Mexican upper classes and the Church; this was rather hypocritical, since concubinage, although illegal in Mexico, was accepted and widespread. The difference with China was that legitimate wives and mistresses never saw each other in Mexico and certainly never lived under the same roof.

In the United States, Chinese migrants tended to end up living in Chinatowns, whereas Mexico had fewer such neighborhoods. Chinese migrants mingled more with local Mexicans, through their mixed unions, their commercial activities serving Mexican customers, and finally, for a minority of them, their naturalizations. Another reason for this was geographical: while almost all Chinese immigrants in the United States arrived through San Francisco, their entry points into Mexico were much more dispersed, including the Pacific Coast for those coming from China and northern California, the Caribbean for those coming from South America, and the 2,000-mile US–Mexico land border for those coming from the south of the United States. One of the only major Chinatowns to develop in Mexico by the beginning of the century was *La Chinesca* in Mexicali, a border town, although other large Chinese communities developed in various Mexican mining towns.

The high level of acculturation of the Chinese in Mexico thus became a distinct feature of this expanding migrant group. This phenomenon was well observed in 1904 by the new Chinese ambassador to the United States, Liang Cheng (1864–1917), another native of Kwangtung province. Liang travelled to Mexico on an official state visit and met Porfirio Díaz, who told him "The Chinese are heartily welcome as their industry, frugality, and ability are valuable in building up the country."[35] Back in Washington, in an article entitled "A Chinese Eldorado," the ambassador summarized the situation of his countrymen in Mexico:

> The Chinese are rapidly becoming a factor in its business life, inclined to become Mexicanized through intermarriage, they stand much higher in Mexico than in the United States and in time will be prominent politically and even socially, the Mexicans being inclined to receive them as equals. In the United States, the Chinese are restricted to narrow limits for their livelihood, while in Mexico every venue is open. The Chinese receive higher wages than the [local] peons and are everywhere recognized as more valuable workers.[36]

A CHINESE ELDORADO

Liang Cheng belonged to a new generation of Chinese diplomats, who were more familiar with Western culture than his predecessors. A member of the first group of Chinese students sent to the US (see Chapter Four), he had attended the prestigious Philipps Exeter Academy in Andover, Massachusetts, where he even became a baseball star. He was apparently asked by President Roosevelt, himself an excellent sportsman, about his school days and who was the best baseball player on his school team. Putting aside his modesty, Liang replied that he himself was, and later reportedly said that "from that moment the relation between President Roosevelt and myself became ten times stronger."[37] However, one diplomat was not enough to change the anti-Chinese stance of Roosevelt, who had often been dismissive of the Chinese people, viewing them as an inferior race, calling them Chinks[38] and "poor trembling rabbits,"[39] and tightening the Exclusion Act in 1902. By contrast, Roosevelt believed that Japan's strong military was a key indicator of the worth of the Japanese, writing of them in 1905 that they were "a wonderful and civilized people" who were "entitled to stand on an absolute equality with all the other people of the civilized world."[40] That same year, Roosevelt brokered the Treaty of Portsmouth, giving Japan free rein to colonize Korea, for which he dubiously received the Nobel Peace Prize. In 1908, before the end of his presidency, Roosevelt also signed the Root-Takahira agreement with Japan and Russia giving Japan the right to govern large areas of land in China's Southern Manchuria,[41] part of his "Monroe doctrine for Asia." This further distressed the Chinese and unwittingly gave Japan a base for their future expansionary policies in China over the following three decades.

7

BOURGEOIS AND MEXICAN

Hing's work takes him all over Mexico. He stays in each city for periods of a few days to a few weeks depending on their size, often renting a room in the house of a local family. He enjoys talking with his hosts and enquiring about their city, while they, in turn, question him about China. In 1898, Hing arrives in Acaponeta, a small town in the state of Nayarit, near the Pacific coast. While he is selling his products there, he lives in the modest home of an old man in the town. In this house he meets a young girl with fair skin, long black hair and intelligent eyes, working diligently in the kitchen. Perceiving his curiosity, his host explains to Hing that the girl, Cruz Rivera Nava, is sixteen years old and a distant niece, who has recently moved into his home. She is an orphan, having lost her mother two years earlier and never having been acquainted with her father. Hing is immediately attracted to this shy young woman.

He has sought a Mexican spouse for years, but whenever he has felt attracted to someone, he has been rejected. Most of the fathers he speaks to simply refuse to see their daughter marry a Chinese man. Hing tactfully mentions to them the betrothal money he is willing to offer—the "Engagement Gold,"[1] as it is called in China, where it is still customary today—but he is then rebuffed with even greater contempt. Hing realizes that being a successful businessman and now a naturalized Mexican is simply not enough to be accepted in his new country. He has considered bringing a wife from China but does not believe any woman will like trading her land there for a lonesome existence in a foreign country, especially since he is constantly traveling for his business. He also wants to fully integrate into Mexico, and feels that marrying a local woman is the best way to achieve this. Besides, he hopes that a Mexican wife will help his business, assuring his clients that he has truly become one of them and is worthy of their trust.

Cruz has never seen a Chinese person before. A few years earlier, the nuns in her Sunday school had explained that the Chinese were yellow-skinned people living far away, ignorant of Jesus, wearing silk robes and pointy hats, but her knowledge of China stops there. Like most young women in Mexico, she only knows how to decipher a few dozen words, the literacy rate in Mexico being only twenty-five per cent at the time, and even lower in the countryside and among women. The price of a newspaper, the main reading material of the laboring class, is higher than the average daily worker's salary,[2] and Cruz has no interest in these, preferring to chat with her relatives after her housework is finished. She is surprised to see that Hing is so well dressed and groomed, unlike some of the men in her town, who have made indecent proposals to her. When he smiles at her, he looks reassuring and respectful. While he asks her about her life, his Spanish, although strange to the ear, is not unpleasant. Yet part of her feels scared: he remains mysterious to her, and she thinks about what strange places he must come from. Besides, he does not seem to know anything about Jesus.

Realizing that his host is poor and cannot afford to take care of Cruz, Hing explains to him that he is a prosperous and recently naturalized Mexican with serious intentions. In addition, he is ready to give him a generous engagement gift if he allows Cruz to marry him. Cruz's uncle is impressed when he sees Hing's naturalization document, but carefully considers his niece's options, pondering what she can aspire to become. He knows Cruz is a serious and charitable person, but he also knows that without the protection of a father, a surname and a dowry, she is unlikely to find a good husband among any of the respectable families in the region. He can only imagine Cruz entering a convent or perhaps becoming a servant in one of the haciendas, and he fears what might happen to her there. He thinks for a whole day about the right course of action, praying to God for guidance, and keeping in mind the money promised. In the end, Cruz's uncle reluctantly agrees to let Hing marry his niece.

Cruz is stunned when her uncle explains to her that she will leave his house the next day to marry Hing. She feels ashamed to be forced into this relationship with a foreigner, but she knows that she can say nothing and that she has nowhere else to go. She also fears that no priest will ever agree to marry them, so that she will be subjected to the double infamy of an illegitimate relationship with a Chinese. She cries as she thinks about the great injustices to which she is again victim: first the absence of a father, then her mother's death, and now this pagan Chinese man. When Hing explains to her that he sells Chinese handicrafts for a living, Cruz is surprised that people are interested in such things, which she finds strange and useless.

There is no wedding ceremony; she simply packs a small bag with personal belongings, embraces her uncle and relatives one last time, makes the sign of the cross before the statue of the Virgin of Guadalupe, and leaves Acaponeta, never to return. From a Chinese perspective, they are now married, Hing having gained the agreement of Cruz's uncle. He sees the marriage as a business transaction, as is customary in China, where spouses, especially second wives or those from poor backgrounds, are bought from a family through a civil contract, without any religious ceremony, marriage certificate or entry in a public register. From the perspective of Mexican law and the Church, however, they remain unmarried. Hing has not felt so happy and light in a long time; he reflects that this marriage is the best deal he has ever made. Years later, one of my aunts remembered, he would even advise his own sons to marry orphaned women, as he had done, so that they would not have to feed additional mouths. He has already led a lonely itinerant life for two decades, feeling the pressure and responsibility to continue the Leung family lineage, knowing that the greatest impiety for an eldest son is to be without sons himself. Over the following months, Hing tries everything to please his new wife, buying her new clothes and speaking with excitement about his plans for his growing business. Although the marriage lacked a romantic beginning, he is nonetheless in love with Cruz and knows how important it is that she now falls in love with him in return.

* * *

From Acaponeta, Hing and Cruz traveled one hundred miles north, settling in the port of Mazatlán, in the state of Sinaloa. This had been

Hing's point of entry into Mexico a few years earlier, and it would now be their first home. Mazatlán was a prosperous city of about 10,000 people on the Pacific coast. During those years, the city experienced strong economic growth, gaining various buildings in the style of La Belle Époque, including a grand theater. Being an international port, it had a small foreign community which, based on the city archives of 1895, numbered 170 people, of which fourteen were Chinese, mostly farmers. The choice of a city with regular ships bound for San Francisco and China as a place to start his family was no coincidence, reflecting Hing's desire to keep a connection with his native country and to source Chinese goods for his business more easily.

There is no wedding photo of Hing and Cruz: they remained officially unmarried most of their lives, which did not bother Hing but remained a burden on Cruz's Catholic conscience. At that time, marriages and births were more a matter for the Church than the state, often only being recorded at the registrar's office many years after they occurred. According to an aunt, Hing and Cruz, probably ashamed of their situation, sometimes sent their maid to register their newborns at the civil registry. Hing did not understand the religion of the Mexicans: how people could invoke God's name to look down on them, or how the Church could have so much power. He saw no harm in his union with Cruz, but did not mind her going to church alone (and later with their children) if that made her happy. Hing came from a land where people's daily lives were shaped by many different rituals, religions and traditions. The Chinese were known to be Taoist while tending their garden, Confucian in front of their sovereign, and Buddhist on their death bed; and Chinese students had a god of literature, soldiers a god of war, and merchants a god of wealth. The fertile Chinese imagination filled every lake and river with spirits, every street and house with ghosts, and every wood and mountain with deities.[3] Confucianism is a moral and practical philosophy rather than a spiritual belief system: although the spirit of Confucius was revered in temples and schools across China, he was not seen as a deity in the Western sense, and his teachings were not in conflict with the other Chinese religious beliefs. Unlike the West, which has experienced so many religious wars, syncretism has been the basis of Chinese society and its stability, with religious authorities rarely sharing political power and religion rarely becoming a powerful state creed. In contrast with most European royal residences, in Beijing's Forbidden City, although there are numerous Buddhist and Taoist shrines, there are no obvious monotheistic religious structures.[4] Ironically, the separation of church and state is enshrined in the US constitution too, but it would bring the US on a very different spiritual path to China in the twentieth century. Hing would remain loyal to the worship of his ancestors all his life, and, being a practical and down-to-earth Chinese, he was not overly concerned about picking the right set of beliefs. He found it easier to change between different divine creatures than to disown his own ancestors. This was the root of his religious tolerance.

Cruz found Hing a taciturn and patient husband, not passionate in his feelings, but devoted and constant in his affection and care for her. She was relieved that he was hard-working and rarely drank alcohol, which she had seen bring misery to families around her. They both lacked a large circle of family and friends in Mexico, and so they now had only one another for support. Hing loved the food she prepared, including two popular dishes among urban Mexicans that reminded him of China, noodle soup and Mexican style rice (*sopa de fideos* and *arroz a la mexicana*). Since the sixteenth century, middle-class Mexicans have eaten rice, another product originating from Asia and brought to Mexico by the Spaniards. Of course, Mexicans prepare rice differently from the Chinese, with tomatoes and plantains for example.

Cruz hated the way some people, especially other women, looked down on them as she walked beside her husband. She knew it was useless to get angry, and she prayed that one day God might forgive her tormentors and her for their sins. She took comfort in seeing how Hing brought money daily to the family, was never violent with her, and was later so loving with their children. Hing hoped that in Mexico, as in China, fortune alone would not only provide protection, more than any government, family or Chinese association, but also pave the way to respectability—which seemed to him to be human nature. He was delighted when Cruz became pregnant, rightly feeling that his mixed child would anchor him even more in his new country.

Mestizos aside, Cruz had never seen mixed-race children before, and she wondered fearfully what her child would look like. She prayed that the child would be healthy and would live a happier life than her own. She asked herself whether the child would be Chinese or Mexican and what language it would speak; she only knew that she would love it either way. She was confident that her parish priest would agree to baptize the baby despite its mixed blood and their sinful illegitimate relationship. In 1899, Hing named his first child Melchor, after one of the three biblical Magi, who brought the gift of gold to the baby Jesus. He also gave him the Chinese name of Meichuk,[5] meaning "beautiful clan," displaying his attachment to his ancestors. In the first photo of the young family, taken around 1903, Cruz is seen smiling, surrounded by her first three sons and Hing's three brothers, all recently arrived from China. Bringing close relatives to Mexico was then quite common among wealthy Chinese, like Hing in need of helping hands to grow their business. While only a few years earlier she had never set an eye on a foreigner, Cruz now pondered how her life had been transformed in many strange ways by her taciturn husband from a distant land.

* * *

From the 1890s, as the Chinese population in Mexico grew, Mexican attitudes towards the Chinese began to deteriorate, with sporadic attacks reported in several cities, including Mazatlán in 1886 and Monterrey in 1894. Public opinion was slowly turning against the "yellow plague and Mongol invasion."[6] In 1899, the Sonoran newspaper *El Tráfico* published a series of articles against Chinese immigrants, describing "the Mongol [as] the ant of the human family," and writing that "the commercial talent of the sons of the celestial empire is superior to that of the Jews," stating further that "he will never gain affection for the country to which he emigrates."[7] One petition signed by 167 dry goods merchants and sent to Sonora's governor complained about Chinese competition. In contrast with the United States two decades earlier, the Chinese were not criticized this time for taking the jobs of the locals; instead, Mexican merchants were worried about the competition posed by wily Chinese merchants.

In 1902, Mazatlán was struck by the global pandemic of bubonic plague, which caused more than ten million deaths worldwide, mostly in Asia. The local government reacted promptly, exterminating all the city's rats and instituting strict hygiene measures. The outbreak was contained but there were 580 victims in the city. Several newspapers highlighted that the plague was brought by ships from San Francisco's Chinatown, as it could be traced to there in 1900 and four years earlier to Hong Kong and Kwangtung, where it killed 60,000 people. Some in the United States and Mexico were quick to blame the Chinese for the pandemic, which confirmed their stereotypical image of the sickly and dirty Chinese opium addict. This plague epidemic combined with the Boxer Rebellion two years earlier marked the nadir of Western public opinion on China.

Incidentally, the old Globe Hotel in San Francisco, where Foon Chuck had studied twenty years earlier, which was now a Chinese boarding house with 300 residents, was the location of the first plague victim in the United States. Chinatown was then quarantined by the government and its few white people ordered to evacuate.[8] San Francisco's Chinese population, outraged by the government order that all corpses be autopsied instead of being sent to China for burial, hid their dead and their sick from American doctors, alienating themselves even further from Americans.[9] A few years later, while traveling through San Francisco, the exiled Chinese politician Liang Qichao noticed not only the wide sidewalks but also the strict enforcement of a ban on spitting on the streets, which aimed to help prevent further epidemics. It would have been difficult to implement such a ban back in his overpopulated country.

Hing, Foon Chuck and the young Chinese community throughout Mexico felt themselves directly affected for the first time by the fear of contagion and the collective xenophobia it brought. Although lasting only a few months, the event induced Hing to move to Tampico, a port on the Atlantic coast, a railway city with a growing Chinese community, and an important point of passage for illegal Chinese immigration from the Caribbean to the United States.[10]

In 1904, a Mexican government commission recommended that immigration from Asia be suspended but its conclusions were not followed. In 1905, an article was published in the *Mexican Herald* stressing that the government's official policy was not to encourage Chinese immigration, which was therefore exclusively the result of private commercial initiatives without government support.[11] In 1908, on the eve of the Mexican Revolution, the first immigration law was passed in Mexico and an immigration service created, three decades after the United States did it. But it was not until 1926 that foreigners started to be properly registered and migrant cards issued.

* * *

Meaning cross in Spanish, Cruz was a widespread Christian name in this religious country. Cruz was later called Abuela Cruzita (Grandmother Cruzita) by her grandchildren, who always spoke of her with affection. My great-aunt Lola always insisted that her mother was of pure Spanish lineage—that is, not mixed with Indians—as if it was essential for her to show that she and her siblings were no less than half Caucasian. Reproducing the same racial prejudice of which she was a victim, my great-aunt saw herself as above the Indians and the mestizos, aspiring to join the white Mexican bourgeoisie. This was a self-deception, as Cruz, although predominantly white, also had some Indian ancestry. For the whole family, Abuela Cruz was a calm, taciturn, loving and pious Catholic woman. The first family photographs show her a little absent: my mother speaks of her as being in "a world of her own." Her illegitimacy, added to her undeclared marriage to a Chinese, led her to lead a relatively reclusive existence, without a social life and striving to remain insensitive to any rejections. She compensated for this by having a great affection for her family. She had little education and showed little interest in learning new things. As Hing became prosperous, she felt his success to be a fair redress from a society that had been neither fair nor kind to her. Over time, she became more assertive and confident and is seen smiling in many photographs in her forties and fifties. This progression mirrored Chinese society, where women gain respect as they advance in age, especially those with male heirs. Cruz by then had ten grown-up children; she bore a total of twenty-one children, so that for more than half of her adult life she was either pregnant or recovering from childbirth, the sad fate of many women at the time. According to one of my aunts, each time Hing returned from a business trip, a new member was added to the family.

His family, even more than his business, was like an anchor for Hing, who never forgot his years of solitude before his marriage. One day, returning from a long trip, he found the door of his home and store locked, throwing him into a rare but uncontrollable rage. When his family came back home, they found the door shattered by Hing's powerful kicks. His anger quickly vanished when he saw them. He behaved like a patriarch, though he was affectionate and enjoyed spoiling his children. He did not hug and kiss them like Mexican fathers—this was not the custom in China—but had his own ways of showing his affection, and the whole family loved him in return. In most regions of China today, the Chinese are not as tactile or effusive in showing their affection to their relatives as in Mediterranean cultures. Their affection, which is no less strong, is often displayed through actions and sacrifices. Decades later, to encourage obedience, my grandmother would often tell me: "Love means good deeds, not good reasons" (*el amor son buenas acciones no buenas razones*), something she probably learned from her father. Hing liked to buy his children toys, trips, and expensive clothes, and to fund their studies abroad. Pablo, one of his younger sons, remembered that he had a gilded childhood: a photograph from 1925 shows him, aged six, next to his father, with an expensive suit and a teddy bear on wheels.

In addition to Mexican food, Hing grew fond of other Mexican traditions, like the many religious festivals, which reminded him of those in Hoksaan. He particularly enjoyed the Posadas, just before Christmas, when processions of family and friends sing and eat together, moving from home to home each night, and the Día de Muertos, the Day of the Dead, when families visit their ancestors in cemeteries, build altars at their homes in their memory and eat with them, exactly like in China. Despite embracing Mexican culture, Hing never got seriously involved in politics, either local or Chinese, since this was not required by his business. He was, though, a respected figure within the Chinese and diplomatic communities, often presiding over large receptions with pomp and ceremony, and was acknowledged as a well-known entrepreneur by the local press. Cruz is never shown in any of the photographs of the large receptions given by Hing: she remained a traditional wife, a life companion who stayed at home with their children. Unfortunately, the prevailing racism of the time did not encourage Hing to go out arm-in-arm with her, which he felt hindered the family's social life. If Cruz had had a large family herself, things might have been quite different and life less solitary for the Leon family.

Hing kept his promise to bring his three brothers to the Americas, of whom the youngest, Tin Po, returned to China, while the other two remained in Mexico. Later, Tin Po established his family in the city of Canton, where he managed a hotel investment. Ironically, while Hing never converted to Christianity, his brother, upon his return to China, married a Chinese Christian. Nothing is known about what happened to the other two brothers, but they never married and according to family rumors they both died in suspicious circumstances in the 1920s, in either an opium or a gambling den in Mexico City. One of my great-uncles remembered how one night he had to pick up one of Hing's brothers, Uncle Antonio, completely drunk at a cantina. Perhaps they both felt that they would never be a match for their older brother or simply did not manage to assimilate into Mexican society.

As Hing's business flourished he was able to send more money to Hoksaan; he was proud to provide a comfortable life to his family back home and to have honored his promise to his mother. With time, Hing started selling increasingly refined and precious Chinese art, soon specializing in luxury items, quite a step up from the cheaper products he used to sell when he first started his business. He baptized his business the Golden Dragon (El Dragon de Oro in Spanish), a symbol of fortune in Chinese tradition. He benefited from a favorable economic environment, as those in the new Mexican *haute bourgeoisie*, born during the regime of Porfirio Díaz, who survived the revolution, built large mansions and palaces in European style, craving luxury items, especially those imported from France and the United States. It was ironic that fashions among the Mexican elite came to be dictated by the two imperial powers which had recently invaded their country. At the start of the twentieth century, as in the United States and Europe, department stores appeared in the main cities around Mexico, many opened by French immigrants eager to import luxury goods into Mexico.[12] While largely ignoring the rural and Indian areas, the Díaz government promoted higher education and the arts, filling cities with beautiful monuments and architecture. By specializing in Asian fine art, Hing filled a market niche and a cultural need which did not exist before his arrival in Mexico, one that fitted perfectly with the aspirations of the new Mexican elite.

BOURGEOIS AND MEXICAN

In the 1920s, Hing asked his brother Tin Po to move to Hong Kong to establish the East Asiatic Trading Company Ltd, sourcing products directly for him, bypassing the San Francisco merchants. This was beneficial for the profits of El Dragon de Oro and for both branches of the family, in Mexico and Hong Kong. From an itinerant business, El Dragon de Oro grew rapidly, and physical stores opened in various cities. Thus, Hing's first three sons were born in Mazatlán, while the middle siblings, including my grandmother, were born in Guadalajara, the second-largest city in Mexico, and the youngest two in Monterrey, the more liberal industrial capital of the north.

It was not until 1924 that Hing moved his family to Mexico City, where he established his flagship store at number fifty-seven on the iconic and elegant Calle Madero, in the historic heart of the city. The capital of Mexico had become by then a sophisticated city of one million inhabitants, including about 3,000 Chinese, a tiny percentage compared to San Francisco a few decades earlier. A railroad advertisement of 1910 described Mexico City in the following way: "The illuminations, parades, exhibitions, floats, historic rides, in combination with the beautiful parks, avenues, streets and buildings of the *Paris of the Americas*, form a set which cannot be replicated."[13] During the Díaz regime, more than eighty per cent of government infrastructure expenditure was spent on the Mexican capital.[14] With a truly cosmopolitan character, Mexico City had various international hotels and restaurants, as well as offices of multinational companies, housed in iron and concrete multi-storied buildings. It was a cultural and leisure capital with countless theaters, museums, coffee shops, cinemas, casinos and social clubs, its streets filled with automobiles and tramways. The Belle Époque buildings of the city date from this period, such as the Fine Arts Museum and the Angel of Independence column. By 1900, already seventy-five per cent of the urban population in Mexico enjoyed public electric lighting, while Mexico City was by some accounts "the best lit-up city on the American continent,"[15] even enjoying an expanding telephone network, appearing to be as well endowed as Paris or London.

El Dragon de Oro's flagship store had more than 300 feet of façade and three floors, which opened onto a large central atrium, with the store itself occupying the ground and mezzanine levels. On the second level was the warehouse and on the third, following Chinese tradition, a family apartment, as it was essentially a family business, all Hing's brothers and later children helping with the various branches across Mexico. A wide range of luxury handicrafts were sold, such as carved ivory items, jade and cloisonné products, bronzes, porcelain, tapestries, table linen, silk products, and lacquered items. My mother remembered a canopy bed, made of ebony wood with carved columns and a roof, which was too big to stay in the store and was kept in the warehouse. Calle Madero was for many years the most elegant shopping street in Mexico City. The flagship store was famous among the city's high society, and had many regular customers. In the 1930s, a time when diplomatic relations were strained between Mexico and China, Hing's business was sometimes an unofficial link between Chinese diplomats and local politicians: art and culture were often able to bring people together when diplomacy failed. El Dragon de Oro also became well known among the Chinese community in Mexico, as a place where overseas Chinese and their families could reconnect with and feel proud of their ancestral culture—long before a Chinatown was established in Mexico City. Often, departing or arriving Chinese migrants came to sell their Chinese objects to Hing, hoping to supplement their savings. Decades later, one of Foon Chuck's grandchildren still remembered their ritual family visits to El Dragon de Oro when traveling to Mexico City, a treasure cave where they were allowed to take what they wanted, since their grandfather was a good friend of Hing. Despite having this physical base in Mexico City, Hing continued to travel throughout the country, now also offering wholesale products to other stores, and selling his brother's products from Hong Kong, thereby amassing a considerable fortune.

1. First photo of Hing, c. 1890, Mexico.

2. Hing's naturalization certificate, 1898, describing him as a native of the Chinese Empire.

3. The Leon family, c. 1903, Mazatlán, Mexico.

4. Foon Chuck and his family, Lily in bottom left corner, c. 1905, Piedras Negras, Mexico.

5. Wong Kingfung, c. 1900, Piedras Negras, Mexico.

6. Wong Yaiwai, c. 1907, Canton, China.

7. Hing with his family during the revolution, Concha (bottom left) and Victoria (bottom right), c. 1916, Guadalajara, Mexico.

8. Meeting at Hacienda Limon, Wong Yunwu (bottom left), Arturo Chuck (top left), General Osuna and Juan Saenz seated, c. 1919, El Mante, Mexico.

9. Foon Chuck (top left) with his brother Yun Wu (top right) and his wife, his nephew Yaiwai (bottom middle) and his son-in-law Ah Kian (bottom left), c. 1924, Hacienda Limon, El Mante, Mexico.

10. Concha, 1928, Mexico City.

11. Hing with his two younger sons, Pablo and Hector, enjoying a gilded childhood, c. 1925, Monterrey, Mexico.

12. Lily Chuck, c. 1929, Mexico City.

13. Leon family, c. 1930, Mexico City. From left to right: Pablo, Lola, Carmela (Alejandro's wife), Alejandro with baby, Jorge, Victoria, Hing, Hector, Yaiwai, Concha, Cruz, Juan, Melchor with daughter, Berenice (Melchor's wife) with baby.

14. Leon sisters: Victoria, Concha and Lola, c. 1930, Mexico City.

15. Hing at the ancestors' village with his brother and sister-in-law, c. 1935, Hoksaan, China.

16. Hing in Western Hills, 1935, Peking, China.

17. Foon Chuck and his family, c. 1930, Piedras Negras, Mexico. Standing from left to right: Ah Kian Lee, Hortensia, Benjamin, Selina, Santiago and Ruben. Seated: Margarita, Elvira, Wing On, Foon Chuck, Cristina and Lily.

18. Yaiwai, Concha with first son, c. 1932, Shanghai, China.

19. Concha in Cheongsam on the left with mother-in-law and sister-in-law in the middle, c. 1932, Shanghai, China.

20. Caricature of Hing in Mexico City's newspaper titled *Business Entrepreneurs*, c. 1935, Mexico.

21. Hing in silk robe, c. 1935, Kwangtung province, China.

22. Leon family house in Tlalpan, 1940, Mexico City.

23. Concha with three children and Chinese family helper, 1935, Shanghai, China.

24. Last family photograph of Yaiwai with Concha and children, 1937, Shanghai, China.

25. My mother, on SS *President Coolidge* bound for San Francisco, USA, 1938.

26. Wong children with grandparents and Felipa, 1941, Tlalpan, Mexico.

27. Foon Chuck with Concha and children, 1938, Torreón, Mexico.

28. Foon Chuck and Hing, 1938, Torreón, Mexico.

29. Leon family, 1939, Mexico City. Concha in mourning, top row, fourth from left; my mother in the bottom row, second from left.

30. Hing and Cruz with sons, 1943, Mexico City.

31. Bust of Hing, 1945, cemetery in Mexico City.

8

THE LAND OF THE CANOES

In 1884, Foon Chuck's US residency permit application was rejected, unsurprisingly given the Chinese Exclusion Act. This gave him a new impetus to expand his business network in northern Mexico, near the border, where he would later establish his family. He moved to Mexico that same year (one year before Hing), and settled just across the river from Eagle Pass, in a small border town of 3,000 people called Piedras Negras, which means "black stones" in Spanish named after the many coal deposits in the region. Like his native village of Chaitong, Piedras Negras is located next to a large river; in this case, the Rio Grande, which serves as the border between the two countries. It was then a new city, founded in 1850 after Texas was annexed by the United States and a new border line artificially formed. Foon Chuck settled in northern Mexico in order to retain ties with the United States and do business with the many US companies in the region. Until 1900, along with El Paso and Nogales, Eagle Pass was one of the only three official ports of entry along the US–Mexico border, all railroad towns, although by 1908 there were already twenty-one, thanks to the growing trade between the two countries.

The border between Mexico and the United States remained porous: many Chinese migrants came to Mexico to be later smuggled into the United States. It is not well known that the Chinese, not the Mexicans, were the first undocumented immigrants in US history. It is estimated that at least 2,000 of them entered the United States illegally between 1876 and 1911, mainly via Mexico,[1] but some estimates make the figure much larger. US lawmakers called for a "Chinese Wall" to be built at the border to keep them out.[2]

People smuggling was lucrative and deadly, with migrants willing to pay as much as $500 to get into the United States,[3] and the desert between San Felipe and Mexicali was called "the Desert of the Chinese" after the many migrants who died during the crossing.[4] In 1907 a US immigration inspector, talking about photographs of apprehended Chinese disguised as Mexicans, found it "exceedingly difficult to positively state whether those are pictures of Chinamen or Mexicans,"[5] probably evidencing the shared ancestry between the Chinese and native Indians. Many of the migrants were smuggled into the United States with the help of the Six Chinese Companies, which maintained arrangements with various shipping companies.

Proximity to the United States and to the many mines and companies in the region was an important reason why more than sixty per cent of Chinese Mexicans decided to settle in the north compared to ten per cent in Mexico City and thirty per cent in the rest of the country.[6] The northern Mexican states, like the American Wild West, were sparsely populated, mostly arid regions, marked by violent historical conflicts with Native Americans, a secular rather than religious culture, and populated by independent and commercially-minded white ranchers, like the cowboys north of the border. The central Mexican states, where many indigenous and mestizo peasants resided, were completely different, with subsistence agriculture, a dense and more urbanized population, and a highly Catholic and conservative culture. The cultural differences in Mexico between the capitalist north and the agrarian south remain to this day. The experience of living in northern Mexico is described by sociologists as involving a "wild pragmatism" and has a more commercial but also at times more violent character, as Foon Chuck would experience.

Driven by his ambition and confident in his destiny, Foon Chuck charted a path in the Americas that very few other Chinese migrants would ever take. Now fluent in Spanish, he courted Mexican politicians to advance his plans. In 1885, only a year after his arrival, he became acquainted with Don Miguel Cárdenas,[7] an ambitious and educated thirty-year-old lawyer, who, almost a decade later, would become governor of the state of Coahuila, one of the richest in northern Mexico. Don Miguel was charmed by Foon Chuck and his fluent Spanish and bold vision of Mexico's future development.

THE LAND OF THE CANOES

Over the next twenty-five years, he helped Foon Chuck with his businesses, until he was ousted from power by the Mexican Revolution. Foon Chuck, just twenty-two years old and freshly arrived, already understood the importance of networking and political clientelism, a lesson he had learned from his Chinese family. Seeking the support of local politicians was a common practice for foreigners in Díaz's Mexico, but this was the first time that a young independent Chinese had engaged himself in it. Political clientelism was another common factor between China and Mexico, a practice that continues to this day in both countries. Despite his young age and inexperience, Foon Chuck showed audacity, maturity and adaptability when he arrived in Mexico.

After he crossed the border in 1884, Foon Chuck recognized the lack of quality services offered to Mexican rail travelers, and he built, acquired and leased various restaurants and hotels along the railway lines of northern Mexico. This became a highly remunerative business. His first hotel was in his new town of Piedras Negras, the Hotel del Ferrocarril, meaning Railway Hotel, which he opened in 1886. He later brought various cousins and his two brothers into the town, building himself a large family house next door to the hotel, thereby beginning a community which would soon grow into a small yet important Chinatown. One of those relatives was Wong Kingfung (黄琼凤), born in China around 1880, her first name meaning "jade phoenix." She was well educated, and learned to speak English and Spanish. A photo taken in Piedras Negras around 1900 shows a resolute and bright young lady, illustrating the progressive mindset of the Wong family. She would later travel around the world, becoming a renowned painter and helping Kang Youwei raise money for his reformist cause in China. All the employees of the hotel were Chinese. There was a small vegetable garden beside the hotel, also cultivated by relatives, which supplied daily fresh products for the clients, a business model which Foon Chuck would soon replicate across the region.

In the decades following the arrival of the railroad in 1883, Piedras Negras experienced sustained economic growth, its population doubling to reach 5,000 people by the start of the century. During this period, a customs office opened and, thanks to advantageous duties rebates, the city became an important crossing point for goods between Mexico and the United States. Close to important coal mines, it soon grew into a prosperous town, its agriculture also benefiting from the mighty Rio Grande, which occasionally flooded. From 1888 to 1911, the city took the name of Ciudad Porfirio Díaz, in honor of Mexico's president, transforming itself from a dusty, desolate, and remote frontier village into a modern town with an electric grid, paved roads and various public buildings. It gained a certain sophistication, with not only products from both Mexico and the United States available but also from Europe, like wines, whiskies, and furniture, brought from the nearby port of Galveston on the Gulf of Mexico. The famous Mexican writer and philosopher José Vasconcelos (1882–1959) grew up in this booming town, where his father was a customs official, and, like Foon Chuck's children years later, he attended a bilingual school in Eagle Pass just across the border.

In 1889 an American consulate opened, housed on the ground floor of Foon Chuck's hotel, which with twenty-seven rooms was the largest in the city, later receiving visits from two Mexican presidents. It lies in ruins today but, thanks to its period architecture, various scenes of the iconic film *Like Water for Chocolate* (based on Laura Esquivel's book) were filmed within its walls. Ownership of the hotel has passed from the Mexican Railway Company to the government and there is, at the time of writing, a project to refurbish it and turn it into one of the city's heritage sites.

Foon Chuck reflected on the differences between his American family in San Francisco and his new Mexican friends. He was surprised by how much more passionate and emotional people in Mexico were. He found the Mexican propensity to hug and touch each other strange, since in many regions of China people rarely touched each other, even within families. This cultural difference could simply be due to hygiene reasons, he thought, the Chinese being historically concerned not to spread germs to loved ones in order to contain the many epidemics that ravaged their densely populated land. He was pleased to find that Mexican women had what he saw as more traditional roles than women in the United States, a situation closer to what he knew from China. He also noted with surprise how much the Virgen de Guadalupe (Mexico's representation of the Virgin Mary) was revered in Mexico, a mestizo symbol of the country, known to be a synthesis between pre-Columbian and Catholic beliefs. He found similarities with Guanyin, the Chinese goddess of mercy, and wondered what impact on women's standing such a belief would have back home. Noting that Christianity was practiced differently across the border, he was himself naturally drawn to the Presbyterian Church of his American family, which was known for reaching out to the working classes and minorities.

Foon Chuck received a job offer from his supplier, the Kim Lung Company of San Francisco, to become its general manager in Los Angeles. He refused, having his eyes now set on Mexico.[8] As in his earlier refusal to his uncle, he showed his desire to remain the sole master of his destiny. Until 1889, he focused mainly on developing his retail and hotel businesses. He then returned to China for a second time, staying for ten months. With the profits he brought back to China, he ordered the construction of a large new home for his family and a school for the village, proud to honor his clan in this way. While in China, he lived with his wife whom he had not seen in seven years. His Chinese biography mentions that he was unable to convince her to move to Mexico with him, but does not mention any children the couple may have had.[9] Foon Chuck discussed with powerful and wealthy people from his family the vast business opportunities offered by Mexico. Impressed by his words, his relatives realized that they had been right to back this promising young man fifteen years earlier, and they agreed that the clan should continue supporting him with capital. His experience exemplified the transnational investment system of the Chinese diaspora, based on trust and loyalty derived from family ties and a community of origin, remarkable at a time when international communications and the banking system were in their infancy.

In 1884, the first coal mine in Mexico opened in San Felipe, creating the Coahuila Coal Company, owned by the American industrialist Collis Potter Huntington. He was also the proprietor of the Southern Pacific Railroad and of various Mexican railway lines, illustrating the control of American rail barons over the Mexican economy. Such foreign owners were less concerned with the returns on their railroad investments, which were low at three per cent per annum, than with their goal of penetrating Mexican markets and mining regions and cutting transportation costs and time, since the Díaz regime granted them reduced tariffs on all products traveling by railroad.[10] Many landowners benefited from the railroads by seeing the value of their land jump, something well understood by Foon Chuck.

Upon his return from China to Piedras Negras in 1890, at the age of twenty-seven, he learned that the San Felipe mine was looking for workers. Having heard that Chinese workers building the Tehuantepec railway line in the south of Mexico had just been laid off, he negotiated an employment contract for a hundred of these workers with the mining company. The Tehuantepec railway was a controversial project, employing hundreds of coolies brought directly from China by a state-owned Mexican shipping company, many coerced or cheated, poorly supplied, and falling ill just a few weeks after their arrival. Of course, underground mining was a hazardous activity, more so than railroad construction, with the constant dangers of explosions and rockslides. However, despite this, the better pay and generally better working conditions at the mine compared to the Tehuantepec railway made the workers grateful to now be working under Foon Chuck's supervision. This first contract being a success, he was asked to find more workers for the mine. Within two years he was supervising 400 miners; but an accident, when a landslide almost took his own life and killed two of his workers,[11] forced him to look for new and safer opportunities.[12] Organizing mining workforces was Foon Chuck's fifth business. He had not foreseen the inherent dangers of the work, and he thereafter discouraged his compatriots from working or investing in mining. History would prove him right: the mines at San Felipe developed a bad reputation for their dangerous conditions, with workers dying of diseases and frequent explosions, including one in 1902 that killed 142 miners.[13]

Although US regulations governing the Chinese became tighter every year, Foon Chuck continued to travel back and forth to the United States for business. In 1892, the Geary Act required all Chinese in the United States to be registered and to carry residency certificates, or else be deported. A decade later, a proposal was put forward to make illegal immigration a criminal act punishable by prison. At the instigation of the Six Chinese Companies, the Chinese migrants refused to register, in protest against the Geary Act, one of the country's first cases of mass civil disobedience. Foon Chuck

THE LAND OF THE CANOES

realized that it was now a matter of survival to improve his status of perpetual alien, becoming one of the first Chinese to obtain Mexican naturalization,[14] only eight years after entering Mexico and seven years before Hing, likely with the help of his friend Miguel Cárdenas. However, as early as 1893, Mexico was informed by the US government that it would not recognize the naturalization of Chinese for the purpose of entry into the United States, which some saw as an affront to Mexican sovereignty.[15] In May 1892, on a business trip to San Antonio, Texas, Foon Chuck was apprehended by US immigration authorities, an event which was widely covered by the US press, the *New York Tribune* reporting that Foon Chuck had assets of more than $100,000.[16] This happened despite the Mexican consul in Eagle Pass certifying that Foon Chuck had a good reputation for his conduct and providing proof to the courts that he was a naturalized Mexican. Although Foon Chuck had enough money to provide a bond, a US law prohibited the Chinese from paying bonds and he was forced to endure round-the-clock supervision at his own expense.[17] Despite acknowledging that he was a merchant and Mexican citizen, the court sentenced him to one hour of forced community work and deported him to Mexico, an event as humiliating as it was absurd for Foon Chuck.[18] In reaction, the *Washington Post* published a scathing article where it proposed, with obvious irony, a "mass exodus" of the Chinese to Mexico,

> [...] as in Mexico the Chinese would be treated with justice, even with liberality. Their industry, their skill, their frugality would be appreciated, and they would find, not only the reasonable recompense of honest toil, but a humane and civilized spirit in their reception by the people. They have been treated here with shameful brutality. They will encounter in Mexico nothing but kindness and encouragement. We hope that the exodus will be consummated and this we hope for their sake as much as for our own. The change will be to their advantage in every way, and it will be to ours in that it will obviate the cruelty and oppression which the new feature of the Exclusion Act provides for, and which, in many parts of the country, would infallibly be practiced. We wear already a sufficient odious stigma in the matter of our dealings with the Chinese; there is no reason why it should be made bigger and blacker and more disgraceful.[19]

Like in many Chinese-Mexican families, Foon Chuck's precious certificate of naturalization was later framed at his home, and is kept to this day as a relic by his descendants. In place of his Chinese surname, Wong, he took as his Mexican surname the second character of his Chinese first name, Chuck, which his Mexican descendants still carry today. This was a common practice for Chinese migrants in Latin America, since in China the surname is always placed first. He was henceforth called Wong Foon Chuck, both in Chinese and Spanish. In contrast to Western culture, this Chinese tradition of emphasizing the family name ahead of the given name shows the importance of belonging to a clan before anything else. The fact that the name Chuck had an easy English pronunciation may also have been a way to get closer to his friends in the United States, as well as differentiating him from the many other Wongs, a more common surname. When his two brothers joined him in Mexico a few years later, they too took the surname Chuck, even though their Chinese first names are not pronounced in this way. Unlike most naturalized Chinese, Foon Chuck never adopted a Spanish first name, something he did not consider necessary to become accepted, and a statement that he wanted to retain his Chinese heritage and culture. This was a courageous act from someone who struggled all his life, despite his naturalization, to enter the United States, where a Mexican name together with his fluent Spanish might have helped.

In 1893, his new citizenship emboldened him to invest in the town of Torreón, in the same state of Coahuila, but further south along the railroad track, 350 miles from Piedras Negras and with a population of 2,700 people, of which only five were Chinese, all operating a family-run store.[20] There he first bought another hotel, the Hotel del Ferrocarril, from the two US railway companies which owned it, with whom he immediately signed five-year lease agreements. This was an innovative financial transaction for the time, known today as sale-leaseback, showing that he was not only a shrewd businessman but also well versed in financial structuring.

In 1895, he traveled through the more fertile neighboring state of Tamaulipas looking for land to buy, as he wanted to develop a farming business alongside his hotels and restaurants. His granddaughter recalls that he always asked the locals where the water stopped during floods in the summer months, making sure that his land was always on high terrain, a habit he brought from his Chinese village. During this trip, he was introduced to a young woman named Cristina Vega Dominguez from Pueblo Viejo near Tampico. Cristina was from a humble background and was barely literate, but Foon Chuck was struck by her ambitious and strong-willed character as well as her intelligence. She was mestizo, her father being a tall and fair-skinned worker and her mother a short and determined woman of Huastec Indian descent. That year, aged thirty-two, Foon Chuck married Cristina in the church, establishing his family on Washington Street in Eagle Pass. With the distance and never having lived much with his Chinese wife, he felt within his right to ignore his first marriage. Elvira, their first child, was born shortly afterwards. Foon Chuck and Cristina had ten children, Elvira born in Eagle Pass and the nine others in Piedras Negras, across the border, since most of his businesses were now in Mexico. In order of birth, his six daughters were Elvira, Lily, Margarita, Rosita, Selina and Hortensia, and his four sons were Arturo, Santiago, Benjamín and Rubén. Being naturalized, Foon Chuck could have brought his Chinese wife from Chaitong, but like Hing he decided instead to marry a Mexican and build a family in Mexico, realizing that the country where he had already lived for twelve years, and where he had established so many friendships and businesses, was the one he wanted to settle in for the long term. However, it is telling that Foon Chuck established his family in Piedras Negras, just across the border, instead of further south in Torreón, where he was developing his business. Maybe he wanted to spread his risks or simply to keep stronger ties with the United States.

Having similarities with Piedras Negras, Torreón was an ideal town for investors. It was located in the fertile valley of the Laguna, irrigated by the Nazas River, and formed the meeting point of two new railroad lines completed in 1888 and bringing Mexico's mining and agricultural products to the US market, one running to El Paso, Texas, and the other to the Arizona border. Chinese and other foreigners flocked to Torreón, including Americans, Spaniards, Germans, French, British and Italians, attracted by advantageous government tax breaks. Local entrepreneurs, such as the family of the future revolutionary leader Francisco Madero, were also active in Torreón, building various modern industries, department stores and banks. The town already enjoyed running water, electricity, a modern drainage system, and even an electric tramway, the third in the country. By 1910, the population of the district had increased to 40,000 inhabitants, up from only 2,000 two decades earlier, including 1,500 Americans and more than 700 Chinese. Now Torreón was called "the most American City in Mexico,"[21] the US government posting a permanent consul in the city in recognition of its growing importance. With its many foreign residents, its status as a capitalist boom town, and a growing urban proletariat, Torreón could be seen then as a perfect example of President Díaz's social engineering project and eugenic utopia in Mexico.

As Torreón became a booming city and most of its land was used by the cotton industry, Foon Chuck struggled to supply his restaurant and hotel, making him purchase six hectares of land on the east of the city in an area called El Pajonal, to create his own vegetable growing business,[22] the first of its kind around Torreón. It served his hotels and restaurants across the state and even exported part of its production to the United States by railway, another highly cash generative business. He then rented parts of his land to other Chinese for them to grow food and cotton. The "Chinese Gardens," as they were later known, quickly became a feature of this growing city. Within a few years, they already occupied an area of 150 hectares[23] and employed a hundred Chinese horticultural workers. Their size and number meant they could not be missed by anyone who visited the city.[24] Foon Chuck retained the largest of these Chinese Gardens, called the Do Sing Yuen, adjacent to La Rosita Ranch. Torreón became known in Chinese as "the City of the Horticultural Garden."[25]

By 1910, Foon Chuck and other Chinese food wholesalers and retailers already controlled the entire production, distribution and sale of daily food to the local population, rich and poor, as well as many restaurants and laundries. Like Foon Chuck, most of the Chinese proprietors came from out of town, many from the ports of Manzanillo and Mazatlán,[26] where they kept their families. This, plus the fact that these companies employed almost exclusively Chinese workers, created resentment among the local Mexican population. Like San Francisco in the previous century, Torreón was predominantly a city of male workers with a chronic shortage of women, another source of anxiety for the local populace.

THE LAND OF THE CANOES

Meanwhile, Foon Chuck's hotel business grew rapidly. By 1901 he already owned six hotels in the state of Coahuila alone, all located along the railway lines,[27] and some under sale-leaseback contracts with the railway companies, including establishments in Sabinas, Jarral, Piedras Negras and Torreón. His business was vertically integrated: he controlled the entire value chain, from the hotels and restaurants to the agricultural companies and other suppliers, which meant he could provide a reliable and unique service to his powerful American customers, an important reason behind his success.

In 1896, two representatives from the Beaumont Rice Company of Texas arrived in Mexico to study an option they had to buy land in the El Mante region, in the neighboring state of Tamaulipas, about 500 miles southwest of Torreón, and halfway towards Mexico City. They sought someone to help them with their assessment, and the American president of the Monterrey Rail Company recommended Foon Chuck, given his recent agricultural successes, his knowledge of Tamaulipas state, and his command of English. Although more than forty miles away from the railway, Foon Chuck immediately fell under the charm of that land, a Mexican "Peach Blossom Spring"[28] (a utopian hidden land of peace and prosperity). In contrast with the arid north, it is at the center of one of the most fertile regions in Mexico, La Huasteca Tamaulipeca, with an incredible level of biodiversity. Driving from north to south on the highway one is struck by how the desert suddenly gives way to tropical vegetation. As one of his granddaughters told me, Foon Chuck found it to resemble the lush countryside of Chaitong, except that it was "covered with lemons and mangoes." Decades later, Rubén, Foon Chuck's youngest son, told passing visitors, who wanted to pick the many fallen fruits, to pick them directly from the trees, such was the abundance. According to a local historian, El Mante was the only city in Mexico to possess a network of clean water canals, still visible and in use today. In the ancient Indian Tenek language this region is called "the place of the canoes,"[29] giving a vivid picture of its hydrography. The land is also archeologically rich, with pre-Columbian artefacts excavated regularly by the locals, showing how people have occupied these lands since remote times, although without leaving traces of larger stone settlements like those of the Aztecs or Mayas. Located at the intersection of five rivers with a high flow rate, Foon Chuck found this land ideally suited for becoming a prosperous agricultural zone, long before any Mexican entrepreneur became interested in the area. After sending his report to the Texas Company, he learned that it had lost interest in the land, since it was located so far from the railroad and seemed to require too much investment. At the same time, he learned that the government of the state of Tamaulipas was now offering to sell the right to use the water of the five rivers.[30]

Chinese civilization is strongly connected with agriculture, its people having been farmers for thousands of years. Its greatest monument, the Great Wall, was built to protect China's agricultural society against nomadic aggressors from the northwest. Agriculture has long had the special patronage of Chinese emperors, who every spring ploughed three furrows of a sacred field set apart for that purpose, the same ceremony being performed in other parts of the empire by the highest officials.[31] Unlike Hebrew civilization with its pastoral tradition, or Greek civilization with its maritime one, China's has always revolved around arable agriculture.[32]

Foon Chuck was a polymath businessman, but he remained a farmer at heart, as his ancestors had been for generations. Missing the rice paddies of Chaitong, he saw nothing dishonorable in agriculture, especially if it was profitable and used modern techniques. Taoist philosophy teaches that, toiling endlessly his fields and being close to nature, only the simple farmer can truly be virtuous, "like a child who has not smiled yet." Important concepts of Confucianism can also be explained metaphorically in terms of agriculture: fixing one's determination on something is like sowing seeds; the reverential attention needed for self-cultivation is the same as watering plants; and weeding is akin to eradicating evil things and selfish desires.[33] In ancient Chinese culture, there were four classes in society: scholars, farmers, craftsmen and merchants.[34] Traditionally, these categories were ranked in order of their economic utility to the state and society. Scholars were placed first, then farmers, because they were considered the main creators of wealth, then craftsmen, and finally merchants, seen as disruptors of the social order by their excessive accumulation of wealth. This did not prevent China from becoming a mercantile-minded society, but emperors always strived to maintain a healthy balance between the four

THE LAND OF THE CANOES

classes. An ancient Chinese emperor once declared that farmers are "the root of all under heaven."[35] By pursuing agriculture, unlike opening a bank or hotel, Foon Chuck saw himself as building something virtuous and meaningful for society, like an industrialist might today. This, he thought, more than anything else, would bring prestige and honor to his clan.

It's worth noting that during the nineteenth century, the soldiers' class in China was at the very bottom of the social ladder, below even that of merchants. This could be partly explained by the fact that the Qing dynasty was the dominant regional power and had maintained peace for more than one hundred years. Moreover, the army recruited among the poorest, the unemployed and even the imprisoned. A Chinese proverb states: "Do not waste good iron on nails and good men on soldiers."[36] This attitude was exacerbated by the fact that the Manchu rulers, whose military tradition contrasted with the literary and administrative skills of the Chinese Han majority, maintained tight control over the army, behaving more like occupiers than rulers. All written army communications were in Manchu, unintelligible to the Han Chinese, while Manchu officers were better treated and paid than their Han counterparts. In contrast to most Western countries then, and like their dynastic predecessors before them, the Qing emperors had also been maintaining a strict monopoly on power by regulating the manufacture and ownership of weapons (and later guns) by the common population, a society marked by the credo "esteeming literacy while despising martiality".[37] It was therefore not surprising that China became so weak militarily, especially compared to other countries where the army was then admired and even glorified, such as Japan and Germany.

Between 1897 and 1899, Foon Chuck acquired with two Chinese partners 1,100 hectares of farmland six miles northwest of El Mante, between the Mante and Guayalejo rivers. His land grew to 1,870 hectares a few years later, becoming the Hacienda Canton, meaning the "Farm of the Province of Kwangtung" (GuangDong Yuan in Mandarin).[38] The Chinese character Yuan refers to a district or academy and therefore the name of his farm in Chinese translated as the Academy or District of Kwangtung, demonstrating his vast and ambitious plans for the land: he wanted to recreate a piece of his homeland in Mexico. Between 1901 and 1907, in association with an American and a Mexican partner, he purchased another 608 hectares further east near the little village of El Limon, alongside the Guayalejo river, along with water rights to the river. This portion of the land became Hacienda El Limon. By 1907, he had managed to cultivate six hectares of irrigated land with corn and rice, as well as 500 furrows of sugar cane, still a small portion of his close to 3,000 hectares.[39] In 1908, he established a partnership with his friend Miguel Cárdenas, now governor of the neighboring state of Coahuila, obtaining in 1909 public funding to purchase 8,883 hectares, which were acquired on behalf of the governor and various local politicians. By 1911, Foon Chuck and his politician partners had become the largest landowners in the region, controlling 19,235 hectares, which were by now producing 150 tons of sugar cane and 281 tons of rice annually.[40] Very little of this vast land was yet suitable for agriculture: it was uneven, covered in dense vegetation and large swamp areas, and lacking infrastructure, hence requiring significant investments. The land was purchased entirely from existing large landowners, mainly from a retired colonel who was now chief of police, highlighting their limited economic value in their existing condition.

In addition to his hotel business, this farm became Foon Chuck's other major commercial venture in Mexico, taking most of his time over the following decades. At thirty-three years old, Foon Chuck had never felt so accomplished in his life, conscious that buying such a vast and fertile parcel of land would have been impossible in his overpopulated province of Kwangtung. He was surprised that Spanish colonists had never exploited the riches of the land before, musing that sufficiently advanced technology may not have existed then to clear, irrigate and level up the land. In contrast with the beliefs of Indian Americans, and even Western philosophy, the Chinese have long had a utilitarian view of nature, in which humans and their environment are always interrelated, nature never excluding human activity but instead embracing it. This large purchase of land by a young Chinese in association with governing officials and with government help may seem strange, but it fit perfectly with Mexican policies at the time, in particular the Land Colonization Act of 1883. As with the conquest of the American West in the

THE LAND OF THE CANOES

United States, the Mexican government aggressively encouraged settlers and entrepreneurs to develop projects on virgin land throughout the country, and hundreds of thousands of hectares were thus exchanged. In 1803, Alexander von Humboldt wrote of Mexico that, "[t]he people [...] know little how to exploit the riches that are presented to them [...]. [T]hey have kept inhabited the most fertile regions and those close to the coast."[41] He observed as well that the state of Tamaulipas was among the least populated in the whole of Mexico,[42] and wrote that "the Indians, indolent in nature and benefiting from fertile lands, do not grow crops beyond their own immediate needs."[43]

Foon Chuck was thus interested in a land that was largely unexploited and whose value few had recognized before. As the future would show, it was a risky project given the lack of infrastructure, the distance from the railway, and the heavy capital investments required. In 1897, he hired the civil engineering company J. C. Abbot to carry out earthworks, and then thirty-two Chinese workers for his Hacienda Canton. After clearing and leveling the land, he ordered the construction of a dam on the Mante River, to be eleven feet deep and eighty-eight feet long, along with eight miles of canals to bring water to his farm.[44] This would be the first and only irrigation project of such magnitude in the region until 1927. Within three years, he imported state-of-the-art machinery from the United States, including the state's first tractors, to set up a sugar factory and process rice, making the operation one of the most modern in all of Mexico. He was also the first farmer in the region to rotate crops. From 1900 to 1910, the population of Hacienda Canton grew from sixty-seven to 438 farmers; he managed to create a vibrant farming community. A local historian has written that those early steps by Foon Chuck marked "the start of the transformation of that region [and] were more powerful than those of the 1910 revolution."[45]

China is believed to be a hydraulic society with its first ancient state and bureaucracy emerging out of the need to tame its rivers. Foon Chuck proudly remembered the rice fields surrounding his home village in Kwangtung province, a region famous throughout China for thousands of years for its irrigation techniques. In the nineteenth century, its agriculture was already among the most

121

modern in China, many farmers having already abandoned subsistence agriculture for sugar production.[46] Foon Chuck was not afraid of an agricultural project like Hacienda Canton: he carried agriculture in his blood, and felt proud to import to Mexico both irrigation techniques and rice workers from China. He had studied ancient Chinese history, and knew that the most powerful emperors were those who could build and maintain large-scale infrastructure work and thus control the enormous human resources required. All Chinese people respect and fear the power of rivers; the first hydraulic engineers were considered masters in their profession. The journalist Malcolm Gladwell attributes Asians' skill in arithmetic and organization to their intensive cultivation of rice,[47] which for thousands of years has required meticulous planning of irrigation and soil preparation.

With a talent for identifying new opportunities and working in a buoyant Mexican economy, Foon Chuck had found the perfect recipe for building a commercial empire. The ingredients were his ability to quickly raise Chinese capital; his mobilization of cheap, efficient and abundant Chinese labor; his connections, both among politicians and business leaders; and finally his organizational skills, which were manifest in his setting up of integrated, modern, innovative companies. From this point of view, Foon Chuck had a definite advantage over most of his competitors, who were not able to raise funds so rapidly given Mexico's underdeveloped banking system.

Foon Chuck realized the extent of his debt to Reverend Loomis for his enlightened education, which allowed him twenty years later to become one of the first Chinese modern entrepreneurs in the Americas. His enterprise was not the only large-scale Chinese business in Mexico, other merchants from San Francisco having also invested in the country, including in mining projects in Sonora and Baja California, in clothes manufacturing, and in retail distribution around the country. However, his rapidly became the largest and most diversified of such companies. The common characteristic between Piedras Negras, Torreón, El Mante, and all the other business locations chosen by Foon Chuck, is that they were all places of high economic potential, where he enjoyed political support, and where few Chinese had settled before him. This demonstrated his confidence in Mexico and his pioneering spirit. During those years, most of his Chinese compatriots settled in the Mexican northwest, in the states of Baja California and Sonora, near Arizona and California, or in mining and agricultural regions where they labored for large Western companies. By contrast, Foon Chuck's three main places of business were in the Mexican northeast, further away from San Francisco. Importantly, this put him in competition with Mexican businessmen as opposed to working for them, unlike many of the other Chinese immigrants. With time, the locations of his businesses all grew into larger Chinese settlements, as members of his family and his Chinese friends joined him. From this perspective, Foon Chuck's experience, like Hing's, was an exception, not particularly representative of the broader Chinese-Mexican community.

Sadly, despite employing almost no Mexicans in his businesses, in an essay on Mexico in 1898 and later in a letter to his friend Tom Leung, Foon Chuck reproduced the same prejudiced and exploitative language towards the poor Mexican class that was common among the wealthy and the foreigners in Mexico at the time:

> The rich lead sumptuous lives and are polite and respectful, even more so than in China. But the poor live in abject misery, their character is deceitful and their look crude [...]. Their addiction to alcohol makes them even rougher [...].[48]

> Today Mexico is a new world. The land is vast and fertile. The natives have very little education, close to foolishness. Only with a bit of talent, ambition, and capital, one can exploit them. Our Chinese people can build a solid foundation for business here.[49]

Over the years, with his marriage to a mestiza, the passage of the revolution, and later the expansion of his agricultural business, Foon Chuck would gradually adopt more enlightened views on the Mexican Indians.

Despite the exclusionary laws in the United States, Foon Chuck's American education meant that US businessmen viewed him largely as one of them, now serving as an intermediary not only between Chinese and Westerners but also between Americans and Mexicans. Thanks to his mastery of languages, he worked at the crossroads of three distinct cultures. Excluded from the United

States, he never abandoned his goal of working with his American friends, even if no longer on their soil. All his life, despite having become a wealthy Mexican merchant, he continued to be restricted under the Chinese Exclusion Act, facing difficulties crossing the border with the United States. US law makers and politicians continued to see the Chinese exclusively on racial grounds, instead of as Mexican, British or Canadian citizens, which many had become. In 1907, despite being already well known in the city, Foon Chuck was refused entry at the Eagle Pass border by an overzealous immigration officer. All he was trying to do was buy some equipment in Eagle Pass before returning to Mexico. He was told instead to enter the United States via New York, since Eagle Pass was no longer a permitted point of entry for the Chinese.[50]

US immigration reports from around 1909 identify a certain Wong Foon Chuck from the state of Durango, and another bearing the same name from El Paso, as traffickers of illegal Chinese immigrants to the United States,[51] but it is doubtful whether this was our Foon Chuck, since his businesses were 500 miles away from those locations. It is possible, though, that his hotels served as places of passage for illegal Chinese migrants to the United States, perhaps also giving them assistance. Despite facing widespread contempt and racism in the United States, Foon Chuck continued to speak better English than Spanish all his life, and he maintained strong friendships and emotional connections in the United States. Thanks to his Christian education there and Reverend Loomis, Foon Chuck retained a kind and forgiving disposition towards the country that would reject him and his people all his life.

The model of economic development of the Chinese diaspora that Foon Chuck exemplified, based on intermediation at the confluence of several cultures and in cooperation with Anglo-Saxon companies, was very similar to that observed in other Chinese migrant communities in Southeast Asia. But this was one of the first such instances, if not the only one, on the North American continent, and was thanks to the friendly policies of Mexico as well as Foon Chuck's bilingual and progressive upbringing.

His successes did not make him complacent, though, and he reflected on the insecure position of his people in Mexico. In another letter of 1903 to Tom Leung, he summarized with great clarity the situation of his business and of his fellow compatriots:

THE LAND OF THE CANOES

You asked about the business of my brothers and I: mainly farm work and hotels. In hospitality, we employ 150 Chinese, and the business outlook is positive. However, the price of silver has fallen, causing us some losses. You plan to send brothers here, anyone who works hard can find work. The salaries, however, will not measure up to the United States. Therefore, Chinese workers generally do not stay long. All they want is to escape and go to the United States. It is annoying [...] I believe that if the Chinese like us, who have knowledge, work hard and diligently, we will certainly surpass the locals in ten years. But if they do not change their old habits like those Chinese in the United States, in less than ten years we will surely end up [excluded] like them. This is the most terrible and frightening thought.[52]

9

A REFORMER IN EXILE

In nineteenth-century China, the modern concept of the nation was less developed than in Europe and the Americas. No equivalent word in Chinese even existed. The term "Chinese nation" only appeared at the start of the twentieth century, being first put forward by the political thinker Liang Qichao. This is partially explained by the fact that the Chinese Empire had been closed for so long and, since the seventeenth century, had been under the rule of a foreign dynasty, the Manchus. Until 1905, this same dynasty, anxious to preserve its ethnicity, prohibited mixed marriages between the Manchu nobility and its Han Chinese subjects,[1] as well as internal Chinese migration to the northern Manchu heartland. The Chinese were thus discriminated against not only in the United States by the white majority but in China itself by the ruling Manchu minority.

Chinese society was also still predominantly rural and hence mostly clan-based, with thousands of distinct dialects and customs; the idea of a Chinese nation made little sense in this context. The word "country" is translated today in Chinese as the combination of the two characters meaning state and family,[2] while the word "nation" is made of those meaning people and clan (i.e. extended family),[3] highlighting the historic connection between these concepts. Another idea, widespread in the nineteenth century and still in vogue in the twentieth, was that the Chinese were like a "sheet of loose sand,"[4] meaning that, unlike the Japanese for example, they were incapable of joining together for work or politics, perhaps as a result of overpopulation. Illustrating this Malthusian mentality, a friend told me in the mid-1990s, during the reform era of Deng Xiaoping, "The problem with us Chinese is that we are just too many."

At the end of the nineteenth century, the low value of human life in China and the lack of solidarity amongst the people, was illustrated by the fact that, as a missionary priest recorded, sinking river boats were often not rescued. The superstitious Chinese feared that "the water spirits should claim the rescuers instead of the rescued."[5] Since the Ming dynasty (1368–1644), fear of rebellions meant that all kinds of associations were banned in China; men of knowledge thus did not become used to assembling in large groups for political purposes.[6] The repressive character of Chinese emperors for centuries was therefore a possible reason for the absence of political consciousness in many Chinese people.

Therefore, it was only by going abroad that migrants first learned both about democracy and, feeling their otherness, about what it meant to belong not only to a family or regional clan but to a broader Chinese community. Facing a hostile white majority in the United States, the overseas Chinese realized that they must organize themselves politically. Hence, at the end of the Qing dynasty (1636–1912), the first national movements and Chinese political parties arose not in China but among emigrants, before spreading to China itself. The idea that the Chinese are all "descendants of the mythical Yellow Emperor"[7] was only born in the early twentieth century—but it became a powerful national symbol.

Kang Youwei[8] was a Confucian philosopher, politician, and reformer of the late Qing dynasty, probably one of modern China's most influential thinkers, compared by historians to a Chinese Voltaire. He was born in 1858 in Nanhai, a few years before my ancestors and not far from their villages in Kwangtung province. The characters You and Wei in his first name mean "he who has achievements." Sun Yat-sen[9] (1866–1925), the father of the Chinese republic, was born nearby. As mentioned earlier, it is no coincidence that the two great Chinese reformers at the beginning of the century were both natives of Kwangtung, since this was one of the regions in China that was most open to the West and its influences, and most distant from the northern capital of Peking.

Kang's trajectory, although very different from those of my ancestors, intersects theirs from three different perspectives. First,

A REFORMER IN EXILE

he was also an immigrant to the New World, even if only temporarily. Second, he too became interested in Mexico, not only for business but also for its politics. Third, he became Foon Chuck's business partner, thus playing a key role in my family's history. Despite his traditional upbringing in a China still living to the rhythm of its ancestral customs, Kang was hungry for modernity and to change the world, confident in his and his country's destinies, not unlike Foon Chuck.

In contrast to my ancestors' farming origins, Kang Youwei came from a family of scholars and officials. Before becoming a political thinker, Kang was already a philosopher at heart, imbued from a young age with Buddhism and the Confucian ideals of service to society. Many Chinese from the gentry at that time revered only Confucius, despising Buddhism and Taoism as mere superstitions.[10] This was not the case in Kang's family. His father died when he was only ten, causing the family to suffer from relative poverty during his youth, which may explain his later ambition to reinstate his family fortune. His intellectual gifts were recognized early on, and he was sent by his family to study the Confucian classics in order to take the Imperial Examination. However, he disliked the required literary exercises, which he found repetitive and only useful to pass examinations, without any practical relevance for the daily tasks of a future public official. He preferred philosophy and Buddhist meditation, and it was during a meditative contemplation that he decided to enter politics with the aim of reforming and saving the Chinese Empire.

From ancient times, the Chinese have believed that public officials should be well-rounded scholars and gentlemen, continually cultivating themselves, and that the study of public administration should thus be accompanied by a private pursuit of literature, philosophy and the arts. In the late Qing dynasty, having beautiful calligraphy was still expected as part of the Imperial Examination, as well as knowledge of poetry, explaining in part the lack of practicality of many civil servants at the time.

In 1879, at the age of twenty-one, Kang traveled for the first time to Hong Kong and Shanghai, where he had a revelation. Seeing the prosperity of the British-administered ports made him realize that Western ideas could not simply be dismissed as inferior, as was the belief amongst most Confucian bureaucrats. Since ancient times, the Chinese had viewed themselves as being at the center of the world, or "all under Heaven,"[11] with barbarians needing to be assimilated into a Chinese culture that was impermeable to foreign influence. In antiquity, the philosopher Mencius (372–289 BCE) reproached his disciple for having abandoned the learnings of China, saying: "I have heard of men using the doctrines of our great land to change the barbarians, but I have never heard of any being changed by barbarians."[12]

In Hong Kong, Kang also had his first exchange with foreign missionaries, another revelatory experience—this time of a religious nature–that had an impact on his later theories. This suggests that the young Chinese elite was not only in search of modernity but also spirituality. According to Confucius, a gentleman has the duty to pass his knowledge to others, and from that time Kang started not only to immerse himself in Western books on politics and science, but also to establish his first schools in China, with a mixture of classic and modern teachings, including physical education, which was a first in the country. Those schools earned him fervent disciples among the most progressive young Chinese men. Endeavoring to reconcile tradition with modernity and Eastern with Western thinking, at the age of thirty he wrote a revolutionary book demonstrating the reforming character of Confucius; his disciple Liang Qichao was inspired to call him a "Martin Luther of Confucianism."[13] All his life, Kang proved to be a visionary thinker, anticipating before others for example that the world would one day be connected by a global telegraph and telephone network. Towards the end of his life, he became excited about the possibility of interstellar travel, even creating an Academy of Travel through the Heavens.[14]

In his late thirties, after more than twenty years of study, Kang passed the Imperial Examination with distinction, becoming a high-level official. It was quite common to pass the examination at such an advanced age, meaning that civil servants had often studied the Confucian classics for most of their lives, which was not conducive to critical thinking. However, Kang did not practice his new profession with much success or zeal; instead he sent several petitions to the Guangxu Emperor that made him famous, especially after China's defeat in its war against Japan and the humiliating 1895 Treaty of Shimonoseki. These earned him an audience with the

A REFORMER IN EXILE

emperor and he became his close advisor. The military defeat against Japan, which was still considered a vassal state, was a surprise to many Chinese bureaucrats, shaking their self-confidence and further putting in question the Qing dynasty's mandate to rule. Inspired by reforms that had been implemented earlier in Japan, the reforms Kang proposed were broad in scope while also reflecting the thinking of an educated Confucian scholar.

In 1898, his ideas inspired a reform movement in China, the Hundred Days Reform, and the young emperor tried—unsuccessfully—to implement the radical changes he proposed in imperial education, the political and military system, and the economy. These included the adoption of a constitutional monarchy, rapid industrialization, and the modernization of the army. Inspired by foreign missionaries, Kang even proposed the establishment of Confucian academies abroad to spread Chinese culture overseas,[15] which the Chinese government would effectively implement more than a hundred years later with the Confucius Institutes of today. The Guangxu Emperor's adoptive mother, the powerful Empress Dowager Cixi, seeing these reform attempts as an affront, responded with a coup, imprisoning or killing the reformers and their families, including a brother of Kang, and even desecrating their ancestors' tombs in Kwangtung,[16] which in a world ruled by spirits was considered the safest way to bring disaster onto one's enemies. After this failure, with the help of the British consul, the heartbroken Kang Youwei was forced to flee China as the empress ordered that he be executed by "slow slicing." Kang and his disciples, including Liang Qichao, spent fifteen years in exile, not returning to China until 1913, after the fall of the Qing dynasty.

In 1898, as he fled China and passed again by Hong Kong, Kang lived with the family of the legendary businessman Sir Robert Ho Tung. From then on, Kang saw Eurasians as part of a possible future for China. Sir Robert's family (he had a Dutch-English father and a Chinese mother) was the first example Kang had seen of a high-society family who, for economic and status reasons, chose to present themselves as Chinese rather than British. Eurasians were less discriminated against in China than in the West, as my grandmother would experience three decades later. The Chinese elite historically had had limited foreign contacts, so Kang was one of the first

Chinese political thinkers and scholars to live for a long period in the West, where he encountered modern European culture.

This culture clash led him to develop a unique set of personal thoughts about the diaspora and the Chinese nation, thoughts which were revolutionary for the time. During his years of exile between 1899 and 1913, he spent twenty-nine intermittent months visiting the United States, Canada and Mexico,[17] studying the workings of their economies and societies. As a Confucian scholar, Kang must have been puzzled by democratic systems, where elected officials were the ones who campaigned the most vigorously, spent the most money and energy on promoting themselves, lacking any sense of modesty and propriety,[18] and were not always the career bureaucrats who dominated officialdom in China. Kang was not won over by democracy. He remained all his life a supporter of constitutional monarchy, and called political elections a "world of darkness."[19] He was perhaps the Chinese writer who traveled the most in his time and had the highest access to power, meeting with monarchs, industrialists and presidents. He had audiences with US President Theodore Roosevelt, the Mexican president, and the King of Sweden, discussing with them how to solve the world's problems.[20] One of his close friends, who introduced him to Mexico and became his daughter's tutor, was the American industrialist Charles Ranlett Flint (1850–1943), the founder of IBM.

Kang wanted the US and British governments to help China establish a parliamentary monarchy. However, since they completely ignored him, he turned his efforts towards the overseas Chinese. He galvanized them by providing these business elites with unparalleled investment and networking opportunities[21] through his Chinese Empire Reform Association,[22] founded in 1899 in Canada. This association claimed that the Guangxu Emperor was weak and was unduly locked up for his alleged role in an attempted assassination of Empress Dowager Cixi. In 1902, Kang also established the Commercial Corporation[23] to invest in companies around the world in order to use their profits to both advance the work of his organization and enrich its members, becoming in a way China's first modern fund manager. This corporation concentrated its investments in the banking, real estate and transportation sectors.[24] The concept of joint investment being widespread in China, especially in the diaspora, Kang managed to raise significant capital from the overseas Chinese communities in North America and Southeast Asia. It was through this corporation that he later invested in Mexico alongside Foon Chuck.

Kang's talents were multifaceted: not only was he a brilliant politician and intellectual, passionate about scientific progress and philosophy, but he was also a businessman constantly looking for investment opportunities, both to promote his causes and for his own benefit. He was a controversial figure in China during his lifetime. Many portrayed him as an avaricious, cunning, egotistical and power-hungry politician who got too close to Japan. His enemies nicknamed him "Wild Kang Fox."[25]

Kang was the first Chinese politician to reflect carefully on the Chinese diaspora, which he compared to the Jewish people as having a common civilization but potentially no physical country,[26] since he feared that, with the dissolution of the Qing dynasty, China would lose all sovereignty to colonial nations or would descend into chaos. While he was in exile, the diaspora became his country. For him, it was essential to preserve this diaspora, unify it and even create a new China abroad, composed of Chinese colonies. What he had in mind was less a political and territorial project than an economic one, finance and trade being the means for the diaspora to survive and prosper,[27] especially given China's ancient banking tradition. His concern about the survival of the Chinese race was shared by all reformers at the time. During his trip to the United States, his disciple Liang Qichao noted that the Native Americans had by now become almost extinct, and he predicted that the African Americans would soon follow the same fate.[28] The implication was that without political reforms the Chinese might also become extinct.

However, Kang was more of a visionary philosopher and less of a nationalist than Liang: he dreamed of a world without borders in which human and material progress would make them obsolete. With the repeated failures of the Qing dynasty, most overseas Chinese felt abandoned and even stateless, knowing that their government was powerless to help them against the racism and violence they faced. Kang offered them a different self-image, not as stateless, scattered victims, but as a strong, organized national group. An important role of the Chinese Reform Association was therefore to defend the cause of the overseas Chinese against discriminatory policies around the world. It had branches in 170 cities in North America, claiming at its peak a membership of more than 100,000 members worldwide,[29] and creating one of the first Chinese political parties. The association published a newspaper, *The Chinese World*, boasting five million readers at its peak,[30] with Kang's exile and outlaw status further increasing its popularity amongst the reading public in China and overseas.

Kang competed for funds and members in the diaspora with the revolutionary leader Sun Yat-sen and his China Renewal Society, which later became the Nationalist Party, or Kuomintang.[31] Although Sun Yat-sen called for a revolution to replace the Qing dynasty with a republic, he coincided with Kang and Liang Qichao in their belief that China was not yet quite ready for real democracy and needed a transitional period under a benevolent dictator. He stated that: "Only the Party has liberty. Individuals cannot have liberty."[32] However, Sun Yat-sen had a very different background from Kang: he did not belong to the gentry but came from a farming family, thus having no incentive to maintain the Qing dynasty. Sun did not have Kang's classical Chinese education, attending Western schools in Hawaii and Hong Kong, and later studying modern medicine. Sun converted early on to Christianity, quickly adopting European-style clothes, while Kang remained a disciple of the Buddha and Confucius all his life, always wearing the traditional Chinese robe of the scholar and a pigtail, loyal to Chinese traditions till his death. Finally, Sun never got close to political power in Peking, spending most of his life in the south or in exile. In Japan in 1989, Sun attempted to approach Kang,[33] who he saw as his elder and as sharing similar goals for China. But Kang rejected his advance, seeing him as a competitor and an opportunist without his intellectual abilities. He further saw Sun as someone who had turned his back on Chinese traditions and the emperor, and he understood him to have a distinct political and civilizational project for China.

Competition between Kang's pro-reform and Sun Yat-sen's pro-revolution factions began on an equal footing. For a time, financial and moral support abroad leant towards Kang's less radical and risky cause; he was seen as the more traditional and established politician.

But as the Qing dynasty lost its grip on power over time, the only alternative to the status quo seemed to be revolution, and Kang's influence began to diminish, especially after the death of the Guangxu Emperor in 1908. The Xinhai Revolution of 1911 led to the abdication of the Qing dynasty and, in 1912, the establishment of a republic under Sun Yat-sen, which lasted only a year. Chinese politics descended into chaos and a long civil war. After the founding of the republic, Kang continued to advocate a constitutional monarchy and Confucian society, even launching a failed coup in 1917. As his political theory was never put into practice, within twenty years he passed from being a visionary reformer to an anachronistic pariah. Indeed, Kang's experience mirrored that of his master Confucius, who also failed to hold an official post and find a ruler to put into practice his theories during his lifetime.

Kang's best-known work was the controversial *Book of Great Unity*.[34] He largely completed it in 1902, but it was not published in its entirety until after his death in 1935. Its basic premise is that the suffering of the world comes from man-made boundaries—of nation, class, race, gender, family, occupation and law. By eliminating these boundaries, humanity can eliminate suffering and enter the utopian era of a unified world, an era of peace, prosperity and equality. The book's title is borrowed from Confucius' concept of the Great Harmony, which exemplifies an ideal Chinese society, while its core philosophy is inspired by Buddhist scriptures and their perspective on suffering. Hence, Kang's thinking constitutes a fusion between two ancient Oriental traditions, mixed with modern ideas about economic and social reforms. Kang proposed the end of private property, family units and political and racial boundaries. Perhaps naively, he saw mixed marriages as the solution to Western imperialism, which put him in conflict with the nationalists, who for some time promoted a China for the Han Chinese race only, excluding all its ethnic minorities.

Unlike the nationalists, Kang was an internationalist but also a political opportunist: he saw no contradiction in supporting a Manchu foreign dynasty or asking for Japan's assistance to develop China. In 1919, he was enthusiastic about the creation of the League of Nations, which he saw as a first step towards his vision of a unified world.[35] Sadly, Kang also theorized a hierarchy of the world's racial groups, but unlike some Western racial theorists at the time who favored segregation or even extermination, he instead proposed racial mixing and assimilation as ways to unite the world. Although, like most of his contemporaries, he had several concubines in addition to his wife, his desire to end traditional family structures defined him as one of the first advocates of women's independence in China. Kang was very close to his daughter, Kang Tongbi, an intellectual who studied journalism in the United States and accompanied him on trips, becoming later one of the first Chinese feminists. Despite or perhaps because of his experience as an investor, Kang saw capitalism as an inherently evil system, believing that governments must establish socialist institutions such as nurseries, schools and nursing homes. *The Book of Great Unity* remains popular in China to this day, with a Beijing publisher recently placing it on its list of the hundred most influential books in Chinese history. Kang inspired China's future communist leaders, including Chairman Mao, one of his admirers.

For Kang and his organization, education had to be the foundation and strength of the future Chinese nation, becoming an essential part of his plan in North America. Set up by local Chinese communities, the Chinese Reform Association's network of elementary schools, in addition to helping children improve their Mandarin, introduced Chinese news to them, while focusing on physical education, ethics, philosophy, Western science and technology. The association funded scholarships, sending students to Japan, Europe and the United States. However, it was only in the United States and Canada that Kang established a network of paramilitary schools organized by US veterans. Kang was not naïve: he understood that before it could reform, the Chinese state must regain strength militarily. More than 2,000 Chinese migrants in the United States, in more than twenty cities—many low-paid restaurant and laundry workers—contributed fifty cents a month to learn military science and tactics, often behind closed doors and in remote locations. These students became Chinese cultural representatives, whose expertise in military marches in American parades earned them rare praise in the generally hostile English-language media.[36] This was perhaps testament to the prevalence of the idea at that time that a country and race's honor depended on its military strength, which surely contributed to the barbarity of two world wars. A few years before meeting Kang, President Roosevelt had declared: "All the great masterful races have been fighting races; and the minute that a race loses the hard fighting virtues, then [...] it has lost its proud right to stand as the equal of the best."[37]

In 1905, Kang made his first trip to Mexico, where he stayed for five months, making his first investments in the city of Torreón in association with Foon Chuck, his organization setting up a newspaper called the *Mexico Morning News*.[38] Kang was aware of theories connecting Native Americans to the Chinese through common Siberian ancestors. He was fascinated by Mexican food and culture, especially the high pre-Columbian civilizations of Oaxaca and Yucatan, which he visited with his daughter and Foon Chuck, looking for similarities between Asian and pre-Columbian architecture. He even took Mayan language lessons, finding later commonalities between Nahuatl, the language of the Aztecs, and Chinese.[39]

In 1907, in Mexico City for the second time, he had a cordial meeting with President Díaz, following which he announced to the press his intention to create a shipping company connecting the ports of Hong Kong and Mazatlán. During this meeting, President Díaz, impressed by Kang's demeanor and ignoring the fact that he was a political exile from Kwangtung, gave him the title of "Chinese prince," causing a spat with Manchu diplomats. Kang explained to the Mexican president his plans to invite new Chinese settlers, and the president reportedly replied that they were welcome, and all the more so if they brought capital.[40] Echoing the views of Chinese diplomats, Kang had high hopes for Latin America as a destination for immigration and colonization, due to its similar climate to China. He found Mexico particularly well suited, seeing it as the place where his philosophy of union between countries and races would materialize. He considered Díaz to be a benevolent and paternalistic dictator, not much different to a Chinese emperor, who would ensure the stability of Chinese investments.[41] Although he deeply admired the United States and its well-functioning institutions and industry, he was frustrated with its anti-Chinese policies. At the same time, his views on the potential for collaboration between the Chinese and the countries of the Americas were in perfect harmony with those of Díaz, despite Mexico's less progressive institutions. In a 1907 interview, asked about the "yellow peril," Kang's answer was as follows:

> There is no yellow peril, there is no white peril, there is no black peril, or brown or any peril, of a particular color. [...] Basically, all races of men are similar if not identical. The great question that is presented to civilized nations today is not whether their unimportant differences will lead them to clash, but rather whether their inherent similarities and oneness will inspire them to unite in the great global work that needs to be done.[42]

10

AN ERUDITE PHILANTHROPIST

In parallel with his business activities, Foon Chuck closely followed political developments in his native country, which he read about regularly in the Chinese international press from his distant base in northern Mexico. He was one of the first in Mexico to get involved in Chinese transnational political organizations. Despite the distance from China and their relative isolation, Foon Chuck and other Chinese migrants managed to keep close political ties with their native homeland. Having seen how well-functioning institutions could contribute to a nation, they hoped to change China from the outside, a country whose failings had forced them into exile but to which they remained emotionally attached.

As early as 1898, Foon Chuck wrote several letters to Kang Youwei, who had just settled in Canada, including a detailed report titled *Outline of the Mexican State*, introducing Mexico's geography, social and economic environment, and business opportunities. As a result, the recently founded Chinese Reform Association in Canada sent two emissaries to Mexico, one in 1901 and the other in 1902.[1] They both praised Mexico as a favorable destination for Chinese business and immigration. At this time, Foon Chuck also became friends with Tom Leung, a doctor of Chinese medicine settled in Los Angeles, who had been a student and supporter of Kang from their days in Kwangtung. Leung became leader of the Chinese Reform Association in North America, and Foon Chuck exchanged several letters with him. A year later, Foon Chuck and other Chinese from Torreón established a branch of the Reform Association, before the highly anticipated arrival of Kang Youwei himself, who visited the city twice, in 1905 and 1907. Not a city with a large Chinese population or one at the center of Mexican politics, the choice of Torreón in the state of Coahuila reflected the economic priorities of the Chinese Reform Association. By 1910, Coahuila only counted 759 Chinese inhabitants, compared to 5,800 in the neighboring northern states of Sonora and Chihuahua,[2] and 13,200 overall in Mexico.

In June 1901, Liang Qitian, a cousin of Liang Qichao and member of the Chinese Reform Association, wrote a long letter about his astonishing first trip to Mexico:

> I have travelled to seven [Mexican] states with only 600–700 Chinese. However, I was well received everywhere and really enjoyed my trip [...]. No highways or railroads reach the Pacific Coast [...]. I visited Wong Foon Chuck's New Canton Farm which makes me envy him very much. The farm has 5,000 [hectares], of which only 600 are currently cultivated. He bought the land at half a dollar [per hectare], and since its founding six years ago, it has cost him $60,000. Within ten years, he could make over $500,000. His achievements are a credit to the Chinese. I also visited his neighbors, local Mexicans within a few meters of his farm, all showed him great respect and were friendly and welcoming. It is really incredible! Local officials invited us to a party and danced until the early morning. I believe that an immigrant could surpass all others here [...]. I am wholeheartedly joyful for him and envy him very much! However, when I think that Overseas Chinese who have ambitions are rare, and many do not have enough capital, I am upset and feel sorry. In Mexico, everyone may be naturalized as a Mexican. Isn't that really a rare opportunity? I vow to make every effort to do this. The damaging behavior of the Chinese here is like in the United States. However, the more than one hundred people under Wong Foon Chuck seem very civilized. Luckily the number of Chinese here is not great [...]. The worry is that, as shipping companies are established, people will keep coming. There are no farmlands or industries to absorb them. I fear the disaster of Cuba will happen again [...]. The Wong brothers are very generous [with the organization]. When we have talented people and sufficient capital, we will do farming [...]. We can entrust the business to Wong Foon Chuck and his associates [...]. I am now raising money for a Chinese Mexican grocery store in Torreón. It is a small business, but profits will be great.[3]

AN ERUDITE PHILANTHROPIST

In 1902, Foon Chuck acquired the new Hotel Internacional in Monclova,[4] Coahuila state, another boom town, halfway between Piedras Negras and Torreón, but with a population of only 5,000. The hotel became one of the most luxurious in northern Mexico, built with red bricks imported from Kentucky and wood from Texas, with eighty rooms, many having their own bathrooms and saunas with running water, a first in the region.[5] This further illustrates Foon Chuck's desire to create innovative enterprises with the latest technologies, demonstrating that Chinese migrants were future-orientated rather than turned towards the past. The ground floor had various lounges and two restaurants with large curtains to separate each table, where large receptions and weddings took place. The hotel became the most prominent and elegant place for the high society of the region, hosting the Mexican president and other senior politicians on official visits to the city. Referred to by the local population as "the hotel of the Chinese," some newspapers suggested that it had special rooms, one for gambling and the other for smoking opium. After nearly half a century of trading, the hotel closed its doors in 1949. Its historic walls still stand today, though they are in a state of ruin; there are plans to transform it into a museum. Like the older Hotel del Ferrocarril in Piedras Negras, it is worth noting that, due to their distinct architecture, two of Foon Chuck's hotels are now considered heritage landmarks, showing these towns' attachment to their history.

In 1904, Foon Chuck used his own money to open a school in Monclova, which he named the Yue Mae School,[6] meaning "school of beautiful education." He opened the school to accommodate his children as well as those of other Chinese migrants in the region,[7] since a Chinese community had already grown around him, other migrants having followed him hoping to make lucrative investments by his side. The school was founded with the direct support of the municipal president of Monclova, demonstrating once again Foon Chuck's influence and the benevolent and enlightened policies of the Díaz government towards some of its migrants. It is probably not a coincidence that Foon Chuck's friend, governor Miguel Cárdenas, was himself a native of Monclova.

The students' costs, food and lodging were funded in their entirety by Foon Chuck as well as other Chinese benefactors. Since ancient times, a distinctive feature of the Chinese peasantry was their desire for their descendants to one day pass the Imperial Examination and become mandarins, thereby bringing honor and wealth to their relatives. This is why most up-and-coming Chinese farming families, even of modest origins, had a strong reverence for education. At the turn of the century, various high-ranking Qing ministers came from destitute families.[8] This mentality continues to this day in all segments of Chinese society, education being regarded as a key for social advancement. A Chinese idiom states that "the value of ten thousand activities is low, the study of books surpasses them all."[9] The school count included twenty-eight boys and four girls. Foon Chuck's four oldest, Elvira, Arturo, Lily and Santiago, attended the school.

One of his first family photos, taken around 1905, shows Foon Chuck with almost Mexican features. In contrast with everyone else in the picture, his daughter Lily has a large smile on her face; she looks even a bit mischievous, a character trait that she kept throughout her life.

At that time, Foon Chuck invited his younger brother, my great-grandfather Wong Yun Wu (meaning "Lively Garden")[10] to join him in Mexico as the director of the school and later to help him with his other businesses. Like his older brother, Yun Wu was well versed in the Confucian classics and spoke English. He gained a reputation for running the school in a strict and disciplined manner, importing to Mexico some attributes of the Chinese educational style. Unlike his two elder brothers, he was less of a businessman and more of an intellectual. Yun Wu brought his Chinese wife, Jovita Woo, to Mexico along with their only son, Wong Yaiwai ("Brilliant Radiance"),[11] my grandfather. The first photograph of Wong Yaiwai, from 1907, shows a thoughtful, calm and taciturn young boy, attributes he would retain all his life, taking after his father. Foon Chuck's older brother had chosen the American name of Joe Chuck Wong when he first arrived in the United States; now his younger brother, arriving directly in Mexico a few years later, was adopting the Spanish name of José Chuck Wong, showing how the geographical aspirations of the family had changed.

The ambitious school curriculum included Chinese, English, Spanish, mathematics, grammar, history, music, geography and physical education, the school having a well-known musical group, one of the first children's brass bands in Mexico. For thousands of years, music has been a core teaching of Confucian education, which views musicality as a reflection of well-rounded individuals and harmonious communities. Like in Foon Chuck's San Francisco school, lessons were given in the lounge of a hotel, the Hotel Internacional, the children's band giving concerts on special occasions for the guests and, years later, even going on a tour in the United States. It is remarkable that in 1904, in a still relatively undeveloped northern Mexican region, a school with such a broad and modern curriculum was founded, under the supervision of the Chinese Reform Association and inspired by other similar institutions throughout North America. The school had six teachers from Mexico, the United States and China, one of whom was taught in Kwangtung province by Kang Youwei himself. To celebrate its founding, on his visit to the school in the spring of 1907, Kang wrote the following poem:

> Keep our home country in our thoughts,
> Keep Confucius' teachings as our aspirations,
> Be focused, be strong,
> Be sharp, intelligent, and erudite,
> Be kind with a noble character,
> Do not forget your origins,
> Do not only worship what is foreign,
> Explore new land, expand the colony,
> Let the development of a New China be your responsibility,
> Is this possible?[12]

In the same period, the Chinese education system was undergoing an unprecedented revolution in China itself, part of a new reform program finally initiated by Empress Dowager Cixi and the late Qing bureaucracy, referred as "New Policies."[13] These reforms were ambitious, also including local elections, new legal institutions, amnesty for all past political offenders (except Kang and his disciples), and special missions sent to the West to study their methods of governance. For their scope and impact, these educational reforms have been called "the most revolutionary act of the twentieth century."[14] In 1905, as Kang Youwei had called for a few years earlier, the 2,000-year-old Imperial Examination system was dismantled, to be replaced by a modern system emphasizing technical, practical and physical education, in contrast with the moral Confucian teachings of the past. In the eyes of Confucian scholars, whose lives seemed to have suddenly lost their meaning, the government had sacrificed the aim of reproducing a Confucian society for the aim of mobilizing wealth so that the state could compete internationally: "the principles of benevolence and righteousness have been put aside to talk about money and profits."[15] Civil servants who had spent most of their lives studying now wondered whether they would have to go back to school, hence their fierce resistance to the reforms. Reform was made even more difficult by the lack of modern teachers in China.

Kang Youwei found himself conflicted, trying to reconcile the views of a Confucian scholar wanting to preserve old wisdoms with his desire to promote a modern and mercantile education and the mindset of Western nations. An important early aim of the reformists' philosophy, developed by the prominent scholar-official Zhang Zhidong (1837–1909), was to retain the substance of Chinese teaching while learning from the West how to apply this teaching in practice.[16] However, this intellectual compromise proved impossible, and so the whole ancient symbolic universe of Confucius and the classic sages with its many traditions was dismantled, making way for a new set of beliefs with a radically different meaning of life for the Chinese.

Importantly, the reforms in China also fostered social change. For example, in 1911 gambling was banned in Kwangtung province,[17] and there were further restrictions against opium smoking throughout the empire. From 1905 to 1910, this vast reform program by Empress Dowager Cixi and her decaying dynasty was truly remarkable, vindicating the earlier efforts of Kang Youwei and the reformists, but it arrived too late to help the dynasty hold onto power, instead precipitating its downfall.

The extent to which Foon Chuck was a polymath bears emphasizing. Besides being a businessman and agronomist, he was interested in international politics, economy, education and art. This was a remarkable intellectual journey for an immigrant of peasant origins who, twenty years earlier, had no credentials beyond his basic education. Letters from friends called him then an "erudite gentleman,"[18] while a remarkable page-long article in the US press of 1905 describes him as "the most progressive Chinaman, a philanthropist, thoroughly Americanized, a student of economic problems, a believer in education and with the most delightful personality."[19]

By then, of course, Foon Chuck had already converted to Christianity, thus managing to reconcile his Chinese beliefs with Western religion. By joining the Presbyterian church of Reverend Loomis and his business partners, instead of the Catholic Church of Mexico, he demonstrated his progressive views, strong loyalty, and continuous attachment to the United States. He had grown up in a land full of ancestral ghosts, but he felt that his new country possessed none, with so many people recently settled, having come from so far away and moving all the time. According to the Chinese Philosopher Mozi (470–391 BCE), spirits are important for a harmonious society, as people will be on their best behavior when they know that spirits are watching them.[20] In a land without spirits, Foon Chuck believed that the worship of a common Christian father was important for society and not in contradiction with the love of his own ancestors back home, nor with the teachings of Confucius. All his life he would encourage his fellow migrants to lead a spiritual life. But, while he now read the Bible, he decided to read it in Chinese translation.

In 1905, Kang Youwei became Foon Chuck's close friend. Kang and his daughter Tongbi used Foon Chuck's home in Piedras Negras as a base during their five-month-long visit to Mexico. During that time, Tongbi befriended Kingfung, who was related to Foon Chuck; they were the same age and shared the same aspirations. Although Foon Chuck's family was not from the gentry, he and Kang were both Cantonese and they had both read Western books in addition to the Confucian classics, although Foon Chuck's level of erudition was much lower than Kang's. Foon Chuck deferentially called Kang "Jung Jeung," meaning General President in Cantonese, showing the political aspirations of the movement. In the twentieth century, a more than 2,000-year-old Chinese philosophy still molded the views of and brought together these two Chinese migrants so far away from their native country. They also both shared a passion for business, which undoubtedly cemented their friendship. Advised by Foon

Chuck, Kang personally tested the market by buying land in Torreón for 1,700 pesos, which he sold a few days later to another Chinese for double, doing the same with a house.[21] He therefore chose this city to be the regional headquarters of the Chinese Reform Association, with nine other branches to be set up all around Mexico,[22] Foon Chuck becoming his main friend and associate in the country. In partnership with a consortium of Chinese international investors linked to the Chinese Reform Association, Kang made major investments in Torreón. In 1906, the Compañia Bancaria China y Mexico, or the Bank of China and Mexico,[23] was inaugurated with 100,000 pesos of registered capital, or $1.5 million in today's money, coming from Mexico, Hong Kong and the United States.

Instead of being controlled via a corporation, more than ninety per cent of this initial capital was owned directly by Kang and his relatives, with Joe Chuck and another partner owning just a handful of shares.[24] Kang was later criticized for this. The first bank in Mexico to be owned by Chinese private capital, it remains to this day the only institution of its kind to have been established. In the fall, after receiving a charter from the government, the bank began selling shares to the public to raise further capital. It then not only served as a deposit bank for Chinese funds from all over Mexico but also engaged in the speculative purchase and sale of real estate. By 1907, the Commercial Corporation and many of Foon Chuck's own associates had become among the largest property investors in Torreón, owning large parcels of land throughout the expanding city. That year, the corporation made paper profits of several hundred thousand dollars from real estate speculation in Torreón,[25] causing its share price to surge.

To promote the sale of land, the bank obtained a government concession to construct a second electric tramway line in Torreón. In 1906, the Compañia de Tranvias Wah Yick was founded to build a tram line from the cemetery in the west of the city to the Chinese Gardens in the east, and in 1907 the bank was granted a shipping concession to start a service from Mazatlán to Hong Kong. These developments indicated the long-term and global plans of Foon Chuck and Kang for their Chinese colony of Torreón. The works on the tram line were delayed due to the economic crisis of 1907, but the following year they were already well advanced with eight miles of track completed, Foon Chuck traveling that year to Baltimore to buy some rail equipment.[26] However, tensions and even outright hostility towards the Chinese were increasing in the city, and the employees of the existing tram line, owned by a consortium of local shareholders, hindered the new tram's progress by preventing the new line from crossing their tracks. On the night of 1 January 1909, under the cover of darkness, hundreds of Chinese workers, recently arrived in Torreón, worked on the troublesome junction. To the surprise of unsuspecting locals, it was completed by the early morning.[27]

To help finance the tram line, the bank sold land it owned along the tracks, but since the money was still insufficient, more shares had to be issued to the public. Chinese investors flocked to the bank due to its early successes in land speculation and the expectation that the finalization of the tram line and new shipping concession would generate large profits. As the promoter and main investor in these companies, Foon Chuck, now forty-four years old, was appointed general manager of the bank and of the tramway company. During those years, Torreón experienced rapid economic growth along with unbridled land speculation, and the resulting rampant inflation angered the local middle class, with sky-high rents forcing many workers to share homes with other families.[28] Many held the Chinese to be the main culprits. In 1907, Foon Chuck wrote to Tom Leung:

> I am astonished by how land prices have increased. When a piece of land is for sale, everyone believes it is too expensive and that nobody will buy it. Yet it can be sold within a minute [...]. I feel this is incredible [...]. A few months ago, I bought with Jiyu [Kang Youwei's nephew] thirty blocks of land in Torreón. We plan to find investors in the United States to build a high-end resort. It will cost 300,000 Mexican dollars [...]. I believe it will be extremely profitable, Jiyu and I are fully committed.[29]

Alongside his work at the Chinese Reform Association, Foon Chuck also played an activist role in Mexico and the United States, where he lobbied for his businesses and the cause of the Chinese. One of his granddaughters remembers that his home in Piedras Negras had a special wardrobe full of black suits and bowler hats for his meetings with US and Chinese politicians in Washington. The Mexican press wrote about the grand receptions Foon Chuck gave for the diplomatic community in Mexico City, to which American diplomats and industrialists were also invited.[30] After his 1904 visit to Mexico, the Chinese ambassador to the United States, Liang Cheng, described Foon Chuck to the US press as "the perfect example of a successful Chinese businessman in Mexico."[31] A few years earlier, Foon Chuck had joined the Masonic lodge of Eagle Pass, taking the highest degrees of the order. That, more than his affiliation with the Presbyterian church, provided him with useful and high-level contacts for his business, both in the United States and Mexico. Curious about learning new things, making new friends, and growing spiritually, Foon Chuck did not see any conflict between his masonic lodge, the Presbyterian church, and Confucian beliefs, regarding all as advancing humanity towards the same goal.

Around 1903, Foon Chuck purchased from an American the most modern laundry in Torreón, which was fully automated and very profitable, demonstrating his interest in new technologies, especially those that facilitated the work of his compatriots. Located eight blocks from his hotel, the Lavandería de Vapor Oriental (Oriental Steam Laundry) had a large wood-burning vat and a staff dining area, and employed twenty people, including a chef to cook for them.[32] In 1908, the newly established Coal Company of La Agujita granted Foon Chuck a concession to operate a general store in the mining town of Lampacitos,[33] another profitable venture for him, for which he was able to use his extensive network of suppliers throughout the state. After his hotels, vegetable farms, and the Hacienda Canton, the Chinese bank and the tramway became Foon Chuck's fourth major business in Mexico. He was already one of the first Chinese multi-millionaires in the Americas.[34] A US newspaper noted that his businesses made $300,000 a year, or more than nine million dollars in today's money.[35]

With his school, his businesses, and his political role in the Chinese Reform Association, Foon Chuck had become a respected leader of the Chinese-Mexican community, not only in Torreón. Migrants went to him for business reasons but also to settle private affairs. Period documents, including letters from friends and family, show his involvement in charitable work, helping the poorest

AN ERUDITE PHILANTHROPIST

Chinese not only in the Americas but also in China, which continued to suffer from various calamities. He always remembered his place in the family tree and kept in mind the Chinese saying, "when drinking water, never forget the source."[36] Today, just a short walking distance from his village of Chaitong, a cluster of more than a thousand beautiful watchtowers and Western style mansions can be visited as part of the UNESCO protected site of Kaiping Diaolou and Villages.[37] Many of these buildings were constructed with the money of Foon Chuck and his clan at the start of the century. Decades later, one grandchild still remembered how sacks of silver were loaded onto carts and ships bound for China, to be used for the Chinese Reform Association or to provide for their relatives, showing the philanthropic nature of Foon Chuck's project in Mexico. Together with other ancient sages, and in opposition to the legalist school, Confucius had an idealistic, if not naïve, view of human nature, believing that power derives almost exclusively from moral character, with good leaders being naturally followed by their people for their good deeds. For him, culture and virtue, rather than force, are the basis for successful rule. This was a thought that Foon Chuck kept close to his heart all his life.

Foon Chuck saw himself as the representative of his Chinese compatriots in Mexico, wanting to promote their immigration to Mexico. He saw no contradiction between being Mexican and helping his Chinese community become larger and more prosperous in his new country. It was obvious to him that Mexico was a large enough country to welcome everyone and that he was contributing actively and positively to its economy, a view which coincided perfectly with those of President Díaz. But his successes also made him many enemies in Torreón, rich and poor people alike, who took a dim view of a foreigner, especially a Chinese, becoming so rich and powerful.

In 1903, in a letter to Tom Leung, Foon Chuck expressed his thoughts on himself and his people, showing his humility and sense of duty:

> Your writing reflects patriotism and sincerity and makes me admire you. Although I am an ignorant person, you praised me with your words. This makes me ashamed. Looking at the situation of our motherland, the country is declining, people are miserable, the economy is exhausted, neighboring countries invaded us and the

whole race is in danger. How can we simply lament and ignore that? if our fellow countrymen do not think themselves as animals [...] they should rise up and work hard to make the country strong and show the world who they are. The heavens do not wish to harm us. How can we blame the Manchu government? The reason the Manchu rulers oppress and harm us so badly is that we reap what we sow. As people of the yellow race and compatriots, we must do some soul searching. Everyone must do his duties [...]. I am not a person who can serve as a pillar of the community. What I can do is strive to offer some assistance. I wish I could express all my feelings, but my inelegant prose fails me.

There were nine banks in Torreón, including one American, one British and one Chinese, reflecting the cosmopolitan character of the city and the government's friendly policies towards foreign capital. The Chinese bank possessed its own imposing building located near the train station and Foon Chuck's hotel, at the corner of Avenida Juarez and Valdes Carrillo Street, which it shared with the tramway company and the Chinese Reform Association. The yellow Chinese imperial flag, with a transverse blue dragon reaching towards a red circle was proudly displayed on a mast on top of its roof.[38] This was where newly arrived Chinese immigrants were welcomed and political and study groups organized, showing the vast and versatile nature of Foon Chuck and Kang's project in Torreón, the association even owning a printing machine to distribute tracts and newspapers to the Chinese population. Kang perhaps envisioned that his Chinese colony in Torreón would one day be a living example of his utopian one-world society. The grand original construction is still intact today; the adjacent building has been converted into a museum, the Centro Cultural Arocena, which traces the history of the Chinese community of Torreón.

In no other place in North America had Chinese migrants reached such a level of power and influence within a local community. The 700 Chinese residents of Torreón constituted "the most prominent foreign colony in Mexico," in terms of both numbers and property,[39] as described by Evelyn Hu-DeHart, the first and most respected scholar on the Chinese in Mexico. They only represented two per cent of the local population but they constituted close to one in ten of its workers, and more than 150 of them were naturalized Mexicans, more than anywhere else in Mexico but the capital. There were larger settlements of Chinese in Mexico at the time, like in the mining town of Cananea in the state of Sonora, where there were more than 1,000 Chinese, but none were as organized, as strategically planned, and with the economic scope and influence of the colony of Torreón. Furthermore, Torreón was like no other Chinese settlement in the Americas because it was not established to serve Western interests, but was instead the only colony set up by Chinese entrepreneurs to develop an economic project of their own. From that perspective, it resembled the large American and European enterprises in Mexico, with a major difference being that it employed Chinese workers almost exclusively, instead of locals or migrants from other nationalities. The Torreón Chinese colony, then, truly stood out and was unlike any other enterprise in Mexico, whether Mexican or foreign.

According to the Chinese ambassador to Mexico, Foon Chuck told him in 1904 that he had been offered the title of mayor of the city of Torreón,[40] although no other records exist of such an offer. But in 1907, for the twenty-fifth anniversary of Torreón, he officially received an honorary distinction from the City's Founders' Committee, being named "one of its favored sons for his civic virtues and effort for the development and prosperity of the city."[41] Despite his business successes, to avoid any appearance or accusation of impropriety, Foon Chuck continued to keep his distance from local Mexican politics, preferring to stick to the commercial sphere and Chinese transnational politics. He even advised one of his employees to refuse the title of mayor that was offered to him in a small nearby village.[42] As the Chinese saying goes: "Men fear fame as pigs fear getting fat."[43]

In the fall of 1907, following a bank run, the New York Stock Exchange fell by more than fifty per cent, triggering a global recession, the Mexican peso losing half its value against the dollar. Reflecting on the close ties of his country with his northern neighbor, President Díaz is believed to have then famously said: "Poor Mexico, so far from God and so close to the United States," an aphorism used to this day.[44] This crisis strongly affected Torreón, which had experienced rampant speculation on land prices and whose economy was largely supported by foreign capital. Land prices along the tram line fell rapidly, causing significant paper losses for the bank as well as massive withdrawals from depositors. Despite the economic crisis, the Mexican government threatened to revoke the tramway's concession if the line was not completed on time. In that year, Foon Chuck had his first disagreement with Kang when he refused—temporarily—to fund the completion of the tramway[45] in order to keep more liquidity within the bank. The following year, Kang decided to sell some land in Torreón to fund other ventures of the Commercial Corporation abroad, but he was opposed again by Foon Chuck,[46] who felt the price was not right, an incident which harmed their relationship permanently. Kang blamed Foon Chuck for the crisis and felt he was dishonestly trying to take control of the bank. The crisis was exacerbated by poor investments by Kang's Commercial Corporation in South-East Asia and an incident of fraud by one of his Asian associates, who was unable to repay a personal loan, creating an overall cash crunch in Kang's organization.[47] Despite these setbacks, the bank continued to sell shares to the Chinese throughout North America, and by 1908 had accumulated assets of nearly a million dollars (about thirty million dollars in today's money), of which $600,000 had been invested in land, buildings and the tram line.[48] Kang's Commercial Corporation initially funded the bank with $60,880; after the bank successfully raised its own capital, it returned $155,000 for the corporation's investments outside Mexico.[49]

In 1907, the recently established Chamber of Commerce of Torreón, in which the family of future president Francisco Madero had an important position, publicly criticized the increased competition from foreign banks, especially the Chinese one. This was the first time that part of the local business elite publicly took an anti-Chinese stance, which did not bode well for the future of the Chinese in the city. Many locals blamed foreign capital, especially Chinese, for rampant land speculation and the resulting crash. Local Mexican industrialists published a rather honest and gloomy manifesto in the newspaper *El Nuevo Mundo*, declaring:

> We cannot compete with foreigners in the field of business. The sad and lamentable fact is that the prostration of our national trade has created a situation in which Mexicans are replaced by foreign individuals or companies that monopolize the market and behave like the conquerors of a defeated country.[50]

AN ERUDITE PHILANTHROPIST

In 1910, during the celebration of the centenary of Mexico's independence from Spain, the Yue Mae School was invited by the Chinese diplomatic legation to participate in the official celebrations in Mexico City. This constituted a direct recognition of the success of Foon Chuck's school and colony by his Chinese peers. It may also have been a political statement by the Chinese, a way of saying that they were happy to settle in Mexico, invest their capital, and contribute to its economic growth, but through their education wanted to preserve their roots and culture. A photo of the Yue Mae School with all its students in uniform captures this historic but also serendipitous moment in my family's history. It was taken on 18 September 1910, at a tea reception provided by my great-grandfather Hing in Chapultepec Park to honor the passage of the Yue Mae School in Mexico City, illustrating the potent symbol that the school had become for Chinese Mexicans. Hing stands on the left of the student group, and on the right stands my other great-grandfather, Wong Yun Wu, Foon Chuck's younger brother, wearing a bowler hat and surrounded by representatives of the Chinese legation. This was the first time that my two great-grandfathers met, unaware that their children would marry twenty years later.

The school's music band of twenty-four students participated in the parades that took place throughout the city, charming spectators on its path. On 22 September, a concert was given at the Presidential Palace of Chapultepec, where Porfirio Díaz organized a special reception for the school, which was officially recognized for its contribution to education in Mexico. The event was widely covered by the local press, including the brilliant piano performance by Lily, Foon Chuck's brightest daughter, to an audience of thousands of diplomats and heads of state, whose applause and praise made her father cry. The Mexican magazine *Historia* recently commemorated this event with an article ironically titled, "The Chinese who Conquered Porfirio Díaz."[51] This celebration marked the culmination of both President Díaz's friendly policy towards foreign investors and Foon Chuck's meteoric rise and remarkable achievements in Mexico. On that day, each of the school's students was a cultural ambassador, showcasing his mixed education and culture in a welcoming, open and friendly Mexico.

However, on the day of the centenary of independence, far from the pomp and splendor of Mexico City, in Torreón the celebrations took a more macabre turn. There, they were accompanied by speeches and demonstrations with a clear anti-foreigner tone, with various people shouting "Death to the Chinese!" In the following weeks several Chinese businesses suffered significant material damage. The last verse of an anonymous poem of the time, entitled "The Unearthing of the Chinese," states:

> Pray to God, man from China,
> With all your heart,
> That they don't come and lynch you,
> If the revolution comes.[52]

Only two months later, the Mexican Revolution began, and Kang Youwei's dream of a multicultural society turned into a nightmare of nationalism and exclusion for Foon Chuck, Hing, and the many Chinese in Mexico.

PART II

A SHATTERED WORLD

11

THE TORREÓN MASSACRE

In the first half of the twentieth century, Mexican politics underwent seismic changes, this period being one of the most eventful in the country's history. The 1907 world economic crisis further increased the inequalities created by the excesses of the Díaz regime, causing famines in the Mexican countryside as well as popular riots, which formed a violent backdrop for the events to come. The Mexican Revolution lasted for a turbulent and violent decade, from 1910 to 1920, with various factions vying for power. It is estimated that more than one-and-a-half million people died in this struggle, or more than one in ten Mexicans. Ideologically, the main themes of the revolutionaries were socialism, anticlericalism and a nationalism that was epitomized by the slogan "Mexico for the Mexicans." The revolution was also characterized by strong anti-intellectual sentiment: it rejected the technocrats and scientists of Díaz's positivist government. The new constitution of 1917 abolished the inalienable right to private property, giving the government the power to reverse the agrarian reforms of the previous regime and thus take back and redistribute land, including that owned by foreigners.

Porfirio Díaz's dictatorship, which lasted more than thirty years, was overthrown in 1911, and his accommodating policies towards foreigners were subsequently reversed. The revolutionaries dreamed of a mestizo nation, but this included only those of Indian and Spanish descent, excluding foreigners, especially the Chinese and those with black skin, with their motto being "for the motherland and for the race." The next ten years were marked by anarchy and extreme violence, affecting both Mexicans and foreigners in the country; the Chinese, though far from being the only immigrant group affected, felt particularly exposed and vulnerable. In 1910, there were only 120,000 foreigners in Mexico. This contrasted with the situation in the United States, where more than thirty-three million Europeans had immigrated to between 1820 and 1920.[1] Their relatively small number made immigrants to Mexico all the more conspicuous, as did the great economic success that many of them—particularly those from the United States—enjoyed, which provoked xenophobic resentment. Large foreign corporations were considered exploitative and colonial in nature. Foreign companies discriminated against local foremen and managers, especially in the railway sector, where the official language remained English and only a third of the engineers were Mexicans.[2]

But the discontent, especially among lower classes, found an easy victim in the Chinese, who were defenseless and had enjoyed obvious economic successes under Díaz. They were thus among the scapegoats of the revolution. This took the form of anti-Chinese movements which organized demonstrations, boycotts and massacres, ultimately resulting in the passing of racist legislation. Some of those movements, like in the state of Sonora, were organized by groups of local businessmen, who wanted to get rid of their Chinese competition. The Chinese were particularly blamed for price rises and criticized for hoarding goods in times of shortage, such as during the crisis of 1907. A leader of the anti-Chinese movement declared that "Mexican hospitality, indolence and indifference have allowed the Chinese to enter the country and prosper to the point that they now menace the economic and cultural strength of Mexico."[3] In fact, the economic weight of Chinese migrants was minuscule compared to that of American and European corporations, but their prominence in the small-business sector made them more visible. In 1920, the total investment of Americans and Spaniards in Mexico was estimated at one hundred million dollars each, compared to fifty million for the British and less than one million for the Chinese.[4] Although the latter figure is probably an underestimate, it illustrates the ravages of the revolution and the economic balance of power between foreign nations and immigrants in Mexico. Like Foon Chuck, many Chinese worked with or for powerful American corporations and were thus found guilty by association.

THE TORREÓN MASSACRE

A satirical skit at the time had a migrant with a heavy Chinese accent proclaim to his Mexican fiancée:

> Mexico is good for foreigners. The Americans have oil wells. The English own large mines, large tracts of land. The Germans have hardware stores. The Spanish are owners of bars, markets, and bakeries. The Chinese own many restaurants and laundries. In conclusion, all the foreigners are making money. So, what are the Mexicans doing? Nothing, because don't you see, they are revolutionaries [...]. All of them with their carbines doing bang-bang here and bang-bang there, that's all.[5]

The anti-Chinese activists' objective was to destroy the ties that had been forged between Chinese and Mexicans over the past two decades, not only between small traders and their customers but also among workers.[6] Despite the many mixed marriages, one activist wrote: "The racial feeling of the Chinese never dies and if some gain Mexican citizenship, it is simply a matter of self-interest."[7] The activists gave racist speeches in which they portrayed the friends of the Chinese, especially wives in mixed couples, as traitors who had sold and disgraced themselves. At first, they encountered significant resistance from the Chinese and their Mexican friends but, with the revolution, the economic crisis, and the consequent social problems, the activists gained increasingly favorable audiences.

The revolution caused the departure of many young men, going to combat and possible death, often coerced into enlisting by both the federal and revolutionary armies. The Chinese—who tended to be either neutral or biased towards the old regime, and stayed out of the fighting—were accused of trying to take the businesses and the wives of these enlisted Mexican men. This situation stood in contrast with those of other Chinese communities in Latin America. In Cuba, for example, the Chinese participated actively in their country's war of independence. Back in Mexico, the Mexican wives of Chinese migrants were criticized for being "dirty, wretched, lazy, and unpatriotic."[8] Many of the anti-Chinese activists were women—Catholic and xenophobic—who wished to protect their sisters or daughters from mixed marriages but also prostitution, which the many single Chinese men were accused of encouraging. Various Mexican women took a leading role during the revolution, including as soldiers, and through the post-revolutionary period, some of them taking an active political role within the anti-Chinese movements. Chinese aid associations were also portrayed as mafias with suspicious purposes, harboring infamous rivalries and rife with opium use. In short, many Chinese migrants, even those who were not wealthy, found themselves tragically on the wrong side of history.

Educated in France and the United States, Francisco Madero, the leading figure of the revolution, and the president of Mexico from 1911–13, did not directly encourage the anti-Chinese movement, but he and his family were originally from Torreón, where they had significant financial interests and competed with foreigners. Foon Chuck's agricultural land was located next to the Metallurgical Company of Torreón, owned by the Madero family,[9] which tried unsuccessfully to buy the Bank of China and Mexico[10] in order to merge it with its own Banco Mercantíl de Monterrey, illustrating the tensions between Mexican and Chinese businessmen in the city. The business interests of one Mexican revolutionary, Francisco Madero, and one Chinese reformist, Kang Youwei, were thus in competition in Torreón, at a time when revolutions were about to happen in both countries. Both Kang and Madero ultimately failed in their political aspirations: Kang backed a bankrupt regime and never gained power, while Madero was assassinated less than two years after gaining power.

As the Mexican Revolution began, insults and aggressions against the Chinese community in Torreón increased. In March 1911, martial law was decreed and the city's population suffered from a critical shortage of food, with hordes of starving inhabitants roaming the streets.[11] On the morning of Saturday, 13 May 1911, a revolutionary force of 4,500 men led by General Emilio Madero (Francisco's brother) attacked Torreón, whose railway was strategically important. In the preceding days, anti-foreigner speeches had been given by local politicians in which the instruction was given to "exterminate the Chinese who are dangerous competitors."[12] Outside the city, the soldiers first invaded the Chinese horticultural gardens, forcing workers to serve them food and using their homes as fortifications, later killing many of them. Late on Sunday night, running out of ammunition, the 670-man-strong force of the Federal Army in Torreón fled, abandoning the city to the revolutionaries. On Monday morning, 15 May

THE TORREÓN MASSACRE

1911, the violence culminated in the massacre of more than 200 Chinese. In total, in only three days, 303 out of the 700 Chinese in the city, as well as five Japanese, were killed, of whom less than ten were women. The victims included 62 traders, 110 farmers, 65 employees, 56 passing travelers, and 10 children.[13] The perpetrators were a mob of 4,000 people, made up of city dwellers, newly arrived revolutionary soldiers, and newly liberated prisoners.

Monday began with the rebel soldiers entering the city at six o'clock in the morning, accompanied by a crowd of men, women and children from neighboring municipalities, and quickly joined by residents of Torreón. Men on horseback forced the few surviving Chinese Gardens' workers to walk towards the city, dragging them by their pigtails and killing anyone who fell along the way. The soldiers first sacked the business district, destroying and robbing the stores, and then attacked Chinatown. The few Asian women in the city were raped, and Chinese men, women and children were indiscriminately killed, their bodies stripped of possessions and then mutilated. The violence intensified over a period of hours until the crowd arrived in front of the Bank of China and Mexico, which was looted and the Chinese imperial flag thrown to the ground. All of the bank's Chinese employees were massacred with machetes, their heads and limbs severed and then thrown onto the street. The other foreign banks, although larger and richer, were not affected,[14] demonstrating the attackers' racial bias. An independent report describes the massacre as follows:

> The town was searched for Chinese and all who could be found were murdered in the most brutal and horrifying manner [...]. In another instance a soldier took a little boy by the heels and battered his brains out against a lamp post [...]. In another instance a Chinaman was pulled to pieces in the street by horses hitched to his arms and legs [...]. No language can adequately depict the revolting scenes which attended this carnival of human slaughter [...]. The mind recoils in horror from contemplation of such an atrocity.[15]

At least nine Torreón residents, including the daughter of a revolutionary leader, risked their lives by opposing the massacre and managing to hide and save 137 Chinese.[16] Based on historical sources, Emilio Madero only entered the city on Monday afternoon, when he decreed the death penalty for anyone continuing with the killings, putting an end to the violence. However, given the importance of Torreón, it is likely that he or other revolutionary generals were present in the city earlier than this. He then gave the order to imprison the 200 surviving Chinese still present in Torreón, who were then beaten and harassed further by some of the same soldiers responsible for the killings. Finally, the Chinese suffered a further indignity when they were forbidden to bury their dead in the local cemetery, the mutilated corpses being thrown into mass graves.[17] The massacre also resulted in property damages estimated at $850,000, or more than $25 million in today's money, the greatest losses ever suffered by the Chinese community in Mexico, destroying the country's most prosperous Asian colony, which would never fully recover.[18] Goods looted from the Chinese during the riots were still for sale in regional markets months after the massacre.

This pogrom was the most horrific incident against the Chinese during the revolution and, after the 1881 massacre of Chinese in Peru, the deadliest in their history in the Americas. The Chinese victims were disarmed and defenseless, putting up no resistance. They were therefore simply murdered, as several independent investigations concluded the following year. This was a premeditated and racist act of mass murder. According to the writer Julián Herbert, the massacre was as much influenced by the violent impulse of the Torreón populace as by the racist views of the local bourgeoisie.[19] On 12 June 1911, three days before the massacre, Woo Lam Po, the secretary of the Chinese Reform Association and an accountant at the Bank of China and Mexico, tried to warn his compatriots of the violence to come. He wrote (in Chinese) a prescient leaflet, which was unfortunately not disseminated in time nor taken seriously:

> Brothers, beware! Careful! This is serious. Many unjust acts occurred during the revolution. We have been warned that before ten o'clock today, the revolutionaries will join forces and attack the city. It is very likely that during the battle a crowd will form and ransack the shops. For this reason, we advise all our people, when the crowd gathers, to close your doors and hide and in no case open your shops for business or go outside to see the fighting. And if your

stores are vandalized, do not offer any resistance, but allow them to take away what they like, otherwise you could put your life at risk.[20]

The Torreón massacre received little attention in the Chinese press but triggered a swift response from the Qing government, helped by a more friendly relationship with the United States and possibly influenced by the large investments of its diaspora in the city. In March 1909, two years before Torreón, President William Howard Taft succeeded Theodore Roosevelt as US president. In contrast to Roosevelt's anti-Chinese sentiments, the new and more progressive President Taft sought a rapprochement with China. Having been the civilian governor of the Philippines, a United States territory since 1898, Taft had a deep knowledge of and keen interest in Asia, proclaiming that the reforms in China were "the greatest movement in the world today, and have the deepest sympathy of America, and that there never can be any jealousy or fear on the part of the United States due to China's industrial or political development."[21] Although the harsh immigration policies remained in place, this diplomatic sympathy towards China initiated under Taft continued until the Communist Revolution of 1949, in part due to the United States' desire to develop new markets and to counterbalance Japan's ambitions in Asia.

After its defeat in its war against Japan in 1895, the Qing government had ordered from Great Britain two armored 423ft battleship cruisers, the *Haiqi*[22] vessels. In May 1911, while the massacre was taking place in Torreón, the Qing government sent one of these vessels to participate in Queen Victoria's annual fleet review in Portsmouth, seeking to gain naval prestige. Later, in September, the *Haiqi* sailed on to New York, where the Chinese admiral was welcomed with great honor by the Taft government, receiving praise in the US press. In response to the Torreón massacre, Chinese diplomats, using their new influence in Washington, sent a US law firm close to President Taft, Wilfley & Bassett, to investigate the events and demand compensation. Their report was completed with the help of the US consulate in Torreón and the testimony of the many US residents in the city.

The use of American lawyers and their new alignment with the Unites States exemplifies China's subtle diplomatic maneuvering at that time. In June 1911, in another tactical move, Wilfley and Bassett's scathing report was leaked to the US press, whose opinion then turned pro-Chinese. Two earlier investigation reports had been commissioned by the Mexican government: the first one tried to shamelessly blame the Chinese for the event and was widely disseminated in the local press, while the second one got closer to the truth but underestimated the number of victims by a third since it excluded the Chinese who were already naturalized. Following the release of the Wilfley and Basset report, more than twenty revolutionary soldiers were judged by Mexican courts for their role in the massacre, but not a single Mexican military leader was ever criticized for the massacre and claims for compensation were rejected.

In September, at the request of the local Qing consulate in Cuba, the *Haiqi* vessel arrived in Havana. This was a show of force, "to encourage Caribbean and South American governments to respect the rights of Chinese overseas workers and businesses, which should not assume the status of second-class citizens because of a lack of government support."[23] This historic event stood in sharp contrast with the situation just decades earlier, when Chinese emigrants were without any diplomatic protection. The Cuban government gave assurances to the Chinese admiral that their military would not take any harmful action against the overseas Chinese. As the indemnity negotiations with the Mexican government stalled, the Qing diplomats leaked to the press the intention for the *Haiqi* to sail towards Mexico to "further the friendship between the two countries," which was received with great approval in the international press. The *Pittsburgh Press* noted sarcastically that the gunboat diplomacy of the Chinese showed how "China is learning,"[24] while in the *New York Times*, US General A. W. Greely opined "that this new assertiveness, coupled with military and educational reforms was 'impressive,' a word he used repeatedly."[25] Due in no small part to the threat from the *Haiqi*, in December 1911, after much haggling, the Mexican government issued an official apology to the Chinese government, agreeing to pay $3.2 million in compensation for the Torreón massacre, to be received by the Qing government and then distributed among the victims. However, since China shortly afterwards underwent its own revolution and regime change, this indemnity was never settled—an example of the impunity which would be a feature of Mexican politics in the twentieth century. As Eric Setzekorn argues, the *Haiqi* incident demonstrated how the late Qing government successfully used cooperative diplomacy and reliance on international law as ways to achieve its objectives, rather than direct aggression. Had the Qing dynasty not been toppled in the 1911 revolution, one wonders how Chinese diplomacy might have developed over the following decades under the influence of these new and more assertive diplomats.

Torreón did not have a particularly large Chinese community compared, for example, with Chinese settlements in the state of Sonora. But it had two distinct characteristics which influenced events. First, the average Torreón-based Chinese immigrant was richer than Chinese immigrants elsewhere in Mexico, and, second, there were fewer mixed marriages in Torreón than in other cities in Mexico. This was because most Chinese businesses in the city, like those of Foon Chuck and the Chinese Reform Association, were not merely family enterprises but were corporations run by professional managers and invested in by Chinese capital from other parts of Mexico and overseas. In this respect, the young colony of Torreón was like no other in North America, having an important financial and (to a lesser extent) political foundation. It stood in sharp contrast with typical Chinese settlements across North America, with their small family-run restaurants, retail stores and laundries, and it involved a completely different type of interaction between the migrants and the local population. Foon Chuck himself did not have his family settled in Torreón but in the border town of Piedras Negras, where they took refuge as the attacks by the revolutionary forces intensified.

From Piedras Negras, Foon Chuck sent an urgent telegram to the Chinese ambassador in Washington informing him of the violence against the Chinese and requesting that he and his compatriots be given right of entry into the United States.[26] Foon Chuck and his family, along with others, were thus temporarily admitted to the United States on humanitarian grounds.[27] In September 1911, in Piedras Negras, an angry mob attacked several businesses owned by immigrants from China and elsewhere[28] who then sought protection at the US consulate. In August of that year, Foon Chuck had been named special envoy and commissioner for the state of Coahuila by the Chinese ambassador to Mexico to investigate the killings in Torreón.[29] In February 1914, the Chinese legation in Mexico again named Foon Chuck special envoy, this time to investigate the situation of the Chinese across the whole country, illustrating the important representative role that he had assumed within the Chinese-Mexican community. This was a dangerous role given the continuing climate of violence. As had been the case for him in China, the main danger Foon Chuck now faced was of being kidnapped for ransom, as happened to many during the revolution.

In addition to the employees of the Chinese bank, a total of forty-five of Foon Chuck's workers were murdered: four from his laundry business, nine from his hotel, and thirty-two from his vegetable farm. Some were his family members. In less than a day, what had taken him decades to build was destroyed. A secret tunnel was subsequently built under his hotel in Monclova to provide refuge in case of further riots.[30]

The Mexican Revolution had disastrous consequences for the economy, contributing to the slow decline of Foon Chuck's various businesses. After land confiscations by the government and costly legal battles lasting into the 1930s,[31] some of the remaining buildings and land in Torreón that he, his partners, and Kang's Commercial Corporation owned, including the bank building and the tramway company, were liquidated for a fraction of their pre-revolution value and at a significant loss. Decades later, one of his descendants, visiting the home of the vice-mayor of Torreón in the La Rosita district, was shown by his host the foundations of Foon Chuck's old farm, hidden in the back of his garden. The neighborhood was now the city's most exclusive, and its tragic history was mostly forgotten. When the revolution began, Foon Chuck was forty-eight, having already lived two-thirds of his life in Mexico. Heartbroken, he was forced to close his beloved school and send the students home, including four of his own children, whom he registered at an American public school in Eagle Pass. He also hired a private tutor so that they could continue to learn Chinese. Unlike him, his Mexico-born children were regarded as Mexicans in the United States, and they were thus allowed into the country as students. In 1914, revolutionary forces destroyed his general store in

THE TORREÓN MASSACRE

Lampacitos, and in 1923 the Mexican government's decision to expropriate US capital from the railroad companies forced him to permanently close his hotels, since they depended on the patronage of Americans.[32]

Despite the Qing dynasty (now with the child Emperor Puyi on the throne) adopting the reforms that Kang Youwei had proposed a decade earlier, its days were numbered, and in the winter of 1911–12 it collapsed in the midst of the Xinhai Revolution. Instead of being hailed as a reformist hero, the financial setbacks of his organization abroad had seriously dented Kang's reputation by the time he returned to China in 1913. The Mexican Revolution forced him to realize that he had put profits and the economy before politics, ignoring the immaturity of the Mexican regime; he acknowledged his own share of responsibility in the death of the Chinese in Torreón.[33] He lost not only most of his investments but also one of his nephews, an employee of the Bank of China and Mexico, who was murdered during the massacre. With few financial resources remaining,[34] he also lost many valuable members of his movement, who were dismayed by the abysmal financial losses. Torreón and the Mexican Revolution thus directly impacted Kang's ability to shape the course of China's Xinhai Revolution. The Mexican Revolution also reinforced Kang's opinion that China was not yet ready for a republican system: he felt that it might not be able to escape the same fate as Mexico.[35] China's turbulent history in the following decades proved him to be, at least in some ways, correct about this.

In 1911, only ten days after the Torreón massacre, Porfirio Díaz fled Mexico and went into exile in France, proclaiming, "They have loosed the wild beasts, let us see now who will tame them." The extreme lawlessness and violence during the following years validated his warning.[36] With no functioning economy and bureaucracy and the country in chaos, the years 1914–16 were the most violent of the revolution. All Mexican cities suffered from the same curses: snipers terrorizing citizens, acute shortages of staples, people scavenging garbage, begging for food, slaughtering pets to eat them, and women prostituting themselves to survive. In the countryside, crops went unharvested or failed, cattle were exported to buy ammunitions, mines were closed, and hunger was rampant everywhere.[37] During those years, most rich Mexicans chose to flee the country with their families, but this was not an option for most of the Chinese, with the United States closed and China in chaos as well. Hing saw all his wealthy clients vanish, making him wonder whether he now had any future in his adopted country.

Aside from its xenophobic character, the Torreón massacre resembled the hundreds of equally murderous peasant revolts and riots that took place during the revolutionary decade, showing the anger of a nation and the injustice of an era. During the 1910s, instead of Torreón producing public outrage in Mexico, anti-Chinese violence spread around the country. In those years, the whole Chinese community in Mexico suffered from frequent and arbitrary assaults, creating an atmosphere of terror and lawlessness.[38] In February 1912, just a few months after the massacre, the surviving Chinese in Torreón, fearing further killings, appealed naively to the Mexican government for protection,[39] a government that no longer existed, just as they might have done to their emperor in China. In 1912, Mazatlán Chinatown, which Hing had left a few years earlier, was looted and 570 Chinese were forced to take refuge in the US consulate; they all escaped with their lives,[40] although nine Chinese were later killed in the city. In 1916, sixty Chinese were murdered in Parral, Chihuahua, by the revolutionary leader Pancho Villa—well known for his hatred of the Chinese—who hanged them by their pigtails and had them thrown into a mineshaft.[41] Later, he ordered his soldiers to eliminate all the Chinese they found and burn their Mexican wives, and in 1917 his troops killed another sixty Chinese, again in Torreón, six years after the first massacre.[42] An American journalist wrote that Villa was "the most natural human being I ever saw, in the sense of being nearest to a wild animal, his eyes are never still and full of energy and brutality, intelligent as hell and as merciless, his hands are like a wolf's. He's a terrible man."[43]

In 1916, in a notable exception to the general Chinese-Mexican neutrality during the revolution, 500 Chinese joined the US troops of General Pershing to fight against Pancho Villa, who had crossed the border to raid American towns. Many of them were not active soldiers but cooks and merchants serving the US army, something Mexicans refused to do, so as not to appear to be traitors. This event illustrates the state of despair of some in the Chinese community, forced to take up arms with a foreign nation to survive. It also illus-

THE TORREÓN MASSACRE

trates their shifting allegiances in the face of racial violence, now siding with their former tormentors in the United States. In recognition for their service, some of those Chinese were later welcomed to immigrate into the United States.

Pancho Villa is a controversial figure in Mexico's history, the perfect example of an uneducated bandit who opportunistically seized the moment and turned himself into a politician and a revolutionary—at least until his assassination in 1923. The Villistas, as Villa's soldiers were called, were reputed to be merciless rapists, murderers and looters, even sacking Mexico City. Three years after his death, Villa's tomb was desecrated and his head cut off and stolen, a violent end for a politician still celebrated today in Mexico, whose life had been largely dedicated to robbing and killing.

Even in the capital city of Mexico, 129 Chinese were assassinated. In Piedras Negras, Foon Chuck's hometown, more than 300 Chinese were killed,[44] quite an extraordinary number given the city's small size, illustrating that it had also become an exit point for refugees fleeing the violence (more than 10,000 Mexicans crossed the Piedras Negras border in 1914 alone). An American family from Eagle Pass remembered protecting and hiding the young Chuck children in their home, when the soldiers of Pancho Villa crossed the border and tried to kill the Chinese in that American town too.[45] Many Chinese were victims of extortion, forced to buy their protection from dishonest revolutionaries, while soldiers' favorite pastime became to rob Chinese merchants, strip them of their clothes, and tie them up to trees.[46] In the large Chinatown of Mexicali, since most of the Chinese there were poor cotton laborers, no large-scale massacre took place, highlighting the economic motivation behind a lot of the anti-Chinese violence. From 1910 to 1919, a total of 814 assassinations of Chinese were documented in various parts of Mexico,[47] a figure that excludes those killed in Torreón, and which was not officially verified and is—perhaps like many statistics at the time—an underestimate, especially given the lack of independent investigations. The figure may seem insignificant compared to the more than a million-and-a-half Mexican victims of the revolution, but they were non-combatants and therefore simply victims of hatred and racism.

If most Chinese were passive victims during the revolution, some got organized and tried to appeal to the authorities to seek redress, in the same way that they would have petitioned mandarins back in China. In 1916, reflecting their Confucian beliefs, the Chinese community of a small Sonoran town wrote the following letter to the state governor, naively showing their blind faith in authority, their political ignorance, and their tragic state of disbelief in the face of unfolding events:

> We, perhaps more than other foreigners, have suffered the consequences [of the revolution]. We have patiently suffered [...] without complaint or protest. As good friends to the Mexicans, we regret everything [that has happened], and all we have left is the latent spirit of work [...] we comply with all the laws, work honestly, and pay our contributions [...] we don't bring harm to anyone, yet we have been innocent victims of the war, [...] without intention to claim compensation, we believe we have the right to be considered with justice to the same degree as everyone else.[48]

Foon Chuck was devastated by the events taking place during the revolution, but Mexico remained his country, even as he retained an attachment to Chinese culture and his people. He still had many friends in Mexico, including revolutionary politicians, and had reinvested most of his profits locally rather than repatriating them to China. Although his children were now studying in the United States, the heart of the family remained anchored in Mexico. He could not consider returning to China in his old age: his Mexican family would not accept it, and how could he keep his head straight in front of his ancestors after such a defeat, even if it was only temporary? He remained pragmatic; he knew that power could pass from one politician to another, and he hoped that new Mexican leaders would emerge, willing to do business with him on the same basis as before. In China, history is believed to be cyclical, alternating periods of chaos and violence with times of civility and peace. Foon Chuck thought of the Chinese idiom that evokes the Yellow River—then known as the "sorrow of China" for its many floods and for changing its bed frequently—which "passes on the east side of the village for thirty years, then on the west side for thirty others,"[49] while life goes on the same way. Foon Chuck was also a farmer, accustomed to the rhythm of the seasons and the whims of the heavens, knowing that more opportune times would come one day.

THE TORREÓN MASSACRE

As early as 1912, despite the events of Torreón, Foon Chuck gave an interview in the *Washington Post* titled "A Bright Future for China," stating his optimistic views not only on the Chinese but also the Mexican Revolution.[50] By then, following his earlier dispute with Kang Youwei, he had become a nationalist, supporting the young Chinese republic of Sun Yat-sen instead of the parliamentary monarchy called for by his ex-partner. In Foon Chuck's mind, those two revolutions, the Chinese and the Mexican, which coincidentally happened in the same year, stood in sharp contrast: the Mexican Revolution was a popular uprising from below, aiming to transform society, whereas the Chinese Revolution of 1911–12 was driven more by high politics. One happened in the oldest country in the world and the other in one of the youngest, yet both revolutions aimed to advance their respective societies towards a more just future. Hence, despite the massacre of Torreón and the widespread violence against his people, Foon Chuck remained optimistic and hopeful that things would turn out for the better for him and the Chinese, in both China and Mexico, thinking of the Chinese adage: "Watch till clouds part to see the moonlight."[51]

Notably, neither the Mexican nor the Chinese Revolution had any meaningful impact on farmers, both countries having to wait more than two decades for meaningful land reforms to happen, under the presidency of Lázaro Cárdenas (no relation to Foon Chuck's friend Miguel Cárdenas) in Mexico in the late 1930s and under the Communists with President Mao Tse-tung in China in the 1950s. For example, during the 1920s in El Mante, after various failed attempts, absolutely no land was distributed to small local farmers, keeping the large landowners in control, Foon Chuck included.[52]

As the revolution began, Foon Chuck's vast agricultural project in El Mante was not yet developed for two reasons. First, the poor condition of the roads and the distance to the railway rendered the estate difficult to manage profitably. Even in dry weather, it took three to four days by cart to transport the products from the farm to the nearest station, even longer for heavy machinery, while during the rainy season, the roads became impassable mud swamps.[53] Second, the sugar refinery project required heavy infrastructure investments, which Foon Chuck and his Mexican associates were not able to carry out alone. Around 1916, encouraged by the oil boom in nearby Tampico, Foon Chuck even started prospecting for oil on his property, but unsuccessfully. For those reasons and due to the revolution, the population of Hacienda Canton decreased from 438 in 1910 to 289 people by 1920, of whom 125 were women. In 1912, his association with his old friend Miguel Cárdenas, now ex-governor, was dissolved without producing any results, both partners deciding to go in separate directions. Foon Chuck kept his two haciendas, El Canton and El Limon, while giving Miguel Cárdenas some of his land and water rights in compensation for his lost investment[54] (they remained good friends). Despite the revolution and these first setbacks, Foon Chuck's conviction about the bright future of the region grew stronger year after year.

Foon Chuck looked for every opportunity to make his El Mante project fulfil its potential. During the revolution, he continued to pursue the patronage and economic support of local politicians, but without success. In 1919, now fifty-six years old and with the revolution coming to an end, he invited a group of influential leaders to his estate for a short vacation, including three state governors, three generals, and various other politicians,[55] such as Juan Saenz and General Gregorio Osuna.[56] During these meetings, his guests became enthusiastic as Foon Chuck presented detailed plans to establish a large-scale sugar cane plantation and sugar refinery, convincing them to buy the land needed for the project. Foon Chuck had not lost faith in Mexico and continued to fight to recover his fortune, which he saw as his destiny and the reason why the Heavens had given him his gift for business. In those years he showed the same perseverance as his old teacher Reverend Loomis. The following Chinese proverb comes to mind: "An army can conquer a general, but no man can steal his ambitions."[57] That same year, General Osuna and Miguel Cárdenas established a new partnership to develop land, which also ended in failure. By 1922, the politicians and generals Foon Chuck had invited earlier had already acquired most of the land of Cárdenas, who had lost all political influence and needed to repay loans (he retained only 341 hectares). With his 2,479 hectares in El Limon and El Canton, Foon Chuck remained the largest landowner in the region.[58] During the 1920s, the new landowners followed his lead and started drying and clearing land to grow sugar cane, but they too were limited by the absence of roads and the need to build heavy infrastructure.

THE TORREÓN MASSACRE

Not all Mexican politicians during the revolution were xenophobic. Venustiano Carranza, the new governor of the state of Coahuila, succeeding Miguel Cárdenas, was the oldest among the revolutionary leaders and was an educated and liberal man from the gentry, with a solid knowledge of economics and current affairs. He was from Coahuila, and became president of Mexico from 1917 to 1920, restoring law and order in the country after the chaos of the earlier years and setting up a new constitution. He was the only Mexican president of the era to openly express his opposition to the violence against the Chinese, for example by standing against the first expulsions of the Chinese from the mining town of Cananea in the state of Sonora in 1920. Carranza had been acquainted with Foon Chuck for many years. In March 1913, Carranza even decided to establish the headquarters of his revolutionary troops at Foon Chuck's hotel in Monclova, showing Foon Chuck's modest involvement in the revolution, in support of its more liberal leaders. Foon Chuck's elder children remembered how during those years of violence, Carranza often sent soldiers to protect their father against possible aggressions from his enemies, including Pancho Villa. It is no surprise then that Foon Chuck called Carranza his good friend and that he kept an optimistic outlook during the revolution, even during its darkest hours. In 1920, with the revolution about to end, Foon Chuck traveled to Mexico City to speak with the president, whom he convinced to extend the railway line to El Mante.[59] Unfortunately, President Carranza was assassinated soon afterwards by a group of generals from Sonora, unhappy with Carranza's more liberal stance and his opposition to the army. Before his death, Carranza publicly declared:

> The evil of Mexico has been and is militarism. Very few civilians have become President. Always generals, and what generals! This must end for the good of Mexico. I want a civilian to succeed me as President, a modern and progressive man [...]. It is time that Mexico begins to live like other nations.[60]

The army's takeover of revolutionary movements would be a pattern in the history of most Latin American countries in the twentieth century. With the loss of his only ally, the last liberal politician standing, Foon Chuck's hopes were shattered again. It was as if the heavens and history had now resolutely turned against him and his people.

12

UNDER THE PROTECTION OF THE GOLDEN DRAGON

In 1920, the assassination of Carranza and the seizure of power by three generals from Sonora marked the end of the Mexican Revolution. Those generals remained in power for fourteen years, until 1934, first under the presidency of Álvaro Obregón and then from 1924 of the populist Plutarco Elías Calles, both of whom pursued anti-Chinese policies. In 1921, the Torreón massacre already forgotten, during a tense meeting with Chinese Chancellor Quang Ki-Teng, President Obregón renegotiated the 1899 Treaty of Friendship and Commerce with China. While keeping the trade clauses in place, the treaty now limited the number of Chinese migrants allowed into Mexico. Although the two countries maintained diplomatic relations, the Chinese consulate closed in 1922, leaving Chinese Mexicans even more abandoned and vulnerable. The treaty was abolished in 1927 under President Calles, and it was not until the Second World War, when Mexico and China became war allies, that a new treaty was signed between the two countries.

The regimes of Obregón and Calles were marked by unprecedented levels of corruption. Obregón put 500 generals on the government payroll, famously bragging that "no Mexican general can withstand a cannonball of 50,000 pesos,"[1] and admitting to a journalist that "Here, all of us are thieving a bit."[2] However, Obregón also led a policy of reconciliation with the Porfirian economic elites, bringing back a feeling of normality in society. For Hing, this meant that his precious wealthy customers returned.

From 1924, President Calles, a bureaucrat at heart, implemented social programs and positive development policies, including in the field of education, the creation of a central bank and the introduction of a minimum salary. But he was also anti-democractic, brutal and vengeful, carrying out violent anticlerical and openly racist policies, including against the Chinese. Following an earlier trip to Europe, he followed the example of fascist dictators there, creating his own anti-foreigner league, the Golden Shirts.[3] As in the United States decades earlier, Mexican populist politicians at the highest level openly supported these xenophobic and violent campaigns, which distracted their voters from a harsh economic crisis, especially in Sonora, while increasing popular support for the government. After the revolution, the government maintained control over the military and its key politicians by providing them with incentives and material means to go into business. The transformation of Aarón Sáenz (1891–1983), the son of Foon Chuck's new neighbor Juan Sáenz, from general during the revolution, into government official and finally into capitalist entrepreneur, provides a prime example of such processes.[4] This was done with the help of the 1917 constitution, which enabled the expropriation of private property for the personal gains of the generals and their cronies.

President Obregón also enrolled writers and painters to his nationalistic and socialist cause, such as José Vasconcelos (see Chapter Eight) and the famous muralist Diego Rivera (1886–1957), who both put their artistic talent at the service of the racist ideologies of the government. Vasconcelos, Mexico's first minister of education, fought all his life to promote literacy, emphasizing the conflict between the spiritual goals of his people and the material and mercantile ones of American capitalism. He believed the pursuit of materialistic ends to be an unworthy goal which dulls the minds and starves the spirit.[5] Despite, or maybe because of his cosmopolitan education in Eagle Pass, he believed that in terms of evolution Mexico was ahead of both its northern neighbor and of China, about which he wrote in his famous and controversial book *The Cosmic Race* that:

> We recognize that it is not fair that some people like the Chinese, who, under the holy precepts of Confucian morality, multiply themselves like mice, come to degrade the human condition, just at the time when we are starting to understand that intelligence serves to restrain our low zoological instincts, contrary to a truly religious concept of life.[6]

As the political situation deteriorated, Hing hid with his family in Mexico's largest cities: Guadalajara, the more liberal Monterrey and finally Mexico City. His clients were the wealthy Mexicans who had somehow survived the revolution, and remained eager to buy his precious products to flatter their egos. Unlike the Chinese in Sonora, since he was selling Chinese art, Hing did not compete with local Mexicans, and so he avoided this source of resentment. Hing and Cruz had a total of ten children together, born between 1900 and 1924: seven sons (by order of birth), Melchor, Alejandro, Agustín, Jorge, Juan, Pablo and Hector, and three daughters, Victoria, Concepción and Lola. The Leon children benefited from loving parents, a close-knit family, and money from their father's business. As they grew up, all the boys and girls worked in one of their father's stores across Mexico. The Leons' childhoods were not about maintaining a balance between cultures, but about blending into Mexican society, while helping their father with his stores. With an orphaned mother and a father whose roots lay in a distant land, the Leon siblings lacked relatives beyond their nuclear family, and this helped them to develop a fierce loyalty to each other during these violent years.

In addition to its xenophobia, Mexican society displayed a bourgeois and misogynistic culture, with the Catholic Church still exerting enormous influence. With unmarried and mixed-race parents, this was not a very tolerant and indulgent place to grow for the Leon children. At the time, being Asian and mixed race was considered an anomaly, even a pathology, in Mexico as in other Western countries.[7] Some described mixed Chinese-Mexican children as "a new racial type still more degenerated than [Mexico's] naturally abject indigenous castes, the product of filthy unions who embody the worst vices and degeneration of both Chinese immigrants and the Mexican lower classes."[8] Those views were influenced by similar ones from the United States, such as from the eugenicist Lothrop Stoddard who, capturing the mood of the era, wrote in 1922 that as modern transport had eliminated the natural barriers to mixing, white supremacy would be undermined by non-white migrants, and if immigration were not stopped, whites would be ultimately doomed.[9]

Isolated and thus conspicuous, the Eurasian Leon children had nowhere to hide from their bullies. Like all Chinese-Mexican children, they suffered daily from countless acts of casual racism and brutality, especially during the revolution; a sad family photo taken in 1916 shows the children with angry expressions, especially the two elder girls. Their visages show not passivity and resignation but instead an attitude of revolt and courage in front of the aggressions they faced, as if the children did not want to give their bullies the satisfaction of seeing them scared. This photograph forms a striking contrast with the one taken a decade earlier (see book cover), in which all the children have confident smiles. Hing told his children stories about his struggles in California, asking them now to show they belonged here by fighting back when bullied at school, like real Mexicans! As the Chinese saying goes, "the heavier the setback, the stronger the courage."[10] In the dystopian racist world they now lived in, where their tormentors made them feel ashamed of their origins, the children accepted this reality as normal, failing to realize that it was the racist bullies instead of them who should be ashamed. During this period, as the children sought the fellowship of the few other Chinese children around, the friendship between the daughters of Foon Chuck and Hing began. Born out of suffering and exclusion, this friendship survived several decades, giving rise to the marriage of my grandparents.

In addition to daily racism and violence, Hing worried about the new anti-Chinese laws implemented by the generals, doubting whether his naturalization could protect him, since it had been signed twenty years earlier by a now-defunct dictator. All Chinese immigrants in the country were now required to be properly registered and granted immigration documents—a sad echo for Foon Chuck and Hing of what had happened to them in the United States four decades earlier. In the early 1920s, Chinese immigrants continued to become naturalized Mexicans at a rate of around a hundred per year, but after 1925, with President Calles in power, this figure dropped sharply, so that there were only three naturalizations in 1931.[11] Hing, feeling the urgency of asserting his Mexican citizenship, finally married Cruz in front of a registrar in Torreón in 1925, after the birth of their last child and twenty-six years after they first met. He hoped that this would further cement his status as Mexican. They did not marry in front of a priest, though, Hing being proud and stubborn, and refusing all his life to be baptized. Surprisingly, the post-dated birth certificate of his daughter in 1929 shows Hing as

UNDER THE PROTECTION OF THE GOLDEN DRAGON

being born in 1866 not in China but in the Mexican city of Torreón, illustrating how far the Chinese had to go to protect their rights. Torreón was chosen as the place of marriage and imaginary birth because its Chinese population was relatively large and they could find more accepting civil registrars there than in the capital city, where they now lived. This was also facilitated by Foon Chuck, who had become Hing's friend and who retained political connections in the state, even after the departure of his political allies.

As was the tradition in affluent Mexican families, Hing's sons all studied in American military high schools, from the eldest Melchor in 1918 to the youngest Hector in 1940. A photograph from the Second World War shows Hing and Cruz proudly surrounded by five of their adult sons, all with martial poses and in military uniform, a sign of the times. This did not mean that the family had embraced militarism though, the sons would remain mellow and gentle all their lives, but was a statement that the Leon children would not be bullied anymore. In 1939, on his way to the Western Military Academy in Alton, Illinois, Hing's son Pablo traveled to the United States with a Chinese passport instead of a Mexican one. Based on a 1909 Chinese law, all children born to Chinese fathers were automatically recognized as Chinese nationals, to strengthen the ties of the overseas Chinese with their motherland,[12] quite a contrast with the earlier Qing dynasty policies, highlighting the progress of Chinese nationalism. Due to the student exemption in the US's Exclusion Act, Hing found it easier to have Pablo go to the United States using a Chinese passport rather than a Mexican one, even though Pablo had never set foot in China, illustrating the absurdity of a world which had erected new barriers everywhere. While Pablo entered the US by train in Laredo, most Chinese immigrants were now entering the United States through Angel Island opposite San Francisco, where more than 100,000 of them had been kept in detention barracks, some for more than a year.[13] Like many of them, Pablo had to prove that he was a student to be allowed in. More than 200 poems written by migrants can still be found in those barracks today, which are now a museum. For example:

> I clasped my hands in parting with my brothers and classmates.
> Because of the mouth, I hastened to cross the American ocean.

> How was I to know that the western barbarians had lost their hearts and reason?
> With a hundred kinds of oppressive laws, they mistreat us Chinese.[14]

In contrast to Foon Chuck's family, Hing's children were not academic and did not attend university. There were few universities in 1930s Mexico, and less than one in twenty Mexicans had a tertiary education. Hing expected his children to become successful businessmen, and advanced studies were not necessary for that. While Hing at first decided to teach them Cantonese, following the Mexican and Chinese revolutions he changed his mind. He saw the situation in China as hopeless, with his homeland vandalized and gradually falling into anarchy after the fall of the young republic. He did not believe that learning the family dialect was worth it: since Mexico was to be their only country, they had to fight instead to secure their Mexican roots.

Hing even formally forbade his children from learning Chinese, fearing they would adopt the bad habits of some migrants, such as gambling, prostitution and opium, vices which may have been responsible for his brothers' deaths. At least, this is the official, face-saving narrative told in the Leon family; the real reason for Hing's prohibition was simply the xenophobia his children faced, since speaking Chinese would not help them become accepted in Mexico. This thinking stood in stark contrast with the views of many Chinese migrants in the United States, for whom teaching Chinese to their children was not only about maintaining their culture but was essential for them to later find jobs in Chinatown, or back in China when they grew up, as they were excluded from most jobs by the white majority. Hing, on the contrary, still viewed Mexico as the only future for his mixed children.

Also, like most Chinese from poor backgrounds, Hing did not receive much of an education, able to write in Chinese but, unlike Foon Chuck, without any emotional or artistic bonds with the language. He had learned to read and write Spanish well, a much easier language, which was enough for him. Learning Chinese would have also been almost impossible for his children without a proper study environment given the difficulty of the language. Juan, one of the middle sons, remembered his father reprimanding him severely when he was caught speaking a few words of dialect with the family cook. The Leon children had ambiguous feelings towards their roots. The essence of their father's enterprise was promoting Chinese culture, but they were not encouraged to learn more about their origins. How could they become effective promoters of this civilization without any affinity and familiarity with it themselves? This was a contradiction that seemed to doom them to failure from the start.

Melchor, the eldest son, oversaw the stores when his father traveled and later when he retired. Alejandro, the second son, became a sculptor and painter. Hing paid for his studies in Italy, but on his return, did not see a future in art, asking him to work instead. Alejandro enjoyed spending his free time sculpting and painting in his large house in Mexico City's Coyoacan neighborhood, a real museum with works of art in every corner. Often lost in creative work, he was one of Hing's happiest children. Slim and muscular, the third son Agustín became an athlete, but caught tuberculosis. Sent to convalesce in Switzerland in the 1920s, he never returned. Jorge Jr, who married one of the maids, had an inferiority complex and was rejected by the other siblings. After his death, his ashes were not admitted by his siblings in the family crypt, reflecting the narrow-mindedness of the Leon family even as they were themselves discriminated against. Apart from Jorge Jr, all the sons, helped by the money and prestige of El Dragon de Oro, married middle-class Mexican women, a happy fate which was not to be shared by their sisters.

While a growing percentage of the Mexican population was mestizo (that is, of mixed Spanish and Indian descent), white Mexicans still represented an overwhelming majority of the urban upper classes, and many still often despised mestizos and Indians, or simply anyone with dark skin. These prejudices remain common today among many white families in Mexico. The three Leon sisters found themselves in peculiar circumstances; they had white skin and shared with the Indians slightly slanted eyes. Any respectable family would hesitate before marrying their heirs to the strange Leon sisters, neither Indian nor Caucasian, fearing that their future offspring would be ostracized. Like their father thirty years earlier, the three sisters were now excluded from high and middle-class Mexican society, despite their refined educations, their distinction, and the family fortune.

The three sisters followed different—but all tragic—paths. In 1932, the eldest, Victoria, married a mestizo with distinct Indian features, who was the curator of the Churubusco Convent Museum in Mexico City. Being almost thirty, this was her last chance to avoid becoming an old spinster. In China, the soul of an unwed woman after her death is believed to be homeless for eternity. They lived together in the former convent, a serene, beautiful, timeless place, which remains a museum today. However, she felt that he did not reciprocate her love and that he was socially below her. In the wedding photo, the parents of both families have stern faces, perhaps due to mutual contempt. Just three years later, after a party at which Victoria believed he cheated on her, she committed suicide. From a young age, Victoria looks sad and frightened in all of her photos. Disillusioned in regard to a society that rejected her, she could not explain the hatred she experienced just for having a Chinese father. Hing was kind, honest and hard-working, but none of his daughter's tormentors were willing to see beyond the shape of her eyes. She also had trouble assuming her role as eldest daughter, scared that she may never fit or belong anywhere. In 1928, the Chicago sociologist Robert Park described the marginal man or woman as being "usually of mixed race and living between two cultures, being comfortable in neither, prone to spiritual instability, intensified self-consciousness, restlessness and malaise,"[15] which accurately and sadly describes Victoria.

Concepción, the middle daughter, married a Chinese gentleman in 1929 and later went into exile with him. She was the freest and most independent of the three, not afraid to challenge the Church, and hating any form of sectarianism. She felt closest to her father and had more pronounced Chinese features than her two sisters. Despite, or perhaps because of this, she seemed more comfortable with her Eurasian roots than her sisters were, even though she suffered from the same racism. Lola, the youngest, was fearless and resolute but also too proud, and never married; she was tormented and embittered by an impossible and broken love with a Mexican of Spanish descent, who broke off their engagement when she was barely twenty years old. Family photographs show three young girls, distinguished by elegant dresses and with delicate features but unable to be fully accepted and to marry those they considered men of equal social status. Similar prejudices limited Eurasian marriages in most Western countries before the Second World War. Only a few generations later would Eurasian women find their own path in society.

President Calles, who implemented racist laws against the Chinese, was himself an illegitimate child, since his parents never married. Although hailing from the more liberal north, he suffered from his illegitimacy all his life, growing up despised in a conservative society. This made him hate the hypocrisy of the Catholic Church and the Mexican elites. His early experience as a state school teacher also put him in conflict with Church education. A reformed alcoholic, he considered liquor salesmen and priests to be equally evil, persecuting both during his regime. Unlike in the United States, Christianity in Mexico was never reformed and hence continued to be associated with and to bear the negative stigma of the various discredited political regimes of the past. After he took power in 1924, he implemented violent anticlerical policies, including strict government control over the clergy, especially in the field of education. This led to a national conflict, the Cristero War, which left more than 100,000 dead, exposing the injustices and latent hatred in Mexican society. Ironically, had Hing not been Chinese, he might have supported President Calles in his views about the Church. In contrast, in Foon Chuck's Confucian and Christian mind, the complete lack of religious principles of the generals now in power set Mexico and its society on a dangerous, unpredictable path.

A promoter of Chinese art and culture, Hing encouraged rich Mexicans to discover and appreciate their refinement. Yet when it came to his children, he knew that they were forever marked by their blood, and even if his haughty customers deigned to buy his products, they would never allow their sons to marry his Eurasian daughters, no matter how rich and respected he had become. On the contrary, he understood that he and his family must now forget their Chinese culture to be accepted in their new country.

Towards the end of his life, Hing bought a large mansion on Avenida San Fernando in the residential neighborhood of Tlalpan, ten miles from Mexico City, giving it the very bourgeois name of Quinta San Jorge, or "the farm of Saint George." To Cruz's dismay, despite their growing family and wealth, Hing followed all his life the Chinese tradition of living above his beloved business. The couple had to wait for Hing's retirement to finally have a home of their own. Originally a seminary, the house had two floors, a gable roof, a swimming pool (which Hing's family never used), and a playground with swings. The gardens were extensive: the family horse and even a domesticated monkey roamed freely, and there was a large orchard and a pond with carp. The upper floor of the house had a large lounge with a ping-pong table and a library. All the floors were made of wood and the kitchen was huge and located in an annex building, which the children were not allowed to enter. The house had two entrances, one for people and the other for cars, with a small lodge next to each. In one lodge lived the Chinese cook Ramon and his family and the other was used for storage. Hing, now wealthy, could afford to eat Chinese food every day. Ramon married Maria, the Mexican housekeeper, with whom he later opened a Chinese café on Calle Dolores, Mexico City's small Chinatown, which developed in the 1930s around a few grocery stores and restaurants. Its relatively late development corresponded to a period in which the Chinese felt the need to live as a community in the face of growing discrimination.[16]

With the revolution long forgotten, Hing enjoyed giving grand receptions for his Chinese and Mexican friends in his new home. He was generous, wanting to be worthy of his first name, which means "something to celebrate" in Chinese. Every weekend, the married siblings came with their families and friends to the Tlalpan house, mixing with Hing's own acquaintances. Each time a new vehicle with guests passed the entrance door, a servant struck a gong, and all the grandchildren rushed to see which family had arrived. Food was served on three large tables, a fourth being added for the children; guests often stayed for dinner, and parties continued late into the night. Food was an important feature of these receptions: at a time when Chinese restaurants were rare, these were opportunities for everyone to taste Cantonese delicacies, often for the first time. As he did with art objects, Hing enjoyed sharing this other feature of his culture with his Mexican friends—something Foon Chuck did too. The children ran around in the garden for much of the day playing team games, and the adults joined them for badminton and ping-pong. My mother wrote that "everything was like a ceremo-

UNDER THE PROTECTION OF THE GOLDEN DRAGON

nial, with flowers, fruits, and gifts." This was proof to everyone that Hing had finally realized his lifelong dream of becoming a respected bourgeois in Mexico, "something to celebrate" indeed.

13

A BUTTERFLY OF THE AMERICAS

Concepción Leon, my grandmother, was born in 1906 in Guadalajara, Mexico's second largest city, and died in 1998 in Mexico City, where she lived most of her life. Concepción was a typical Christian name given in honor of the Virgin Mary. Her birth certificate, only registered in 1929, the year of her marriage, designated her as of Mexican nationality and "mixed-race," or mestiza. Mixed-race in Mexico usually meant that one was a descendant of a Spaniard and an Indian; even today the civil registry fails to offer a Eurasian box to tick, meaning that no statistics exist on the Chinese community's demography, nor on any other ethnic minorities. Concepción's siblings and friends, including her future husband, referred to her affectionately as Concha or Connie, common diminutives of Concepción. Like most young girls, she finished her formal studies at the age of sixteen. Decades later, seeing me spending my time buried in books, she told me once that I had a very ignorant grandmother. But I did not see it in that way at all. For me, she had traveled extensively, spoke with distinction and in a refined Spanish, and possessed a magnificent prose, writing poetic letters to my mother. In her early photographs she looks like a thoughtful teenager, but with deep melancholy in her eyes, introverted, aware of her differences, unsure where life will take her in this post-revolutionary Mexican society.

My grandmother did not feel particularly Mexican or Chinese; this was of no concern to her. I remember her as being a bit distant, as if her environment could not affect her, much like her mother Cruz. A habit formed during the revolution was that she seldom made eye contact with strangers, minding her own business, only opening herself up to close relatives and friends. During her upbringing, her Chinese side was hidden, Hing wanting his children to become entirely Mexican. All her life, she felt close to her father, proud of his business achievements, his tall and distinguished stature, the beautiful Chinese objects he sold, and his differences. She would not have traded him for any other father in the world. She was a silent girl and always discreet, often telling me: "If you have nothing nice to say about someone, then just keep quiet." In the 1920s, with the xenophobia of the revolution fading, that noble character made her lasting friends among the most liberal girls in her high school in Monterrey. I never heard her gossip about anyone; she did not relish the scandals of others and she hated all kinds of hypocrisy. While spending my childhood summers with her in Mexico, she never pronounced a single inappropriate word or even raised her voice, under any circumstance, in front of me or anyone else. She was a perfect lady, her character influenced by her parents—she had Hing's classical distinction and calm, and Cruz's discretion and piety—but also by Mexico City's stifling and conservative society. There, people stayed in their place, rarely crossing class barriers, everyone remaining overly aware of who one's parents were and where they came from. Perhaps thinking of her sister Victoria, one day she told me that it is not proper to marry above or below one's rank, since one must avoid being despised by one's in-laws.

Concepción, or Concha, met my grandfather, Wong Yaiwai, Foon Chuck's nephew, when she turned eighteen. She began traveling around the world with him, first to the United States, then years later to Japan and Hong Kong, on her way to China. By going abroad, she discovered her own beauty and thus became a little coquettish, as can be seen in her photographs. As a teenager, she was not considered beautiful among her friends, interracial marriages being still taboo. But everything changed when she and Yaiwai discovered one another. This relationship transformed her, not only physically but also in her feelings and opinions, changing her perspective on herself, Mexico and China. In her old age, she still often stared at herself in the mirror, combing her hair for a long time, struggling to imagine her own advanced age. All her life, even when old and destitute, she was always impeccably dressed in clothes that were not ostentatious or expensive, but discreet and dignified.

A BUTTERFLY OF THE AMERICAS

Born in 1902, four years before Concha, Yaiwai grew up in the city of Canton, near his ancestral village of Chaitong. Because of the revolution and the closure of the Monclova school, he did not stay long in Mexico, returning to China with his parents. He left Canton at the age of eighteen to attend university in Shanghai, where he had a cousin. After graduating three years later, he moved to the United States in 1923 to further his studies. It was easier then for young Chinese to get US student visas from China's north, rather than from Kwangtung province. From that date, he traveled back and forth across the US Mexico border, since his parents had resettled in 1919 at Hacienda Limon. With the acute dangers of the revolution in the past, and with ships available again after the First World War, Foon Chuck had invited his younger brother Yun Wu and his wife to join him again. No doubt encouraged by his friendship with President Carranza, he felt confident that Mexico had changed for the better and the worst was now behind them.

Most Chinese universities were only founded at the start of the twentieth century, replacing the two-millennia-old Imperial Examination system. During his reform attempts, Kang Youwei was behind the birth of China's first university in Peking. After the failed establishment of a republic in 1912 and with the country now divided among regional warlords, the young Chinese universities became places of intense ideological reflection and spiritual quests to find the soul of the new Chinese nation. With the dynasty's repeated failures and the fiasco of the first republic, China experienced an existential crisis, many doubting that their traditional and ancient Chinese culture had anything of value to bequeath. In 1919, aspirations for a new China crystallized in the May Fourth Movement, when Chinese students mobilized to protest the Paris Peace Conference. Despite the conference's principle of self-determination and China having joined the victorious alliance, the conference granted the German concessions in Shantung province (Shandong in Mandarin) to Japan. The student movement then took a broader perspective, going beyond anti-colonialism by calling for democracy, social reforms and the utilization of science, giving rise to the foundation of the Communist Party in 1921 in Shanghai. This movement called for the replacement of classical Chinese writing by a new and simplified vernacular, first developed by Liang Qichao a few years earlier. In 1923, under the influence of these ideas, Yaiwai, then twenty-one years old, left Shanghai's Fudan University to study a postgraduate degree in Philadelphia.

After perfecting his English, Yaiwai attended the University of Pennsylvania, earning a degree in architecture in 1929. Founded in 1868, the University of Pennsylvania's architecture department educated the first generation of Chinese architects, who dreamed of building a new China. Before the twentieth century, the idea of architectural design did not exist in China: Fengshui masters were considered more useful than architects, and were required to follow classical rules, with building decisions taken by government bodies. These Penn students established the first independent and modern design firms in the country.[1] They included Liang Sicheng (1901–72), considered the father of modern Chinese architecture, who graduated a year before Yaiwai, and I. M. Pei, who stayed briefly at the school and forty years later designed the Pyramide du Louvre in Paris and the Bank of China building in Hong Kong. Liang Sicheng was Liang Qichao's eldest son, demonstrating the common aspirations among the Cantonese elite at the time. In Philadelphia, Liang Sicheng became Yaiwai's friend; he later became famous as the first modern architect to study and classify ancient Chinese architecture, and continued to be active both in contemporary practice and scholarly research. Towards the end of his life, by then vice-director of the Beijing Planning Commission, he worked tirelessly to defend the old capital, unfortunately in vain, against Chairman Mao's architectural follies.[2] During the Cultural Revolution, he ended his days forgotten, like other Chinese intellectuals whose talents were wasted in this period of history. Among the University of Pennsylvania's twenty-two Chinese architecture graduates in 1920–40,[3] Yaiwai was the only one shown as a resident of Mexico.[4]

Yaiwai's early photographs show someone who was relaxed, but with a certain idealism, ambition and self-confidence, contrasting with Concha's domestic and secluded life in Mexico. During his travels to Hacienda Limon, Yaiwai was reunited with his cousins—Foon Chuck's children—who were delighted to see him again, especially Santiago, two years his elder, who was studying in the United States too. Santiago and Yaiwai spent considerable time together in Hacienda Limon and the United States. In Philadelphia, personal photographs show Yaiwai developing friendships with American and overseas Chinese students, his professors and their families and even his American landlady.

For any young Chinese, studying at an American university was an exhilarating experience, full of new freedoms. Before the 1929 economic crisis, Yaiwai wondered how the United States, then at a peak of its power, managed to be so strong when its people, adults and children alike, seemed to be mostly preoccupied with how to entertain themselves after work or on weekends, quite a contrast with his struggling countrymen. Yaiwai took many photographs of his campus on Poverty Day, when all the students of this wealthy university dressed up in rags and partied all day, thinking how absurd and incongruous this scene would look in China. Unlike other places in the United States, its best universities remained liberal and welcoming to foreigners. This did not mean that their foreign graduates would ever be employed by US corporations or that the restaurant signs stating "No Orientals or Colored allowed" had disappeared. In a 1927 survey, only twenty-seven per cent of Americans were willing to accept Chinese as fellow workers, and only 11.8 per cent as friends.[5] However, by the 1920s Chinese restaurants had become ubiquitous in many cities in the United States, with the American Chemical Society even advising Americans, especially children and invalids, to eat Chinese food for their health, and Louis Armstrong naming his first composition "Cornet Chop Suey."[6]

Yaiwai was now fluent in three Chinese dialects, Sze Yap, Cantonese and Mandarin, as well as in Spanish and English: he was a true citizen of the world, and the Chinese idiom, "to have four oceans as your home,"[7] described him perfectly. Despite the Chinese Exclusion Act, his university years gave Yaiwai hope that a world without racial barriers would emerge one day, as imagined by Kang Youwei.

Nevertheless, just after his arrival in the United States, Yaiwai witnessed the extension of the Exclusion Act to include all Asian people. After 1882, recognizing the need for cheap labor for certain sectors of its economy, the United States had replaced Chinese immigrants with Japanese ones. By 1924, the Japanese immigrant population in the United States had reached 275,000, more than double the Chinese.[8] In contrast with Chinese migrants four decades earlier, the Japanese were directly sponsored by their government and screened before departure, and many were more literate than their Chinese counterparts. They were later allowed to bring their wives, and the Japanese government encouraged them to form families abroad, seeing them as its representatives to the world; women soon accounted for thirty-nine per cent of Japanese immigrants into the United States. At first, the Japanese government was confident its citizens would avoid the fate of the Chinese, whom they held responsible for their misfortunes: the Japanese consul to the United States stated in 1884 that, "It is indeed the ignominious conduct and behavior of indigent Chinese of inferior character [...] that brought upon [them] the contempt of the Westerners and resulted in the enactment of legislation to exclude them from the country."[9] However, like the Chinese, the Japanese were restricted from becoming naturalized Americans and were soon condemned as even more dangerous than the Chinese because of their willingness and ability to assimilate into society with their families—ironically this was exactly what the Chinese had earlier been reproached for not doing. After the First World War, a newspaper tycoon testified before congress that: "Of all races ineligible to citizenship, the Japanese are [...] the most dangerous to this country [...]. They come here [...] for the purpose of colonizing and establishing permanently the proud Yamato race."[10] In 1924, a new Immigration Act stopped any further Asian immigration into the United States, extending the ban that had been placed on the Chinese four decades earlier, history having come full circle.

Yaiwai's best friend at university was Ah Kian Lee, whom he had first met in Shanghai and who was from a prominent Cantonese family close to Chiang Kai-shek, the Nationalist leader of the Republic of China and Sun Yat-sen's successor. Yaiwai and Ah Kian were like brothers and were inseparable. Yaiwai invited him to Hacienda Limon, where he befriended Yaiwai's cousins, soon developing an affection for Margarita, Foon Chuck's third daughter, whom he married a few years later.

In the meantime, Lily Chuck, Margarita's elder sister, had left the family home in Piedras Negras and was studying at Mexico City's music conservatory. Lily had become an excellent pianist, in addition to speaking English and Cantonese perfectly. In Mexico

City, she lived with Hing, who was a good friend of her father. The Chinese bourgeoisie at the time was relatively small, and continued to shrink over time, and Lily naturally became a close friend of Hing's three daughters, especially Concha. Foon Chuck and Hing had by now known each other for decades; they were, of course, both from the Sze Yap region, and the bad treatment of the Chinese in Mexico had brought them even closer, since they were now among the handful of remaining Chinese-Mexicans who had arrived in the 1880s. Concha was drawn towards Lily, a few years her elder, admiring her bright mind, education, artistic inclination and independence. Lily was different from Concha's siblings and her Mexican friends, with a more idealistic, romantic and artistic mindset, and Concha dreamed of becoming like her one day. In her character, Lily resembled her aunt Kingfung, another artist and emancipated Chinese young lady who had lived in Piedras Negras. Lily treated Concha like a younger sister but also learned from her how to dress and how to dance, learning steps like the Foxtrot and the Two Step, since Mexico City's social life was more sophisticated than that of Piedras Negras.

One day in 1924, while in Mexico City to visit her sister Lily, Margarita (accompanied by Ah Kian, who was now her fiancé) was introduced to the Leon family's children. Ah Kian immediately fell under Concha's spell, another young Eurasian about to turn eighteen and Lily's best friend. Thinking that she would make a perfect fiancée for Yaiwai, he asked for her picture, deciding to play the matchmaker. Back at Hacienda Limon, Ah Kian spoke of Concha enthusiastically and used her photograph to convince Yaiwai to travel to Mexico City immediately. This unsolicited visit did not surprise Hing, who was already familiar with Yaiwai's father and uncle. Hing was delighted to converse in the Sze Yap dialect with someone who had just returned from China, yet he was surprised by Yaiwai's optimistic outlook for their country, which was torn apart by a cruel civil war. After chatting for a while, Yaiwai respectfully expressed his desire to meet Concha, bringing a large smile onto Hing's face. My mother tells me that when Concha met her future husband it was love at first sight, or "falling in love in one look,"[11] as it is put in Chinese.

Like Ah Kian, Yaiwai was delighted to have found a Chinese-Mexican fiancée: he hoped she would bring him closer to Mexico while being sensitive to his heritage. Believing their love to be predestined, he thought of the Chinese saying: "Fate has us meet from a thousand miles away."[12] It was indeed a match made in heaven, Concha being as eager to learn about China as Yaiwai was about Mexico. She felt proud to become the fiancée of Lily's cousin and to be joining the Wong clan, which was so well known within the Chinese community.

Concha had never imagined that Chinese-Mexicans could own such a large farm as Hacienda Limon, and she immediately fell in love with its wilderness, wide rivers and secluded creeks, which were so different from her home above El Dragon de Oro in the capital. Concha was introduced to Lily's other siblings, and she too began to travel between Mexico City, Hacienda Limon, and the United States. For Concha, who had so far been confined to the capital, this experience was rich and revealing; her photographs from this time show a radiant and flourishing personality. Like a butterfly leaving its chrysalis, she now moved among a circle of more cosmopolitan and educated people, determined to take full advantage of her new situation. Concha had not imagined that the Chinese could be so cheerful and cultured. Hing was a kind but austere figure, who never read or talked about China or politics with his family, treating Cruz like a housewife. Yaiwai, on the other hand, was always speaking to her passionately, teaching her English and Cantonese words, and expressing his love for her in this way. Concha could not believe that Yaiwai and her father were from the same country, since they acted so differently. For her, China had represented everything old and traditional, like the objects her father sold; but now she found herself with a Chinese fiancé (and later husband) who was so liberal—more even than most of her acquaintances in Mexico. She was surprised that her fiancé, a long-time student, could cook so well, much better than her, something unthinkable in Mexico. She also loved the United States, where everything was so modern and where Yaiwai's college friends, free-spirited and relaxed young people, treated her so gallantly. It was as if an entirely new universe, whose existence she had not even suspected, had suddenly opened up to her, full of possibilities.

After being engaged for four years, Concha and Yaiwai married in Mexico City in 1929, at the ages of twenty-seven and twenty-three respectively. An aunt tells me that their relationship was consummated long before the wedding, showing a modern side to Concha. While she chose Yaiwai for being a gentleman, she was warned by members of her own family and by respectable friends that she was going against the grain and risked losing everything by marrying and emigrating to such a remote and dangerous country. This did not scare her: she was thirsty for adventure and the discovery of new worlds. Having heard tragic stories about China, she had a hunch that a country that gave birth to her beloved father and husband must have good sides too, and she was curious to discover them. Moreover, the lives of her two sisters showed the difficulties Eurasian women had in trying to earn their place in Mexican society. Concha was also greatly influenced by Lily. Like her, Concha proved to be a courageous and free-spirited woman, deciding to follow her instinct and the voice of her heart.

She had a civil marriage, not a religious one, since Yaiwai was not a Christian. Her brother Melchor and Lily served as their witnesses. Well before the excesses of Mao's Cultural Revolution, the Chinese Nationalist government of Chiang Kai-shek, who was a Christian, at least in name, launched violent campaigns in the 1920s to eradicate superstitions and destroy old places of worship in China.[13] The aim was to build a new modern nation. Of the one million temples in China at the turn of the century, more than half had already been closed or destroyed when the Communists took power in 1949. Many young Chinese intellectuals, Yaiwai among them, were decidedly anti-religious or atheist: he never joined the Presbyterian church of his cousins. Concha never felt close to the Catholic Church either, religion being for her a matter of faith and action rather than ceremony.

Strangely, there is no wedding photograph of the young couple. Holding a strictly civil wedding was almost unheard of at the time, and Yaiwai's parents would have probably felt out of place. Another reason for the lack of a photograph could be that both Chinese and Mexican traditions dictated that children should marry in sequence of birth. Since Concha's older sister Victoria was still single and had no engagement within sight, Hing worried about bringing bad luck onto his daughters by organizing a big wedding ceremony for Concha, going against all rules of propriety. Concha's civil marriage made a strong contrast with Victoria's religious ceremony two years later. These two unions would lead them in completely opposite directions. In 1935, now living in Shanghai and learning of her sister's suicide, Concha could not help but feel guilty for having married before her. Of course, she was unaware of the tragic fate that also awaited her.

14

THE GREAT PLUNDER

The state of Sonora, which borders the US state of Arizona, was not only the Mexican state with the largest number of Chinese immigrants but was also the birthplace of the generals now in power in Mexico. The region has a long history of violence, mainly against its native Yaquis, who suffered genocide during the so-called Yaqui Wars, which began in 1533 and continued until 1929, although the Yaquis have continued to suffer from discrimination to the present day. Sonora remains one of the Mexican states with the highest homicide rate per capita, due largely to drug-related crime[1] near its US border. In 1920, the Chinese accounted for less than two per cent of the Sonoran population but represented the largest group of foreign nationals and more importantly were in control of the small groceries trade, arousing resentment from the locals.

Before turning revolutionary and politician, Plutarco Elías Calles began his career as a teacher in Sonora before going into business, suffering from various failed ventures, and never making any money.[2] Descending from an old and ruined family of landowners, these repeated failures made him resentful of newly rich Mexicans and foreigners, and he vowed to use the powers of the revolution and politics to avenge himself and his fellow Sonorans against those he believed had rigged the system in their favour. Like Madero earlier, here was another Mexican politician developing resentment against foreigners for their business success.

In the early 1920s, a series of strict anti-Chinese laws were put in place in Sonora. They banned mixed marriages and put obstacles in the way of Chinese companies, prohibiting their owners from living in their workplace, preventing them from selling foodstuffs, and requiring that a minimum of eighty per cent of their staff be Mexican. These laws even ordered the segregation of Chinese in certain neighborhoods and prohibited them from entering restaurants or holding positions in the civil service. Some anti-Chinese activists called for these laws to apply not only to alien Chinese but to those who had become naturalized Mexicans. The laws enabled dishonest Mexicans to take over Chinese businesses, which were unable to conduct their trade any longer. At the beginning, many Chinese merchants, who were often unfamiliar with the Western legal system, disobeyed and circumvented the laws by finding loopholes, such as arguing that their employees were business partners. They found the new laws as absurd as they were unjust, and hoped they would not be enforced. A foreign missionary at the turn of the century observed that: "[The Chinese] will do as they are told, when they consider it right; but when they consider it wrong, no power on earth can make them obey orders."[3]

Law 31 of the State of Sonora of 1923 prevented mixed marriages, even for naturalized Chinese, and consented to the absolute dissolution of previous mixed Chinese-Mexican marriages. Even some naturalized Chinese ended up being deported and a case was referred to the Mexican Supreme Court, which refused to rule. These laws went further than the similar laws in the United States four decades earlier. It was tragic that this happened in a racially mixed country like Mexico, which also suffered from exclusion not only within its borders against its native Indians but also from its northern neighbor. These laws highlight how fascism had become a global phenomenon, not only affecting Europe and Asia but Latin America too. Anti-foreigner laws, albeit less severe, were passed at the federal level, including the Immigration Act of 1926 and a regulation in 1931 limiting Chinese immigration. The sudden change in policy—from a welcoming policy to one of rejection—represented a shock and trauma for most Chinese Mexicans, who were firmly settled in their new country, forcing them to find ways to assert their Mexican citizenship.

Now approaching his sixties, Foon Chuck continued to closely follow international geopolitics. In November 1921, he wrote a remarkably prescient and bold article for the United Press about the threat to the world of a militaristic Japan and the importance of maintaining an independent China to counterbalance it. He proposed that this policy be financed by a Chinese government bond backed by a land or salt tax to prevent China from falling into Japanese hands, which, he said, would cause "the greatest bloodbath that the world has ever known."[4] Although he received multiple accolades for the article in the United States and China, showing his expertise in foreign affairs and economics, tragically, his voice was not listened to by those who mattered. Furthermore, due to the Chinese Exclusion Act, there were few others like him, who understood both continents and were willing to stir public opinion towards peace with righteous and liberal voices. Foon Chuck exemplified the positive role that migrants can have in fostering dialogue and goodwill between nations. Without the Exclusion Act, one wonders whether a vibrant and enlightened Asian diaspora might have been able to stop militarism and war in the Far East.

In the 1920s, as the Chinese Reform Association had dissolved, two Chinese movements competed for Chinese Mexicans' support and funds: the Kuomintang (Sun Yat-sen's Nationalist Party) and the Chee Kung Tong (or Chinese Freemasons), which supported the return of the Ming dynasty (1368–1644). Since 1900, many young intellectuals had become Ming loyalists—even Mao Tse-tung flirted with the movement in his youth. The Chee Kung Tong had a longer history and more members, while Kuomintang followers were usually more educated and better informed. Trying to earn funds for their causes, both organizations got involved in illegal activities, like opium and gambling, often making the headlines in Mexican newspapers and further alienating themselves in the eyes of the population, what Evelyn Hu-DeHart describes as "self-inflicted wounds" for the Chinese community.[5] As in the United States earlier, although the Chinese in Mexico were facing increasing exclusion, instead of coming together both societies fought each other violently. There were dozens of victims on each side, including the Chinese leaders of both organizations in Mexico. In 1928, Chinese transnational organizations like the Chee Kung Tong congratulated President Calles for his time as president, even though he had been openly anti-Chinese. Like Foon Chuck, unless they chose exile, Chinese activists had no choice but to engage with the same politicians who threatened their existence.

During that decade, 1,500 miles away from Sonora, Hacienda Canton continued to grow and prosper, producing sugar, rice, vegetables and sesame seeds, among other products. The US consul general, passing through the region, noted that "the Chinese are really responsible for the prosperity of El Mante."[6] Hacienda Canton employed Chinese and Mexican laborers and supervisors almost in equal proportions,[7] both groups working in harmony together. Besides producing for the Mexican and US markets, it also grew distinctively Chinese vegetables for the consumption of the local Chinese community, like bok choy, gai lan, bitter melons and Chinese cabbages, which were fermented in large salty vats and left to dry on ropes, to the surprise of Mexican visitors. Importantly, Hacienda Canton was not only a commercial business but a place where Mexicans and Chinese coexisted, a contrast with the Torreón horticultural gardens earlier, which had been exclusively Chinese. Foon Chuck had learned from his experience there, and sought to avoid another tragedy.

In the 1920s, a prosperous Chinese community of hundreds of settlers grew in El Mante: besides Foon Chuck at Hacienda Canton and Limon there were also other farms owned by his Chinese associates, some in partnership with Mexicans. However, as early as 1925, worried about the hostile political environment for the Chinese in Mexico and the new exclusionary laws, Foon Chuck approached Aarón Sáenz, a close ally of President Calles, a member of both his government and his family, his sister having married one of the president's sons[8] (and, incidentally, a Presbyterian on his mother's side). Sáenz's family had become one of the largest landowners in El Mante and Foon Chuck offered to sell him Hacienda Canton for what he called a "very reasonable price."[9] A fine political analyst, Foon Chuck foresaw that Sáenz would grow into an industrial baron and that the environment would only get worse for the Chinese. Another reason may be that, struggling to recover his investments in Torreón, Foon Chuck was running out of fresh capital to invest in El Mante and thus preferred to sell. But with the generals in firm control and Foon Chuck lacking leverage, the negotiations went nowhere.

Foon Chuck saw new opportunities when President Calles drew up a plan to build new dams throughout the country to increase agricultural production. The president visited El Mante for the first time in 1926, accompanied by General Osuna and the newly formed National Commission of Irrigation. Shortly afterwards, when Rodolfo Elías Calles, the president's son, visited the region, Foon Chuck innocently invited him to Hacienda Canton, leaving him impressed by the number of workers packing tomatoes and winter vegetables for the US market, a business which would unfortunately not be profitable due to high transportation costs.[10] Maybe Foon Chuck was hoping that the new president would purchase his farm, not realizing then that he had inadvertently let the wolf into the sheepfold. That same year, President Calles' family purchased directly from the government a large parcel of land, previously owned by Miguel Cárdenas, thereby establishing his own farm, Hacienda Mante, which would grow to 2,228 hectares, making him the second largest landowner in the region, right behind Foon Chuck. President Calles developed his hacienda in the following years, but, according to a historian, it was "created with the support of subordinates and partners who were getting or had become rich through presidential favor and were grabbing public property."[11] Thus, fifteen years after Torreón, Foon Chuck again found himself on the wrong side of Mexican politics—ironically because of his own astute business choices. President Calles had settled near Hacienda Canton of all places, just as he himself had, three decades earlier, settled near President Madero's estate.

Foon Chuck asked the generals to speak on his behalf to President Calles and present him with his plans for the region. A month later, General Osuna returned with an engineer from the New York construction company J. G. White to prepare a feasibility study to build a large dam upstream on the Mante River; Foon Chuck lent him fifteen workers to launch the topographical studies.[12] The construction took place between 1927 and 1929, when a dam fifteen feet high was completed, along with 120 miles of canals capable of irrigating an area of 20,000 hectares,[13] including one leading west to Hacienda Canton. In 1927, by order of the government, work on a new railway line and a motorway going to El Mante also began, the new train station even being named after the president. All these infrastructure projects were financed exclusively by public money, despite being for the private benefit of the ten families owning eighty per cent of the land in the region, including Foon Chuck. As a result of the new infrastructure, from 1929 to 1938 the proportion of cultivated land in the region increased from sixteen to seventy-six per cent.[14]

In 1930, to fund the construction of a large sugar refinery—as had been imagined by Foon Chuck two decades earlier—the main landowners, after refusing an expensive loan from an American financier, turned to the Bank of Mexico, an institution founded by President Calles in 1925. In breach of its public mandate, the bank was coerced into approving the loan under pressure from Calles himself, while the bank would develop a bad reputation for providing loans to the generals in power.[15] The loan was made to the newly formed Al Mante Sugar Company, with 2.3 million pesos in capital and controlled by all the large landowners, whose properties were then mortgaged to the bank. Foon Chuck owned ten per cent of the company's shares, while the Calles, Sáenz and Osuna families together controlled more than fifty per cent.[16] By 1932, the loan exceeded 10.7 million pesos,[17] representing more than four times the company's capital. Seconded by Aarón Sáenz, Rodolfo Elías Calles became its only administrator from 1930 to 1936. In 1931, the sugar refinery was inaugurated, employing 500 workers, while the plantation employed about 5,000.[18]

During a full decade, 1924–34, President Calles and his political allies managed to maintain themselves in power, partly by killing those who opposed them. A prominent journalist wrote of President Calles that, "although not bloodthirsty, killing did not bother him and he disposed of the lives of others with supreme indifference."[19] Álvaro Obregón, President Calles's predecessor as president and now his rival, met the same fate as Francisco Madero and Venustiano Carranza, being assassinated in Mexico City in 1928, just after having won the presidential election of that year. Some claimed that President Calles was involved in the conspiracy.[20] Emilio Portes Gil, a close friend of Calles, became president instead, with Calles retaining an official advisory role while unofficially remaining the real power behind the government.

Gil, as governor of the state of Tamaulipas, had in 1926 tried unsuccessfully to enforce the same anti-Chinese laws that existed in Sonora, to get rid of the 2,000 Chinese in the state. Unlike in Sonora, the Chinese in Tamaulipas were mostly farmers and workers instead of merchants, creating less resentment from the local population. But in 1929, due to the economic crisis in that year, a general climate of animosity towards the Chinese began to affect the entire state of Tamaulipas, El Mante included. In his book *Paisanos Chinos*, based on government archives in both Taiwan and Mexico, the historian Fredy Gonzalez describes in detail the events that took place in El Mante the following year. Local government officials first harassed Chinese business owners, raised their taxes, and carried out surprise inspections at their homes. Many supporters of land reforms in Mexico wanted to ensure that the fruits of Mexico's economic development remained in the hands of ethnic Mexicans, and, being so visible, Hacienda Canton aroused their anger. The state's new governor declared publicly: "The government is determined not to allow the El Mante region to be infested with foreigners."[21]

Soon, allegations surfaced that a Chinese farmer in Hacienda Canton had shot a Mexican thief on his property, angering locals, who asked the state government to help them get rid of these unwanted aliens. In September 1930, all the Chinese farms and businesses, including Hacienda Canton and Hacienda Limon, where Foon Chuck now resided, were raided by immigration officials, searching for contraband and demanding passports. Around 130 workers were detained and sent to the state capital Tampico, 120 miles away. While they were in prison, their businesses and homes were looted, with losses estimated at half a million pesos. The governor also ordered Chinese companies to suspend their activities within four days. Although the detainees had valid immigration documents, these were never verified, the detention apparently being directed by Rodolfo Elías Calles himself.[22] The Chinese government's representative in Mexico visited El Mante and sent an official letter of protest, after which the detainees were released. The Chinese diplomat was in direct contact with former-President Calles instead of Gil's new government, knowing well who was behind the events. However, after their return, thirty workers were detained again, on the orders of the former president's son, and forced to sign a letter pledging to leave the area. Further raids followed. The expelled workers were later allowed to remain in Mexico, which proves that they were legally working in the country and suggests that there were ulterior motives behind the expulsion.[23]

Gonzalez's book demonstrates that these events were less a case of the nationalization of foreign businesses, land reforms or spontaneous xenophobia, than a case of the systematic looting of Foon Chuck and the Chinese for the benefit of Calles's landowning friends and relatives.[24] Foon Chuck's strategy of partnering with the generals had failed, and they now had their eyes set on his two Haciendas. In 1932, Hacienda Canton was expropriated for not paying its river water usage rights[25] and sold to Calles, Sáenz and General Osuna in a public auction five years later. Being the oldest farm in the region, with large areas already opened to agriculture and the most extensive hydraulic infrastructure,[26] it was a coveted prize for its future owners. The fact that the National Commission of Irrigation only started collecting water usage rights from landowners a year later[27] demonstrates the dishonest motives behind the expropriation. Foon Chuck was allowed to keep part of his smaller Hacienda Limon but without any water rights. Having finally seen his vision come true, thirty-four years after visiting El Mante for the first time, this dream was now taken away from him. The Chinese population of the state of Tamaulipas went from 2,100 in 1930 to only 950 a decade later.[28]

As in 1911, when soldiers first attacked his farm in Torreón, twenty years later Foon Chuck's properties were again the first target of violence and expropriations. A pioneer in his business activities, he would also be among the first victims of anti-Chinese discrimination in Mexico. He was now an old man, who had lived through the Torreón massacre and the horrors of the revolution, and now the same populist politicians were continuing to mistreat his compatriots, driven by jealousy and greed as much as by xenophobia. Despite support from the newly formed Mexican Organization of Overseas Chinese[29] and from the Chinese legation to Mexico, which tried every diplomatic channel possible, Foon Chuck felt powerless. He knew well how politics and power worked in Mexico and the futility of his struggle, but he fought to the end. If only China was a powerful nation, he thought, he might get at least fair compensation. He was not only dealing with unjust laws, but with dishonest businessmen doubling as powerful politicians. Since his arrival in Mexico forty years earlier when he began courting local politicians, he had known well the risks he was taking. However, encouraged by his friendship with liberal leaders like Governor Cárdenas and President Carranza, he did not expect Mexican politics to turn so volatile and openly racist. Whereas he knew how to relate to the young Christian technocrats of Porfirio Díaz, he did not feel any connection with the generals now in charge. The former spoke the language of economics and progress, but the generals now spoke the language of militarism, xenophobia and dishonesty, something his Confucian and Christian education had not prepared him for.

Reflecting on his predicament, Foon Chuck found solace in Confucius: "When the Way prevails in your own state, to be poor and obscure is a disgrace. But when the Way does not prevail in your own state, to be rich and honored is a disgrace."[30] Like other intellectuals in those days, facing the rise of fascism and militarism, spirituality and education were what allowed his inner light not to be consumed by a world politics which lacked human decency and justice. His thoughts turned to the concluding words of Reverend Loomis' book *The Profits of Godliness*: "Surely godliness is profitable; it is a pearl of great price."[31] Foon Chuck found it particularly tragic that his nemesis, President Calles, was himself a former teacher, not understanding how such a noble occupation could give rise to such a violent politician, now focused on reforming Mexican society into his image.

In 1931, in addition to being administrator of El Mante Sugar Company, Rodolfo Elías Calles became governor of his home state of Sonora. He now publicly declared that he would "not tolerate any Chinese in the whole state," echoing words pronounced in Tamaulipas one year earlier. The events in El Mante thus served as a rehearsal for the expulsion of the entire Chinese population of Sonora to the United States, the first large-scale expulsion of a Chinese diasporic community in the twentieth century. This was preceded by an aggressive campaign of intimidation, a boycott of Chinese stores, and expropriation of Chinese-owned properties. As in El Mante before, the campaign was a way for dishonest individuals to steal from the Chinese, who were forced to close their businesses. Several stories of small family successes thus ended in tragedy. Another community which was expelled from the state by the generals was the Catholic priests, but, unlike the Chinese, they would be allowed to return later.

At first, many Chinese left Sonora voluntarily, as the hatred against them became intolerable. Several mixed families fled, fearing for their children, the Mexican wives preferring exile to separation from their families. But in the end, more than 2,000 remaining Chinese[32] were forced, some at gunpoint, to cross the United States border with their families, after being stripped of what little property they had left. They were then deported to China with their Mexican families from the port of San Francisco, by and at the expense of the US government. The expulsion from Sonora led to the collapse of the Sonoran economy, as well as to critical articles in the US and Chinese press and protests in China against the Mexican government.[33] The former president Calles could not have been clearer when he wrote to his son Rodolfo in 1931, shortly after the expulsion, without an ounce of irony or shame:

> [You need to reach] a complete renunciation of any egoism and personal interest, and to do a work of real altruism in order to benefit all in the communities of your state [of Sonora]. Only this will justify the fact that you left your personal situation and future, which you were building for you and your family in El Mante [...]. I am aware of the way the Chinese problem has been solved [in Sonora], which must certainly have left a difficult situation given the flight of foreign capital [...], which will need to be replaced little by little by Mexican capital, even if in smaller amounts [...]. [Many] local families, which had not found their place in the economy of the state before [...] will soon fill the void left by the businesses of those foreigners [...]. In our situation of economic crisis, agriculture must save our country [...]. [We] need to aspire to make our nation independent, economically and politically.[34]

On the other side of the Pacific, the minister of foreign affairs of the Nationalist government, then based in Canton, denounced the expulsions as an act of barbarism, comparing it to the pogroms against the Jews.[35] The Chinese government sent its own investigative team, whose report was published by Reuters, claiming that "20,000 Chinese have been expelled from the entire country following a wholesale theft of their properties."[36] As a result of the anti-Chinese campaigns and expulsions, the Chinese population of Sonora and of the neighboring state of Sinaloa fell from 5,800 people in 1927 to less than 300 by 1940, so that less than one in twenty Chinese remained.[37]

In a tragic irony that is forgotten by many today, just as the Chinese from Sonora were deported to the United States, a much larger wave of Mexicans had been deported in the opposite direction. Before the Mexican-American War of 1846–48, all the states from California to Texas belonged to Mexico. With the Treaty of Guadalupe Hidalgo of 1848, the United States annexed from Mexico a total area of 0.87 million square miles, or about fifty-five and forty per cent of Mexico's and the United States' respective pre-war territories—more than it would ever again annex in its history. The South Carolina senator John Calhoun subsequently argued against further expansion given Mexico's Indian and mixed-race population: "Ours, sir, is the government of a white race. The great misfortunes of Spanish America are to be traced to the fatal error of placing these colored races on an equality with the white race."[38] In sad echo to those words, the main victims in these sparsely populated annexed territories would be the Comanches, whose population of 20,000 in 1840 became almost extinct thirty years after the annexation.

Mexico and the United States both had populations of around six million in 1800, but by 1900 Mexico's population was fourteen million while the United States' had swelled to eighty million, illustrating the latter's much more dynamic economy and immigration policies. After the annexation, 100,000 Mexicans continued to live on the US side of the border, guaranteed under the treaty to receive the same rights as US citizens. However, like the African Americans, their US citizenship was only in name, and many of them, having been dispossessed by the US government, suffered from racial segregation and intimidation, and were restricted from voting and exercising their rights as Americans.[39] Until the US Immigration Act of 1924 (which also banned all Asian immigration), Mexicans were allowed to cross the border freely. Indeed, in the decade following 1910, during the Mexican Revolution, 350,000 Mexican immigrants found refuge in the United States,[40] including Foon Chuck's family, while the population of Mexico's border states was temporarily increased by two million refugees fleeing violence in the south. Unlike the Chinese, these Mexicans were welcomed by American businessmen, all finding jobs in the thriving US economy during and after the First World War. An American landowner stated that "Mexicans possess unique crouching and bending habits that whites do not, and its male workforce is docile and easily managed,"[41] a claim reminiscent of the racial discourse used towards the Chinese decades earlier.

By 1929, much like the Chinese before them, Mexicans represented sixty per cent of the railroad workers in the United States. But from 1929 to 1935, hit hard by the economic crisis, the United States deported more than 82,400 Mexicans, raiding dance halls, private homes and public spaces throughout the country. Another 200,000 left the country voluntarily due to unemployment, adverse policies and xenophobia, meaning that a total of around 300,000 Mexicans moved back to Mexico, with a peak of 130,000 in the year 1931 alone.[42] Those deported represented twenty per cent of the entire Mexican immigrant population in the United States, including Mexicans who had become naturalized Americans. Indeed, sixty per cent of the deported Mexicans had US citizenship by birth, showing how the US government thought of migrants strictly in terms of race, instead of citizenship. The *Los Angeles Record* wrote of "a terror reign" for the Mexicans and "deportation mania."[43] The returning Mexicans struggled to find work in Mexico, also in economic crisis, creating even more hostility towards the few remaining Chinese Mexicans, and the *New York Times* reported in 1932 from Mexico City that repatriates were "almost starving."[44] This was a traumatic and humiliating event for Mexico.

The decision of the Mexican generals in 1931 to deport the Chinese to the United States took place in this context, and was influenced by political and economic considerations. There were large US investments in the state of Sonora—much larger than those of the Chinese—but the Mexican government feared alienating the United States and did not want to see those investments repatriated to the north. It thus found it easier and politically more rewarding to prey on the small community of defenseless Chinese traders and workers, whose assets were much easier to confiscate.

The abuses committed in Sonora against the Chinese extended to neighboring states like Sinaloa but did not affect the whole country in the same way. Overall, in just three years, three-quarters of the Chinese immigrants in Mexico fled the country, suffering significant economic losses. They continued to leave until the late 1930s, when President Lázaro Cárdenas (in office 1934–40) expropriated the land and businesses of most foreigners—especially Americans—in retaliation against the earlier expulsions of Mexicans from the United States. Violence, adverse legislation and economic crisis resulted in the official Chinese population in Mexico falling to only 4,800 people in 1940, down from 24,000 in 1926, thus ending for many an adventure that had lasted nearly forty years.[45]

This exodus out of Mexico was proportionally much larger than the exodus from the United States half a century earlier in the wake of the Exclusion Act. This difference can be explained by five factors. First, the scope of discrimination, racist legislation and deportations faced by the Chinese in Mexico was greater than in the United States. Second, the Chinese Mexicans were wealthier, so the impact of the confiscations was greater; and confiscations of property never happened in the United States on the same scale, since the US had only wanted to get Chinese workers out of the job market, not to steal their few possessions. Chinese merchants remained, in principle, welcome in the United States. Third, due to the 1929 crisis, the economic conditions in China in the early 1930s, especially relative to North America, were better than at the time of the Exclusion Act five decades earlier, meaning that the Chinese were more willing to return. Fourth, the Chinese migrant community in Mexico counted many families which were deported all together, whereas the United States had mostly single Chinese migrants. Finally, unlike their compatriots in the United States, the Chinese Mexicans lacked the equivalent of San Francisco's Chinatown, where Chinese immigrants in the United States could find refuge. The only shelter they had against racial violence in Mexico were the steamships that took them back to China.

Six decades later, in the 1990s, 2,500 Korean grocery stores were looted in Los Angeles and other cities in the United States, causing more than $500 million in damage.[46] These riots were motivated by a lack of economic empowerment in local communities and resentment towards an up-and-coming migrant group that was not fully assimilated and was believed to be advancing at the expense of locals. Manila in 1603, Torreón in 1911, Sonora in 1930 and Los Angeles in 1992 demonstrate a recurring theme of violence against successful

Asian migrants across centuries and continents. Beyond the obvious xenophobia, one can also find resentment, envy and possibly frustration from the perpetrators of the violence, in front of a group of successful migrants with a distinctive culture, who are not always willing, able or allowed to assimilate in their host country.

As a result of the discrimination in Sonora and the north of Mexico more generally, some of the remaining Chinese there moved to other places in Mexico that were considered safer, such as Mexico City, where Hing had moved to a few years earlier. These Chinese migrants tended to belong to the middle classes, since Chinese laborers had mostly already been forced out of the country by laws prohibiting them from working in Chinese businesses. After this difficult period, many of the surviving Chinese in Mexico tried to forget and even hide their origins, for example by adopting entirely Mexican names. Those naturalized Chinese-Mexicans who had left the country temporarily during the violence struggled to prove that they were Mexican when they wished to return, with many finding themselves stateless. The 1936 Mexican Population Act established quotas for immigration from countries other than Spain, requiring new migrants to invest at least 10,000 pesos in Mexico to be allowed into the country. After almost fifty years in the country, the families of Foon Chuck and Hing found themselves among the rare surviving members of a once vibrant community, unsure what the future held for them and their children in Mexico, but conscious nonetheless that it remained their only country.

15

A CONFUCIAN AND AMERICAN LEGACY

The dramatic events afflicting Foon Chuck and the Chinese communities in northern Mexico had a profound impact on his family. The closure of his school forced him to abandon the more traditional Chinese path he had initially imagined for his children, causing them to instead assimilate rapidly into Mexican society, while at the same time retaining Chinese traits. Although he had his children relatively late in life, Foon Chuck saw himself as a traditional family man. While he was concerned about his children's education, he delegated it to others since he was often on business trips, and he was remembered as being largely an absentee father. Despite this, his children and grandchildren inherited his character and philosophy: like the Chinese say, "blood is thicker than water."[1] Responsibility for their education thus fell on their schoolteachers as well as his wife Cristina, who knew well her husband's devotion to erudition and ensured that all her children became well educated.

Of their ten children, nine survived until adulthood: their daughter Rosita died from a disease at a young age. Born between 1895 and 1920, the nine surviving Chuck children had radically different childhoods and life paths—depending on the year of their birth—due to the turbulent political events of the period. The children grew up mainly in the family residence in Piedras Negras, only spending occasional holidays in El Mante, where Foon Chuck spent most of his life after the revolution. Despite its closeness to Cristina's native city of Tampico, Hacienda Limon never became the family home due to its remoteness from American schools and universities, which all the children attended. Foon Chuck was fond of El Mante but knew that his children would receive a better education outside of this rural and isolated region. Before the revolution, a proper Chinatown grew in Piedras Negras, with many relatives, associates and employees of Foon Chuck moving there. However, through the revolutionary period the small Chinese community rapidly dwindled, and the younger Chuck siblings grew up in an increasingly all-Mexican environment, although they did learn to speak Cantonese.

After her marriage to Foon Chuck in 1895, instead of a honeymoon, Cristina was sent directly from Tampico to her new home in Piedras Negras. She was accompanied by a cousin of Foon Chuck, Mrs Wah, who did not speak a word of Spanish, and who all the siblings called "The Madame" on account of her oriental manners, which seemed to them both refined and ethereal. Cristina was rapidly integrated into the Wong clan and taught about Chinese customs and traditions. Surrounded by Chinese relatives, she quickly learned what was expected of her, having no choice but to pick up some Sze Yap dialect to survive. Living in a Chinatown in an arid region of northern Mexico, so far from her tropical Tampico, Cristina wondered what strange world she had entered. Later, being so close to the United States, she learned English, often receiving her husband's American guests, including members of the Presbyterian church, whom she found so different from Catholics. In the marriage's first years, she was worried her children would be taken away from her and sent to China, as she had seen happen to nephews of her husband; but she was determined not to let this happen. She made sure that her children became as Mexican as they were Chinese. Over the years, conscious of being the Mexican root of her family and amid increasing anti-Chinese violence in the country, she had the fortitude to grow into a respected matriarch. Between 1905 and 1930, family photographs show how she transformed herself from a mostly illiterate girl into a confident and distinguished woman, after years of sharing her life with an erudite husband among his Chinese relatives and American friends, at the crossroads of three cultures.

With Foon Chuck mostly away and Cristina still finding her feet, the two elder children, Elvira and Arturo, experienced traumatic childhoods, marked by the absence of both their parents, the strict discipline at their boarding school, and the violence of the revolution during their teens. While the Yue Mae school had a modern curriculum, the requirement to learn written Chinese was a heavy burden on the students, especially when they were so far away from China and in addition to the many other school subjects; some older students wondered about the practicality of a strict Chinese education in the Americas. Being all boarders, the students felt a deep sense of alienation, far away from their families in the desolate and arid city of Monclova, studying a curriculum like no other in the country. Few kept fond memories of those years.

Arturo and Elvira grew up under the constant pressure of proving themselves to their prominent and demanding father, while being essentially rootless, unsure whether they were Chinese or Mexican. As a result, both grew into asocial and bad-tempered adults: Elvira was known as the Dragon Lady and Arturo ended his life isolated and lonesome. In addition to her studies, Elvira had the responsibility of taking care of her younger siblings, which she did with great diligence and love, acting as a second mother to them. Elvira was born at a time when women were heavily discriminated against in both Mexican and Chinese cultures, and she suffered from this too, growing inhibited as a result. Elvira was the only child to be born in the United States, and thus to be a born American; she later married a Chinese American from San Antonio. Their only son, Wing On, Foon Chuck's first grandchild, also married a Chinese American, becoming an engineer and later in his life a lawyer in California, helping immigrants with their legal affairs, often for free, something Foon Chuck would have been proud of.

Arturo was the first child born in Mexico: Foon Chuck felt that Mexico would offer better opportunities to his children than the United States. He believed that being born in the United States and having American passports would be useless, since the Americans would only look at his children on racial grounds, as they had done in his case. Of all his sons, Arturo was the only one not to pursue higher education in the United States. Scarred by the revolution, he had a soft, rebellious and introverted personality, preferring to stay in El Mante all his life. In a group photograph of Hacienda Canton from 1919, Arturo is shown with an expression of deep melancholy and insecurity, being unable to bear the heavy expectations of Foon Chuck towards his eldest son. Arturo wanted only to be a philanthropist like his father, but there was not much money left to give;

he was unable and unwilling to assume the role of a businessman. Foon Chuck never trusted his eldest son with money, nor with the family's businesses, and Arturo grew to some extent isolated from his siblings.

The middle daughters, Lily and Margarita, suffered from the revolution in their teens but had the chance to grow up with a mother who had become more assertive and with elder siblings to protect them. Although they spent only their early years in the Chinese school, their tutors in Eagle Pass made sure that they spoke perfect Cantonese, while enjoying a more liberal education in their American secondary school. Lily became one of Foon Chuck's favorite daughters and he made sure that she received a refined and classical education, including music, the arts, and languages. Ahead of their time, Lily and Margarita were far from being frivolous young girls; they were instead academic, both studying seriously. Lily studied at a conservatory in Mexico City, later becoming an accomplished pianist and a professional translator. Nonetheless, she had a bohemian side to her personality and among all the siblings was the one who felt the greatest attachment to the arts. Some photos from around 1930 show her in colored and exuberant dresses, rare at the time in Mexico.

The persecutions they suffered in their teens made Lily and Margarita mature earlier than other children, turning them into sensitive young ladies. Their humanistic, trilingual and religious education did not help them make sense of the violence surrounding them in Mexico but, on the contrary, made it seem even more tragic. Like their elder sister, fleeing a xenophobic Mexico, Lily and Margarita married Chinese gentlemen, but from mainland China instead of the United States. Lily married a Chinese diplomat in Mexico, who was also a captain in the Nationalist army, and, as mentioned earlier, Margarita married Yaiwai's Cantonese friend Ah Kian; both of these men were close to Chiang Kai-shek. During the war of resistance against Japan, Lily accompanied Ah Kian's mother, a prominent bourgeois lady, translating her speeches to raise funds for the Nationalist Party. The two sisters later moved to China with their husbands, who were both killed during the civil war, not leaving any descendants. Lily died from diphtheria in China during the war and Margarita in New York City a few years later, having found it difficult to settle back in Piedras Negras, both socially and due to immigration problems, since she had now taken the Chinese citizenship of her late husband. It was not surprising that the three elder Chuck daughters were left with no choice but to marry Chinese gentlemen and follow similar paths of exile. Due to their lives' circumstances, they became the most Chinese among all of Foon Chuck's children.

The middle boys, Santiago and Benjamín, seeing how their father fought for his businesses' survival, became Foon Chuck's most fearless and ambitious children. Born in 1900, Santiago was a dynamic, bright and sporty young man, known to mount a horse in one jump. He was, not surprisingly, Foon Chuck's favorite son. He played a similar role to Elvira among his siblings: in the absence of their father and of Arturo, the younger siblings followed Santiago's lead; he was like a second father to them, carrying their lunch when they crossed the border bridge with Eagle Pass every morning on their way to school.

Foon Chuck wanted his sons to pursue higher studies in the United States, knowing that they would receive a better education there. In the 1930s, tertiary education was still nascent in Mexico. At the same time, north of the border only one in five Americans attended university, showing Foon Chuck's progressive mindset. Since he had just lost his fortune, Santiago and Benjamín struggled to pay for their studies, completing their degrees in the 1930s, Santiago at Purdue University in Indiana, and Benjamín at the University of Texas. Santiago was forced to study and work at the same time and only finished his degree in his early thirties. Cristina had no choice but to give Benjamín her last savings so that he could complete his degree a few years later. Santiago first studied engineering but switched to agronomy at Foon Chuck's request. In those exclusion years, the two brothers wondered which origin made them more undesirable in the United States, Chinese or Mexican. But his family background did not stop Santiago from briefly dating an American girl: he had the reputation for being quite a catch.

Back in Mexico, the two brothers benefited from the lack of qualified engineers, pursuing brilliant careers as executives in large enterprises, Benjamín even working for some time as an engineer at El Mante Sugar Company in the 1950s. Despite the loss of their family fortune, thanks to their good manners and American higher education, they both married into distinguished bourgeois families, proving that Eurasians could successfully assimilate into Mexican high society. The two may also have benefited from their father's personal acquaintances within the bourgeoisie of northern Mexico. Like their father before them, they found themselves strong-willed and formidable spouses. In 1948, Santiago died of cancer, not yet even in his fifties, a couple of years before his father. After his death, a heartbroken Foon Chuck preached to Santiago's widow the importance of educating her children, since a career in business is uncertain, and, while inherited money can be lost or taken away, a good education cannot. She followed his advice, and years later Santiago's eldest son was named vice-rector of Mexico's best university, the Tecnológico de Monterrey, while all of Benjamín's children became doctors, carrying their grandfather's name with pride.

Foon Chuck's two youngest daughters, Selina and Hortensia, became academics, again demonstrating the intellectual orientation of the family. One day, a Chinese suitor interested in Selina approached Foon Chuck, who told him to speak directly with her since she was free to choose as she wished. Both sisters were devoted Christians, finding in their religious communities a helpful shelter from the racism still pervasive in Mexican society. However, unlike their elder sisters, since xenophobia had now passed its peak they married Mexican gentlemen in the 1940s: Selina's husband was an academic living in the United States and Hortensia's was a journalist. After living for some years in the United States, Selina returned to her native country, where she became a headmistress, running several high schools in northern Mexico and passing away in 2015 at the age of 107, fondly remembered by generations of students and her daughters, who became teachers too. Hortensia, the youngest, having learned to speak better English than Spanish, became a renowned English teacher. Sadly, neither sister taught their own children foreign languages, probably partly due to fear that they would be discriminated against as the sisters themselves had been. Their children, though, did learn other languages by themselves. All the children raised loving and Christian families, just as Foon Chuck would have wished for them.

Rubén, the youngest son, pursued an engineering degree in the United States, but his studies were interrupted by the Second World

A CONFUCIAN AND AMERICAN LEGACY

War when his father called him back to Mexico, afraid that he would be drafted into the US army. Foon Chuck was now retired, and with all his daughters married, Rubén was entrusted with the task and honor of taking care of his elderly father, from whom he inherited a fondness for agriculture, for El Limon, and for the United States. He later took over the little that was left of his father's land in El Limon, where he ran a small orchard and later a trailer park for American tourists. He married an American woman, who lived with him in El Limon before dying a few years later without giving him any heirs.

After her death, Rubén followed Santiago and Benjamín, getting remarried to a courageous and resolute Mexican woman, but unlike the older brothers' wives, Rubén's came from El Mante and from a humbler background. Widowed at a young age, and with limited resources besides her rifles and courage, she fought for her four daughters' education in that rural and still often violent part of Mexico. When she turned eighteen, Rubén's eldest daughter, now studying away from home and missing her family, begged her mother to allow her to come back to El Limon, unwilling to let her mother and three younger sisters sacrifice themselves for her. But her mother forbade it, telling her that her new and only home was her path to university—exactly as Foon Chuck would have wished for her. Against all odds, inheriting her grandfather's intellect and courage, she later became, like her cousin before her, a renowned professor at Mexico's most prestigious university.

During and after the Mexican Revolution, the Chuck siblings continued to cross the border bridge daily to attend school in Eagle Pass, growing up as Mexicans but with an American education. Despite finding in the United States a welcoming haven during the revolution and a place to pursue their higher education, they did not try to settle there. In the 1930s this would have been difficult, at a time when the United States had just expelled its Mexicans and Mexico was about to expropriate most American interests in the country. Besides, Foon Chuck's vision was never for his children to move to the United States; instead he wanted them to study there in order to later help develop their home country, their only one, as he did earlier—while never forgetting their Chinese roots and Cantonese dialect. This vision was successfully fulfilled by each of his surviving heirs. Years later, a maid recalled how she had been scared when, new to the household, she heard for the first time the siblings speak Cantonese together: to her it sounded as though they had all suddenly caught a strange throat disease.

Contrary to Chinese tradition, with the exception of Rubén in El Limon, the loss of the family properties meant that none of the sons pursued a career in their father's business; nor did they become merchants. Instead, they pursued intellectual professions, and, like their father, followed Confucius's instruction that: "The officer, having discharged all his duties, should devote his leisure to learning. The student, having completed his learning, should apply himself to be an officer."[2] This is followed to this day by many Chinese students, ever eager to find stable government jobs.[3] Another reason for this may have been that, unlike the Leon children, none grew up learning their father's skills. The desire of many Chinese to have their children take on government or intellectual professions as opposed to becoming entrepreneurs continues to this day. In Foon Chuck's case, if none of his children inherited his business acumen, they certainly inherited his erudition, sociability and reverence for education, all speaking three languages, playing musical instruments, and becoming leaders in their communities. With mainland China rapidly closing its doors, none of Foon Chuck's surviving children or grandchildren traveled to or kept any connections with China—unlike Lily and Margarita—all becoming prominent Mexicans, with their Chinese culture slowly fading away. In different times and circumstances, they might have developed much stronger ties with the country of their father, something he would certainly have wished for.

In the mid-1920s, Foon Chuck brought to Mexico a son from China called Angel Chuck Wong (黄有恒) or Wong Jauhang in Cantonese, the two characters of his first name meaning "who has perseverance." Angel was born in the city of Canton at the start of the century, later moving to Hong Kong where he completed his studies. By the time he moved to Mexico, Angel was already married in Hong Kong and had four daughters. Foon Chuck brought Angel to Mexico because he had had an argument with his eldest son Arturo, while Santiago was still studying and not ready yet to succeed him. Already in his sixties, he also wanted to establish stronger links between his Mexican family and China. According to Foon Chuck's grandchildren, Angel was an adopted son, and was rapidly accepted into Foon Chuck's Mexican family. Adopted Chinese sons enjoy the exact same rights, privileges and duties as born ones; they often already have the same surname, being adopted from within the extended family.

Angel first settled in El Mante, where he helped Foon Chuck with his farm, marrying a local woman as his second wife. After the expropriation, the young couple moved to the port of Acapulco, where Angel opened a Chinese restaurant, distancing himself from his half-siblings in northern Mexico. In addition to his daughters in Hong Kong, Angel raised four mixed children in Acapulco, the elder one becoming an accomplished athlete, competing for Mexico in the Olympic games. Angel ended his days in Acapulco, never moving back to China, but remaining active in the local Chinese community. All of Angel's children carried the surname Wong instead of Chuck, and both branches of his family, in China and Mexico, keep contact with each other to this day, even as they are now scattered around the world, all revering their grandfather's memory.

The Chuck siblings remembered their father as a meticulous, organized and strict person, a bit distant and not as affectionate with them as he would later be with his grandchildren, as is often the case in China. He was always impeccably dressed and groomed even in the hot countryside of northern Mexico. Before arriving at Piedras Negras from El Limon to visit his family, he sent a telegram with the exact time of his train's arrival, so that someone would be at the station to pick him up. As in most Chinese homes, family life was centered around daily meals, taken together around a large table with all the dishes shared in the middle in Chinese fashion. The children remembered their father as a fantastic chef but, towards the end of his life, as the only one to use chopsticks, as all his descendants by now ate with forks and knives. In his later years, Foon Chuck enjoyed walking on the streets of Piedras Negras with his grandchildren, but strictly forbade them to eat street snacks outside, a well-liked custom in Mexico. Food was, for him, to be taken only at the dinner table at home. He wanted to infuse his children and grandchildren with Christian principles as well as the five Confucian virtues of benevolence, righteousness, propriety, wisdom and fidelity,[4] teaching them to be discrete like himself, disliking any kind of publicity. His grandchildren remember him as a generous grandfather, always arriving from El Limon with boxes of tropical fruits and sending them sweets from the grocery store of one of his Chinese associates in Tampico.

Although Foon Chuck attained a certain fame, he remained an austere person throughout his life, never forgetting his humble origins and not spending his money on frivolities or jewelry for his family. Frugality is a trait of most Chinese migrants, related to their farming roots: Confucius said that "luxury leads to laxity while frugality leads to rigidity, and it is better to be rigid than to be lax."[5] In the eighteenth century, the British ambassador to China, Lord McCartney, while visiting the Peking court and reflecting on what Britain might be able to export to China, noticed the simplicity of the Chinese people and their limited wants, with the poor wearing cotton, the rich silk and everyone eating rice.[6] This frugality can also be observed in politics: from ancient Confucian writings to recent times, Chinese politicians in official decrees strive to reach a level of "moderate affluence"[7] for their society, one where all their subjects have enough to eat to live harmoniously.

Other than his books, one of Foon Chuck's only personal possessions that has survived in the family is a golden ring, with the Chinese characters for luck in Cantonese engraved on it.[8] This is suggestive of his simplicity and shows that, despite his conversion to Christianity, he retained Chinese superstitions. Located on Calle Estudios in front of the train station and the hotel, the family home in Piedras Negras was bourgeois and comfortable but none of his children remember luxuries. If in Chinese culture the concept of sin is absent, a similar role is played by the concept of immoderation.[9]

A philanthropist at heart, Foon Chuck sent many of his profits to China, either to his political organizations or to help his family in Chaitong. None of his money was spent on spoiling his children, and, for that reason, all of them grew up aware of the sacrifices their father made for what he considered just causes. Like other children of Chinese migrants, they often did not understand why the family's money was sent so far away, to a country and relatives they had never seen and would never meet. With such distance from China, like most second- or third-generation migrants, they could not appreciate their father's deep roots in Chaitong—built at a time

A CONFUCIAN AND AMERICAN LEGACY

when the family was working in the rice paddies from dawn to dusk, fighting floods and typhoons together. All their lives, though, their father's actions made them value their education more than money and their spiritual possessions more than their earthly ones. Like their father, they tried to follow the following teaching of Confucius: "The noble man cares about virtue; the inferior man cares about material things."[10] In the Chuck family, built at the crossroads of three cultures, the teachings of Confucius and Jesus Christ blend together to become one.

16

THE ROARING THIRTIES IN SHANGHAI

While his cousins pursued their studies in the United States, newlywed and recently graduated, Yaiwai launched his architectural career in Shanghai, where he had studied earlier and where much remained to be built. China was his only option, with the Western world struck by an unprecedented economic crisis, the United States closed by the Chinese Exclusion Act, and Mexico equally intolerant of Chinese immigrants, with the family on the verge of losing Hacienda Canton. As for Concha, she had never felt so enthusiastic. She was delighted to discover the world and to be on the same path as her cousins Lily and Margarita. She wondered though how the Chinese would view a Eurasian woman like her; this was her first journey to Asia, the mysterious land of her father and husband. In 1931, after a one-year trip via Honolulu, Yokohama, Hong Kong and Canton, where Yaiwai had various cousins, the young couple finally arrived in Shanghai.

Leaving the China Sea, their boat entered the Whangpoo River, passing first a long range of warehouses, docks, mills and shipyards, before a multitude of foreign warships came into view, from every colonial nation on earth, among which floated hundreds of Chinese junks. After a sharp turn, the city skyline appeared, with the imposing granite and marble buildings of the Shanghai Bund. Upon disembarking, Concha was struck by the docks' chaos, noises and smells—a mix of rotten vegetables, fish, oil and sweat. Automobiles, buses and trucks slowly made their way through an ocean of coolies, rickshaws, pushcarts, peddlers and beggars, and occasionally, Englishmen and silk-gowned Chinese merchants.

Located on the Yangtze River's estuary, Shanghai provides its inhabitants with strategic access to the remote interiors of China.

For this reason, the British decided to settle there in 1843, after the First Opium War and the Treaty of Nanking, which gave them the right to legally reside on Chinese soil. Later, the French and Americans joined them, creating the International and French Settlements, transforming Shanghai over the years from a small Chinese port into a world metropolis. Legally, although these Settlements were not colonies and were only leased from China, foreigners enjoyed extraterritoriality, meaning freedom from Chinese laws. Thus, ironically, foreign expatriates were free from Chinese laws inside the Settlements, while in North America Chinese immigrants were deprived of the rights conferred by those same foreigners' laws. In another cruel irony, whereas to begin with the Settlements were reserved for foreigners, from 1854, for purely commercial reasons, they started welcoming Chinese people, who, if they wanted to reside in them, had to pay increasingly high rents to their Western landlords. Following the Taiping Rebellion, the Chinese started to outnumber the foreigners and, by the turn of the century, they accounted for ninety-seven per cent of the Settlements' population. The International Settlement was autonomous, controlled by a municipal council run by an elite of Western businessmen, not by functionaries from Paris like the French Settlement. For that reason, it rapidly became a capitalist paradise with money reigning supreme. A historian sums it up well: although being populated almost exclusively by Chinese, "there was no other city in the world, where foreigners wielded such independent power in a country that was not their own."[1] However, by the time Yaiwai and Concha arrived, things were starting to change. In 1930, the International Settlement municipal council had just accepted for the first time five Chinese representatives.

The city owed its success to the security it offered to both foreign and Chinese merchants against bandits and rebellions, but also against the abuses and corruption of Chinese officials. With a Chinese legal system giving local officials significant autonomy and leeway, especially those further away from the provincial capitals, the Chinese business world is still known today as a place "under the rule of men, not the rule of law."[2] Shanghai therefore attracted merchants from neighboring regions such as Ningbo but also more remote ones like Kwangtung. In the 1880s, the early commercial boom of Shanghai

THE ROARING THIRTIES IN SHANGHAI

was initially led by guest merchants from the provinces of Kwangtung and Fukien (Yaiwai thus had various relatives who had already settled in the city). On his return from exile in the 1910s, Kang Youwei settled in Shanghai, too, where he amassed a fortune through real estate speculation. Kang had three large mansions in the city, proving that this time, contrary to his earlier foreign ventures, he got the timing of his Chinese investments right. Like Kang, most powerful politicians owned a mansion in the Settlements, Shanghai being China's most modern city and a magnet for any ambitious Chinese, young or old, looking to the future, giving birth to the saying "East and West, Shanghai is the best."

Shanghai was also a magnet for hundreds of thousands of poor peasants, victims of floods, drought and famine. In the 1930s, China's rural economy was in crisis, exacerbated by the Sino-Japanese conflict, providing a constant supply of refugees to Shanghai. The year my grandparents settled in the city was particularly miserable, with the flooding of the Yangtze River causing more than two million deaths, one of history's worst natural disasters. Like in today's China, the poor migrants constituted a social underclass, being denied access to most of the city's facilities and the conveniences of modern life, and suffering social discrimination, exemplified by its 100,000 rickshaw pullers, 40,000 dockworkers and an army of 20,000 professional beggars, who fought ferociously for their territory. Most stores had to pay a beggars' fee to avoid harassment. At the turn of the century, temporary laborers, vagabonds and unemployed people with their families made up nearly one fifth of Shanghai's population, or one million people,[3] living in insalubrious shantytowns made of straw huts along the city's many creeks or at its periphery.[4] As had been the case for the overseas Chinese earlier, migration was the only escape from starvation. Nowhere was the contrast between China's past and its future more dramatic than in Shanghai; and nowhere was the divide between the country's rich and poor more vivid. In years of famine, the city's charities and the police picked up hundreds of corpses from the streets every morning. Feudal China had produced inequalities since ancient times. The famous poet Du Fu (712–770) wrote: "Behind the vermillion gates meat and wine go to waste while out on the road lie the bones of those frozen to death."[5]

Yaiwai and Concha settled in what had become the ultimate cosmopolitan city, a town of migrants and fusion, rightly called the "Paris of the Orient." Greater Shanghai's population grew from just one million in 1880 to nearly five million in the 1930s, including 75,000 to 100,000 foreigners, making it the eighth most populous city in the world, with a staggering eighty per cent of its population being migrants, mainly from other Chinese provinces. Like the overseas Chinese, they too kept strong ties with their rural villages, wishing to be buried at home when they died. The unique status of the Settlements—not really colonies but not entirely part of China either—made them a haven for exiles without visas, such as the White Russians and Jews fleeing the violence in Eastern Europe. Shanghai became a fashionable stop for the world travelers of the day, such as Charlie Chaplin, Albert Einstein, George Bernard Shaw and the Duchess of Windsor. Of the metropolis, Aldous Huxley wrote: "In no city, West and East, have I ever had such an impression of dense, rank, richly clotted life. Old Shanghai is Bergson's *elan vital* in the raw, so to speak, and with the lid off. It is life itself."[6]

With half of China's modern factories,[7] Shanghai also became the country's industrial powerhouse, as well as its financial center and one of Asia's largest commercial ports, receiving more than half of China's imports.[8] Two-thirds of Shanghai's total population lived in the two foreign Settlements, and such an expansion put pressure on space, leading to rapid land price inflation. When Yaiwai and Concha arrived, land prices had tripled in the previous five years, making central Shanghai more expensive per acre than Park Avenue or the Champs-Élysées.[9] This resulted in the construction of Asia's first high-rise buildings, including banks, clubs, hotels, department stores and the famous Shanghai terraced houses in its narrow and congested alley-lanes where multiple families shared the same dwelling.

In 1931, Yaiwai and Concha moved into a new one-story home with a garden at 43b Edinburgh Road (now Jiangsu Lu). It was located one mile west of the International Settlement's formal border but within its administrative authority. In a leafy residential area, the house was typical for the affluent Shanghai class, and was called a Yangfang, or Western home, in Chinese. Their neighbors were an American family, the Stearns, and the famous writer Lin

THE ROARING THIRTIES IN SHANGHAI

Yutang (1895–1976). My grandparents owned a sidecar and a private rickshaw, which Concha used every day. Since Concha was Chinese-looking but did not speak the language, Yaiwai was scared to let her wander alone in the hustle and bustle of Shanghai. She felt uncomfortable at first using a human-powered vehicle, but she quickly found out that their private rickshaw puller was among the relatively privileged ones. Like the Chinese immigrants to the Americas before them, public pullers were usually unable to form or support a family, dying young of injuries and sickness. Until the Second World War, with the absence of horse cars, sedan chairs remained widely used all over China: the son of a missionary famously begged his parents to be left in China when he was told that there were no chair-bearers in the United States.[10] Having suffered from the Mexican Revolution and witnessed the anger of a poor populace, Concha found the destitute class in Shanghai poorer yet strangely more submissive and accepting than in Mexico. She was scared to imagine what a popular revolution might look like in China.

Yaiwai immediately opened his architectural practice, and their first son was born in 1932, followed in quick succession by a younger brother in 1933 and my mother in 1935. Concha grew very fond of her missionary neighbors, the Stearns, while the children of both families often played together, attesting to the cosmopolitan nature of the city. When they were not in the garden or the nearby fields, Concha often strolled in nearby Jessfield Park (now Zhongshan Gongyuan). My mother later told me that the hospital where she was born and the house they owned at Edinburgh Road had both been designed by their father. Shanghai was an architect's dream come true, and Yaiwai had high expectations for his career there. The city adopted the latest fashions, was famous for its innovative architecture, and had a booming construction business. With its futuristic sophistication, Shanghai's skyline was a mix of architectural styles, including Art Deco, Gothic, Baroque and Romanesque. The Chinese architect I. M. Pei wrote that he discovered his vocation in Shanghai in the 1930s by "seeing the future." He recalled playing billiards while looking at the Park Hotel across the street, then under construction, which became the tallest building in Asia. The Hong Kong and Shanghai Bank building was described as "the most sumptuous building from the Suez Canal to the Bering Sea,"[11] the Daxin department store had China's first Otis elevator, the Shanghai Club had the world's longest bar, and the Wing On department store included several restaurants, extravagant cabarets, a Chinese opera, movie theatres and a rooftop garden.

In the photos from that period, my grandparents exude happiness with their newborn children and the exciting prospects opening for them. Yaiwai's parents and sister had also moved to Shanghai, settling in a new house in nearby Yuyuen Road, and so did their cousins Lily and Margarita Chuck, creating a small group of women in Shanghai advocating the cause of the Chinese Mexicans. In 1931, when the expulsions from Sonora occurred, prominent merchants from the French Settlement contributed money to help support their returning compatriots,[12] likely encouraged by my grandparents. Hing also made the trip for his grandchildren's births in 1932 and again in 1935. After living for fifty years in Mexico, Hing felt proud, both of his daughter's family, and of seeing how Shanghai showed resolutely the future to China. It seemed that Yaiwai had perhaps been right to be so optimistic about the future of his native country ten years earlier. Hing sent a letter to the whole family in Mexico, writing that he now had a Chinese granddaughter who smiled at him all the time. The eldest son, only four years old, in addition to Spanish already spoke Cantonese, Mandarin, English and even a few words of Shanghainese.

Historically, Shanghai is a city where Western and Chinese worlds collided and, despite its cosmopolitan nature, racial tensions still existed. While Western ways of life were welcomed and foreigners usually felt at home, many anti-imperialist movements began in the city. Until 1927, some public gardens in the International Settlement were still forbidden to "dogs and Chinese,"[13] which had shocked Yaiwai a few years earlier, even though any signs advertising this rule had been removed decades earlier. Various clubs and venues in the Settlements were still reserved for white people, making Yaiwai feel like a foreigner in his own country and showing the absurdity of a world about to be thrown into the flames of nationalism. Many Westerners maintained a patronizing and distant attitude towards the Chinese, avoiding learning the language or doing anything that might signal them as "going native." The historian Rebecca Karl speaks of the "great unevenness"[14] of that era, when foreign communities in China became increasingly privileged while Chinese migrants in the Americas experienced increasing discrimination.

Things started to change in 1927: after a struggle with the Communists and secret, grubby negotiations with the underworld and the financiers who controlled the Chinese districts of Shanghai, the Nationalist government of Chiang Kai-shek formed a Greater Shanghai Municipality, federating all the districts surrounding the International Settlements. The Nationalists' objective was to slowly absorb the foreign Settlements by building a Chinese city around them, one with better infrastructure, the same rule of law, and an independent municipal government, solving the problem of sovereignty that had burdened China for decades. This grand architectural plan was a dream for any architect; it would later be resumed during the reform era of the 1980s.

Shanghai had a split personality, being now both a Chinese city under the control of the Nationalists and an international-treaty port under the control of foreigners. As an overseas Chinese returning from the United States, Yaiwai felt perfectly suited to navigate between those two worlds. The overseas Chinese, who were almost all Cantonese, were the most adaptable of all Shanghai's capitalists, quick to exploit new ideas to their advantage.[15] To add to the city's complex social texture, in business too, internal Chinese migrants retained close ties with their native provinces. Replicating the organizations of their overseas compatriots, Shanghai had more than a hundred native place organizations[16] or guilds, with certain trades often monopolized by internal migrants coming from one particular province. The Cantonese in the city were well known for their influence in the tobacco, silk, foreign grocery and shipping industries, while Yaiwai used his network of Cantonese friends to advance his architectural practice. In Shanghai's "Who's Who" and celebrities lists, one's family name was always preceded by one's native village.

A city of migrants, Shanghai was ideal for a Eurasian woman like Concha. She believed all her life that she was an exception, an anomaly, but Shanghai was full of Eurasians like her, many in prominent positions, suggesting a cosmopolitan future for China. Since their first arrival in Shanghai in the 1840s, the practice of having a Chinese concubine, but not a wife, was widespread amongst British merchants, giving rise to the first generation of Chinese Eurasians, and putting these merchants in conflict with the clergy and missionaries. Interracial marriages remained taboo for both Chinese and Westerners well into the twentieth century.

Like Foon Chuck, many of the Shanghai and Hong Kong nouveau riche were compradors (agents for foreign investors or trade organizations), having made their fortunes as intermediaries between Western and Chinese merchants. Working at the confluence of these two cultures, many were either Eurasians themselves or had mixed families. In Shanghai's high society, a Eurasian woman with a Western education like Concha was a trophy to be prized and put on display, and Yaiwai felt proud of his wife. Concha had had to wait until she was twenty-seven to find a place she could finally call home. Like her, women from all over China moved to Shanghai, confused about their roles in a changing society and fleeing traditional ways of life, all in search of a new freedom. They were little different from the political dissidents arriving in the foreign Settlements seeking refuge from prosecution. Thus, for the first time, my grandmother felt proud to be both a modern woman and of mixed blood, realizing at last that she had been completely ignorant of her father's culture until now.

Still, Concha could not help but feel the conflicts inherent in her origins. Sometimes she felt more Western and was conscious of the privilege she enjoyed through her European heritage and relative whiteness; at other times she felt more Chinese and was aware of the culture of her young family. She never felt this conflict in Mexico, a country with few Eurasians besides her siblings, which made her feel more Chinese and conscious of being different and alien there. Ironically, it was only by moving to China that she became more conscious of her Mexican side: the different societies worked like mirrors reflecting and deciding what Concha was and was not.

Concha later remembered the many nationalities in Shanghai: the elegant French and Russian stores on Avenue Joffre; the American and Chinese bookstores on Fuzhou Road, where ancient books were more expensive than newer ones; the various British clubs; the Japanese in North Sichuan Road; the Sikh policemen who directed all the traffic; all those foreigners, like her, having made of Shanghai their permanent home. With Yaiwai and her in-laws, she traveled on weekends around Shanghai, touring ancient monuments, visiting the new capital of Nanking, the gardens of Soochow, and the West Lake in Hanchow, sending photographs to her siblings in Mexico, who had no idea of China. As she did this, she recalled some of her classmates at school, just a few years ago, who had been so condescending towards her, pitying her for her origins. She could not believe her eyes: she was living an oriental fairy tale.

Shanghai was not only an exuberant but also a scandalous city, a place where money could provide the most exotic of pleasures, but also where sharks awaited the unsuspecting businessman. A newcomer from the countryside seeing the big city for the first time described it as expensive, foreign, irrational, petty-minded, impersonal, depraved, and chaotic, with shameless prostitutes[17] who were called "little salty water sisters"[18] (which in Chinese sounds like "handsome maid"), alluding to their relationships with foreign sailors, or "Sing-Song girls" in the case of higher-end courtesans. One person in 130 was a prostitute in Shanghai, compared with one in 580 in Berlin, 430 in Chicago and 250 in Tokyo.[19] Shanghai's dark side could be witnessed first and foremost in its factories and workshops, which had appalling conditions no longer tolerated in the West, including thousands of child workers. The city's underworld was prominent, and involved, among others, anti-leftist secret societies with opaque ties to both the Japanese and Nationalist governments. This was an ideal place for amoral entrepreneurs and adventurers with dubious business practices to amass quick fortunes. In Shanghai, everyone was in search of either survival or success; everything was for sale, from the flesh of a country-girl-turned-prostitute to the muscles of a rickshaw puller. Chen Duxiu (1879–1942), the communist intellectual, described Shanghai as "an evil empire where human dignity is crushed by greed and lust and Chinese pride is trampled by barbarian foreign devils."[20] If Shanghai had all the comforts of a modern city, like running water, gas, electricity, telephones, streetcars, automobiles and air conditioning, these luxuries were reserved for the wealthy. The middle class still awoke in their alley lanes to the sounds of the nightsoil collector and the roosters' crow and the smell of coal like in their rural villages, using public bath houses and hot water stores for heating and cooking.

But Shanghai was a capital of light as well as darkness, symbolizing modernity and representing China's future. It was a laboratory for new ideas, with China's first modern newspapers, stock exchange, and film studios. Its freedom meant that it soon replaced Peking as China's publishing center; Shanghai's culture was seen as vibrant and liberal, but also commercial, whereas Peking was conservative and traditional.[21] This dichotomy remains true today in the arts, society and politics. Shanghai was a city of intellectuals, home to the famous writers Lu Xun, Mao Dun, and Lin Yutang, and had an associated political history. In the 1930s, Shanghai aspired to show the way to the whole of China, a role it regained during the reform era in the 1990s, after having been dormant for nearly sixty years, punished by the Communist regime for its earlier excesses.

Impressed by her surroundings, Concha was determined to become a Chinese wife and mother, quickly adopting her new country's customs, and taking lessons in Cantonese and cooking, learning recipes that she would remember all her life. While influenced by Western modernity, Shanghai people, like those of Hong Kong today, remained fiercely Chinese in their daily lives. With the high density of its alley lanes, Shanghai was a paradise for itinerant vendors and peddlers, many just teenagers, who brought their trade to Concha's door: there were dentists, blacksmiths, cobblers, fortune tellers, tailors, seamstresses, librarians, and hawkers carrying portable kitchens on poles offering snacks all day. She welcomed them daily, often with some extra coins, as they reminded her of El Dragon de Oro, and how her father had started his business in Mexico.

In various photos, Concha wears the typical Shanghai dress, the cheongsam,[22] suggesting her new aspirations along with those of her new country. Like today, Shanghai people had a reputation as fashion snobs, most residents cutting their own clothes and spending large parts of their income on them. Cantonese people, who put food above all else, would joke that "A man from Shanghai would rather put oil on his head than in his food."[23] All around China, Shanghai's fashions were the model. The cheongsam was a Shanghai creation. Originally a kind of Manchu attire, Shanghai tailors transformed the cheongsam into a longer, figure-fitting, one-piece garment with a high neck, an asymmetric left-over-right opening, and a skirt extending below the knees. By highlighting women's bodies, cheongsams became a symbol of Chinese women's independence and emancipation.

THE ROARING THIRTIES IN SHANGHAI

The cheongsam is what Concha wore when she and Yaiwai went out in the evening to trendy restaurants and nightclubs, including the glitzy Paramout and Ciro's Club, with its bar in the dance floor, its VIP rooms, and its famous Taxi Girls for hire, more extravagant than any place in Mexico or the United States. The newly opened Cathay Hotel had 214 rooms, with marble baths, silver spigots, an internal telephone system, and purified water pipes. Concha was surprised to hear jazz music being played around Shanghai almost as much as in Philadelphia. In China, in 1930 as well as today, money was something to celebrate and display, not to hide like in Mexico after the revolution or in the United States during the Prohibition Era. Yaiwai found much truth in the saying that "A Shanghai man acts like he has $100 when he has only $1, while a Cantonese acts like he has only $1 when he has $100." This rowdy ostentation and extravagance were not to Yaiwai's taste, who was under the austere influence of Foon Chuck, but he nevertheless felt proud of his country's progress. Shanghai people, like today, were known for their boldness in business and life, "casting away gold like throwing out dirt."[24]

In contrast, photographs of Yaiwai's mother and sister show them in traditional dresses with serious expressions, portraying a more conservative and austere world for Chinese women. Unlike her female cousins in Mexico, Yaiwai's sister was raised in the traditional way: she was taught from a young age not to raise her voice or to leave the house alone, and she learned to cook, to sew, to always be obedient and modest, and to wear plain and dignified clothes. While her father sent Yaiwai to study abroad, he left her in China, failing to realize that the progress of Western society was directly linked with the emancipation of its women, as Liang Qichao had just asserted in *On Women's Education*, blaming the Chinese national weakness on the absence of academic achievements by the country's women. If Concha had always felt that Mexican woman were treated as second-class citizens, she now realized that they were in fact more liberated and independent compared to Chinese women. For that reason, she became a more assertive and self-conscious woman in Shanghai, which sometimes became a source of friction with Yaiwai. It would take several generations for Chinese women to play a more public and liberated role in society and, as Chairman Mao said, to "hold half the sky."[25]

Unfortunately, dark clouds began to accumulate on the horizon. In 1931, the Japanese invaded Manchuria, creating the puppet state of Manchukuo and gradually nibbling away more territory. Ten years after the May Fourth Movement, Chinese students reacted violently with protests across the country, in Shanghai in particular, and boycotted Japanese products. In 1932, in the International Settlement, just a few months after Yaiwai and Concha's arrival, a monk from an ultra-nationalist Japanese sect was killed, causing retaliatory assassinations by the Japanese army and riots across the Chinese city. Tolerating no dissent, the vengeful Japanese attacked and bombed Shanghai's Chapei district. That same year, in only two months, 35,000 people were killed in Shanghai, mostly civilians. Presaging further horrors, one writer reflected that "for the first time, the world could marvel at the results of combined artillery and aerial bombing in a thickly populated peaceful city."[26] Japan being unwilling to declare war on the Western powers, the International Settlements, protected by foreign garrisons and the local police, were largely spared violence, at least for the time being, but the entire Chinese section of Shanghai gradually fell under Japanese control. Most Westerners in the Settlements continued their lives unaffected. During those years, an expatriate wrote: "For a long time, during the years of the Japanese occupation of [Peking], Westerners lived there unaffected. Nevertheless, their life was like that of a man who, although physically comfortable, knows he has a deadly disease."[27] Despite these incidents, my grandparents remained hopeful that they had made the right choice by settling in Shanghai, the Great Depression barely touching the city and the property boom continuing as before. But over the next four years, ignoring the Japanese aggression, Chiang Kai-shek, the head of the Nationalist government, concentrated his efforts on his struggle against the Communist Party, instead of uniting the country against the common enemy. In 1935, the year of my mother's birth, the Japanese already formed the largest foreign contingent of Shanghai's population, holding a large share in its economy.

* * *

Over the years, the Japanese advance and war prospects mean that some construction plans across the city begin to be shelved, but

32. Chinese classroom in Imperial China.

33. Ross Alley, or "Gamblers' Alley," c. 1898, San Francisco, USA.

34. "A picture for employers. Why *they* can live on 40 cents a day, and *they* can't." *Puck* magazine, 1878.

35. Anti-Chinese riots in Denver in October 1880, illustrated diary of Franck Leslie.

36. El Dragon de Oro store, 1930, Mexico City.

37. The main building of Hacienda Canton, c. 1922, El Mante, Mexico.

38. Kang Youwei, c. 1905.

39. The Hotel Internacional, c. 1910, Monclova, Mexico.

40. Hotel La Española, formerly Compañía Bancaria China y México, c. 1920, Torreón, Mexico.

41. A cart carrying victims after the Torreón massacre, 15 May 1911.

42. Yue Mae School, Hing (front, left corner) and Yun Wu (front, fourth from right), 1910, Mexico City.

43. President Álvaro Obregón with Chancellor Quang Ki-Teng at the National Palace, 19 February 1921.

44. Plutarco Elías Calles at the National Palace, 1924, Mexico City.

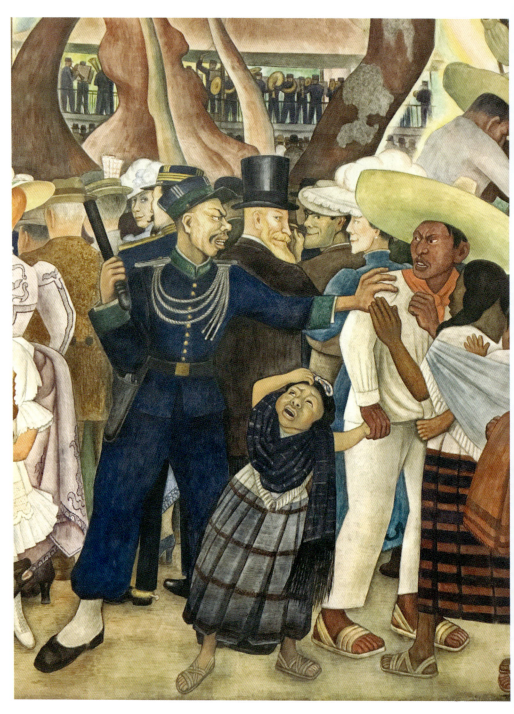

45. Detail depicting a Chinese police officer in Diego Rivera's mural *Dream of a Sunday Afternoon in Alameda Central Park*, 1947.

THE ROARING THIRTIES IN SHANGHAI

Yaiwai manages to keep himself busy, one of his projects being a new mansion for Shanghai's new mayor, recently appointed by the Nationalists. Nevertheless, he becomes increasingly worried about how he is going to provide for his family. He also feels terrified for them, the cruelty and sadism of the Japanese occupiers being well known, compared to which the worst abuses in the United States against his people are just child's play. The Japanese call the Chinese "the ignoble race" and "inferior animals."[28] Despite being a supporter of the Nationalists, Yaiwai feels little in common with its politicians and generals, knowing their cause to be just but finding them corrupt, power-hungry, violent, and unable to unify the country behind common ideals. Although he feels affection for his father and uncle, he does not want to become a merchant—and who would buy and sell in a world at war? He does not see himself in any of these roles, feeling like a lamb surrounded by wolves. Even if able to emigrate, he cannot imagine being given any work as an architect in the United States or Mexico. At the same time, he finds it unbearable to see China so weak, corrupt and vandalized by the Japanese aggressor, feeling surrounded by walls of hatred in all directions.

* * *

In July 1937, the Japanese army continued its advance in the north, quickly invading Peking, confident it could take the whole of China in only three months. In Shanghai, a flood of panicked refugees entered the foreign Settlements seeking asylum, and the numbers increased in the following months (soon numbering hundreds of thousands), with most settling in new shantytowns. From August to November 1937, more than a million Chinese and Japanese soldiers clashed in the Battle of Shanghai, which historians compare to Stalingrad; more than 300,000 soldiers were killed, mostly Chinese. Even if the foreign Settlements remained intact, from August 1937, thousands of foreigners started to leave the city, particularly women and children. The ones who remained lived each day as though it was their last. China's defeat in December resulted in the withdrawal of all Nationalist troops, leaving the Japanese with total control over the Chinese section of Shanghai and a free route towards Nanking, just 200 miles away. The worst atrocity occurred in the latter city that month, when over six weeks the Japanese army massacred 260,000 people, mostly unarmed civilians, and raped more than 80,000 women.[29] This barbaric episode, known as "the Rape of Nanking," was an orgy of mass murder, showing the cruel and demented attitude of the Japanese army. When I was a child, my relatives often repeated to me, to make sure I never forgot and would later tell my own children, how Japanese soldiers held killing contests, threw babies in the air to catch them with their bayonets and mutilated women. The Shanghai Settlements had by now become an island surrounded by murderous Japanese troops, who demanded that every Chinese entering or leaving the Settlements bow in front of their new masters, or be beaten and killed.

* * *

Realizing that the world that had looked so magical and promising to him only a few years earlier is now doomed, Yaiwai falls into despair. He is besieged by hostile forces everywhere,[30] with nationalism and racism in Mexico and the United States, and now the threat of a militarist Japan in China. To a liberal intellectual, the state of the world seems absurd. Instead of the united world dreamed of by Kang Youwei and which Yaiwai too had hoped for, it is now as if many countries have agreed with each other to take the path of exclusion and hatred.

Even as he finally obtains his long-awaited immigration documents for Mexico, there are too many tragedies for one soul to bear: having been diagnosed with liver cancer, he passes away in January 1938. On his deathbed in his Shanghai hospital, sensing that China may be lost forever and that his three children may never return, Yaiwai writes on a piece of silk, in Chinese characters, their names, those of their ancestors and of their native village, so that they will never forget their roots as they grow up so far away from their birth-country. My family will keep this piece of silk carefully framed, to pass it on to our descendants.

My grandmother's feeling of grief is impossible to describe; Yaiwai is her other half. Before leaving this world, he tells her that they will be together in spirit forever and that she must remain strong for their children because from now on she will raise them alone. On

THE ROARING THIRTIES IN SHANGHAI

the back of the last family photograph, Concha writes the following words shortly after his death: "The last portrait we took together with the beloved and unforgettable 'Little Father,' my noble and ever courageous companion, who now enjoys the eternal life and the happiness that never ends." In March 1938, as the Japanese forces continue their advance in Shanghai, my widowed grandmother and her three children board the American liner SS *President Coolidge* to return to Mexico. Their Shanghai home is sold for a pittance, a fraction of what it had cost Yaiwai to obtain the land and build it a few years earlier. My mother has just turned three, and my grandmother carries her husband's ashes in one of her trunks. At the tender age of thirty-two, her whole world has collapsed under her. For decades, the orphaned family will wonder what their lives could have become without that fateful Japanese invasion.

Before they depart, Concha receives a letter from Hing, which mentions that Yaiwai's father Yun Wu would be within his rights, based on Chinese custom, to ask for one of Yaiwai and Concha's children to remain in China with his grandparents. But Concha is too modern and attached to her children to allow that to happen. Heartbroken, Yun Wu does not insist either on keeping Concha or one of his grandchildren in China; he knows well that his country has nothing to offer them for now. Devastated by the death of their only son, Yun Wu and his wife Jovita leave Shanghai to settle in Chaitong. It could have been predicted—thereby sparing more than 10 million Chinese lives[31]—that the Japanese would ultimately be unable to control such a hostile and vast country as China. After the inevitable Japanese defeat and the later Communist victory, Yun Wu moves to Hong Kong, bringing with him his only daughter, whom my mother will only meet again four decades later.

17

BETWEEN EAST AND WEST

Between 1930 and 1935, already in his sixties, Hing returned to China three times. Since becoming Mexican in 1898 and thus in principle being allowed to travel freely, the political environments in China and Mexico had not been stable enough to undertake the trans-Pacific journey, with both countries experiencing revolutions and China facing a civil war. Despite his naturalization, due to Mexico's xenophobic policies, he never felt certain that he had the appropriate documents to be allowed back, and so he preferred not to take the risk of being rejected at the border and losing everything. Like political refugees today, Hing felt trapped, unable to visit his native homeland for most of his adult life. However, after 1930, with a more stable political situation, his daughter Concha in China, and his eldest son in charge of the business, Hing returned to China to visit his ancestors' village, explore the country, and stock up on merchandise for his stores. He was returning as a wealthy man: photos show him in Hoksaan with his youngest brother, and he is not "in silk robe," but in an elegant three-piece suit, leather shoes, and Panama hat.

* * *

Whereas fifty years earlier he had left China destitute and despised, his compatriots now treat this old and distinguished gentleman with deference. He is now one of the overseas Chinese, or Huaqiao;[1] in Chinese the word is made of the characters meaning China, person, and lofty or proud. Hing first goes to the cemetery of his village to bow before his ancestors' graves, thanking them for his good fortune. After forty years, he is moved to see his extended family again and eat a genuine bowl of rice. He marvels at and discovers for the first time high-end Cantonese cuisine, unavailable in Mexico, which he could not afford in his youth, making him feel like a stranger in his own land. Following Chinese tradition, he distributes small bundles of coins carefully wrapped in red paper to his younger relatives, wishing them luck and giving them his blessings. They in turn bow in front of their uncle, wishing him life for a hundred years and that his "fortune be as boundless as the East Sea."[2] They feel honored to meet him for the first time, having heard of his rags-to-riches life in the New World. Hing has not felt so happy in a long time. After so many years abroad he had forgotten how old age is revered in China, where respect for the elderly is a sign of a superior civilization. So-called lesser cultures, such as the nomadic civilizations of the north, were seen as valuing only physical strength, demeaning their elders, and not providing a proper environment for their care.

After spending time with his family, Hing travels around China, visiting sites such as Yantai and Peking, where he is photographed admiring the Summer Palace, the Temple of Heaven, and climbing the Eastern Hills on a sedan chair. He realizes how vast China is—so much larger than Hoksaan and even the province of Kwangtung, the only places he previously knew. He brings back from his trip a delicate jade figurine in the shape of a dragon (which will remain in the family), which has a label in Spanish that reads "Piece of a stone pillar found on the ground of the Old Summer Palace in Peking in 1935." China's most precious stone, jade has been revered for thousands of years, as, according to the philosopher Xunzi (310–237 BCE), it exemplifies all human virtues: "smooth and refined like humaneness, hard and inflexible like justice, ordered in regular patterns like knowledge, breakable but not bendable like bravery, and with its cracks and flaws always showing like sincerity."[3]

* * *

Hing never brought his wife or Mexican children to China. Apart from Concha, he kept the two worlds separate, El Dragon de Oro being the only link between them. It was only after the Second

BETWEEN EAST AND WEST

World War that his son Melchor, now in charge of El Dragon de Oro, traveled to Hong Kong. He was the only one of Hing's sons that still remembered well the Cantonese dialect he had learned from his father. One possible explanation for Hing's desire to keep the two worlds separate is that he may have had a Chinese wife, and although he never lived with her, he would have preferred to keep the two family branches separated, understanding how uncomfortable his Mexican Catholic family may have felt knowing about his earlier marriage. Whether or not Hing was married in China, had any children there, and what may have happened to them, is now lost in history. His eldest relative alive in China at the time of writing, the grandson of his younger brother, believes it is unlikely that Hing had a Chinese marriage.

* * *

Returning to his native country so late in life, Hing has complex feelings. He feels enthusiastic to finally discover China's heritage sites, which he had no idea existed when he left the country the first time. Gradually, his profession had opened his mind to the richness of his ancestors' crafts, and he had become a connoisseur of Chinese art. But seeing his family again leaves him melancholic about the ancient world he has left behind. Although rich and respected, something he could never have become by staying in China, he has lost part of his identity in the West. A famous poem by He Zhizhang (659–744 CE), "On Returning Home," describes an old man returning home after many years of absence:

Left home young, I return an old man.	少小离家老大回
My native tongue has not changed, but my sideburns have grown thin.	乡音无改鬓毛衰
Children see me but do not recognize me.	儿童相见不相识
Smiling, they ask from where I come.	笑问客从何处来

Hing wonders why such an ancient land did not allow him to build his fortune there, forcing him into exile. Why does China remain so crowded, unstable, corrupt and difficult to live in? He bows in front of his ancestors' graves one last time, asking forgiveness for moving away and no longer worshiping them. In Chinese tradition, the eldest son is responsible for the ancestors' cult and for raising sons to carry on that duty after him. A photo is taken in 1935 of Hing celebrating his birthday in Hong Kong, surrounded by his extended family and myriad friends, no one else suspecting that the patriarch being celebrated is a Mexican businessman. In another photo he is dressed in a traditional silk robe in his ancestral village, finally fulfilling his lifelong dream of returning as a wealthy man.

In 1938, learning of Yaiwai's death, Hing sends a telegram to Concha asking her and her three orphaned children to return to Mexico, sending money for the voyage. Despite the tragic circumstances, more than eight years after Concha left Mexico, Hing is delighted to see his daughter and grandchildren again, insisting that they live with him and Cruz above his store. So late in his life, knowing that he will never go back, it is as if China is coming back to him. Concha keeps her Mexican passport, but her three children, born abroad of a foreign father, travel with Chinese documents. Using Hing's influence, they are quickly recognized as Mexicans but, like him years earlier, they must modify their place of birth; hence, my mother and her brothers are officially born in Mexico City instead of Shanghai. As soon as they arrive in Mexico, they travel with Hing to Torreón to pay their respects to Uncle Foon Chuck, the clan's eldest, now seventy-five years old. Foon Chuck has the five of them photographed, wishing to immortalize the moment and honor the memory of Yaiwai, who, through his studies and work, has brought honor to their clan. This is also the first time he meets the grandchildren of his younger brother, whom he has not seen in almost ten years and will never see again. This touching photograph of Foon Chuck with my widowed grandmother is often used by historians in museum exhibits and conferences to depict Foon Chuck's supposed "Chinese family," ignoring its true significance.

Concha and the children move in with Hing above El Dragon de Oro. In the first weeks there, forming what is probably her first memory, my mother holds the dining room table tightly, crying desperately that she wants to return to her Chinese home with her father, a world she has now lost. But as her memories of Shanghai gradually disappear, her sense of loss fades as well. Despite the circumstances, my mother forms fond memories in her early years in Mexico, now being able to play with not only her two brothers but so many cousins, especially her uncle Melchor's children, who are the same age as her and with whom she will remain close all her life. Unlike the isolated existence of Hing's children, this next generation is blessed with countless cousins and uncles. My mother will, many years later, proudly tell me that she is, among all the grandchildren, her grandfather's favorite. Hing always treats her with more affection than the others, for she is an orphan, a girl, and his only Chinese granddaughter.

A year later, Concha and her children move to Monterrey, the country's third-largest city, where she runs a branch of El Dragon de Oro, helping relieve her sadness. Benjamín Chuck is also settled there, and supports her affectionately: he is delighted to meet his Chinese nephews. Hing, now nearly seventy-five years old, visits them one day; my mother has vivid memories of him walking in his suit with his hat and cane, which he swings rhythmically, a true gentleman, with a demeanor at once natural and aristocratic. Since the death of Yaiwai, Hing is the closest thing she has to a fatherly figure, and she speaks of him with affection. One day, Hing slips and fractures his hip, but he soon recovers and walks again, as if nothing has happened. He is a typical Chinese migrant, not the kind to ever complain about his fate.

Business turns out to be difficult in Monterrey, and Concha, like her father before her, must travel throughout northern Mexico and knock on people's doors to sell her goods. She often travels with her young daughter, my mother, which will spark in her an early passion for traveling. In 1940 the store is forced to close, and Hing asks Concha to return to Mexico City to live with him and Cruz in their new home in Tlalpan. Like before, despite the circumstances, he is happy to see them return. Now almost eighty, Hing misses his daughter and Chinese grandchildren, wanting to spend his last years with them. Without my mother's asking him, he teaches her to read the time on the big clock in the living room, and is in general eager to participate in her education. My mother begins to study in a Catholic nuns' school in Tlalpan. After only a week, she skips a grade, and she then stays at the top of her new class despite being two years younger than her classmates, having taught herself how to read with her brothers, without any adult helping her. She walks home from school along an unpaved road, which floods with small streams when it rains on summer afternoons. To avoid getting wet, she must use her school bag as a bridge to cross streams. Seeing the scene, Hing exclaims, "So smart my daughter!" That same year, Concha, on Hing's advice, hires a Mexican governess, Felipa, to help her take care of her young children. Like her, Felipa is a widow, but without children; she is an austere, Catholic, loving person and the family grows very fond of her, cementing them rapidly into Mexican life. Felipa lives with them in Tlalpan, becoming a trusted family member.

* * *

Hing had by now retired, and his son Melchor proudly maintained his legacy in both politics and business. He became chairman of the Mexico City Aviation Association, recently founded to help China in its war of resistance against Japan, pledging to donate the profits of El Dragon de Oro to the war effort. In 1941, at one meeting of the association, Melchor personally donated the equivalent of 200,000 Chinese yuan to purchase an aircraft for China, for which he received a telegram of appreciation from Chiang Kai-shek himself.[4] Melchor had earlier given each of his children a Chinese first name, though these were quickly forgotten. Although Hing had forbidden his children from speaking Cantonese, this episode shows the Leon family's continued connections to China, especially in those times of war against Japan and with the recent return of Concha from Shanghai. In May 1942, Mexico officially entered the Second World War, a few months after the United States, transforming its economy over the next few years. This damaged El Dragon de Oro significantly, since it was unable to source Chinese products from Hong Kong anymore, and the whole country was now focused on the war effort. The store quickly lost all of its clients, who were no longer interested in buying Asian products. Hing witnessed his business deteriorate quickly. Unsure about the outcome of the war, he worried whether Melchor and his younger children would be successful in saving the business and succeeding him.

* * *

Many first-generation immigrants, even as they enjoy good retirements in their adopted countries, find that as they age and have more free time they become increasingly melancholic when they think of their country of birth, wanting to live and die where they grew up. So it is with Hing. Despite having lived his early years in destitution and later made Mexico his country, part of his heart remains in China, of which he retains many memories. According to a famous Chinese saying, "falling leaves always land near the roots of the tree."[5] But for Hing it is impossible to maintain that connection: with the world at war, he knows he will never be able to return to China to see his younger brother and join his ancestors for his final trip. Seeing his homeland vandalized and on the verge of another civil war makes him even more melancholic about a world he has forever lost.

One day in 1943, Hing's eldest son, now carrying the heavy burden of running the struggling business, arrives in Tlalpan to give his father his weekly allowance. But instead of handing it to him, he throws the money on the table, telling him with frustration: "Here it is, for you to spend on your useless children!" This leaves Hing speechless and shaken, wondering what he did wrong that his children speak to him in such an unfilial manner. In truth, Hing continues to host expensive family parties and distribute money to his younger children, as he has always done. But there are too many of them and the money amassed all these years disappears quickly.

One Sunday in April 1944, all the family and friends are gathered around him to celebrate St George's Day. For dessert, large watermelons are served on a fountain in the garden. Hing is seventy-eight years old, and today is a symbolic day for him: not only is it the day of his patron saint but the number four in Chinese is pronounced like the word death and, therefore, April 1944 is a month that represents death. My mother, nine years old, suffers from angina and is watching the party from her upper-floor window. Suddenly she sees her grandfather in her room, which surprises her since he rarely climbs the stairs. She will later remember with emotion that he hugs her, saying goodbye to his Chinese granddaughter, one of the last people he sees. He goes back down the stairs, takes a digestive liquor, forbidden to him as he has a mild skin infection, and excuses himself from the party, taking his leave in the library. A few minutes later a loud bang is heard. Concha rushes to her room in tears, immediately changing herself into black clothes. Her father has just shot himself in the throat. Years later my mother will tell me that "Grandpa Hing never did anything halfway." He has chosen to die on a day that is significant in both the Western and the Chinese calendars—quite appropriate for a Chinese-turned-Mexican. This is not a Catholic way to end his life, but if he has adopted many of Mexico's traditions, religion is not one of them. Suicide is not condemned in China as it is in the West, and Confucian principles even consider it to be honorable if it is done to protect one's dignity and virtue.

The next day he is brought to his cemetery where there are five graves, one in the center for him and Cruz and one at each corner for his children. Hing has prepared everything. "Let the young people live!" he had repeated to Concha a few days earlier. With eight surviving children and already more than ten grandchildren, the next two links in the chain of the Leon family are assured; he has done his duty and is ready for his voyage to the afterlife. Contrary to Chinese tradition, for his last trip, he leaves instructions that he be buried not in a silk robe but in a three-piece suit and not in his native village but in Mexico, which has become his new home and where he hopes all his descendants will one day join him in his grave. Hing is certainly not expecting to come back to haunt his family, like those ghosts of Chinese migrants who are lost in a foreign land, longing for their bones to be shipped across the ocean. The Leon children mourn their beloved father, who has worked tirelessly and selflessly all his life, never failing them and without ever asking for anything in return. Hing may have given them too much, failing to instill in them the sense of sacrifice, discipline and hard work that comes from growing up as a destitute young man. Ironically, he toiled all his life so that his children would become true Mexicans, not migrants like him, which unfortunately also meant that they grew up without the migrants' values of struggle. A few weeks later, his son Alejandro lovingly carves a beautiful stone bust of his father, which still stands proudly today above his grave in his verdant cemetery in Mexico City.

The writer Lin Yutang notes that, for Chinese people, the world is full of spirits, but unlike the powerful Greek gods having fun on Mount Olympus, the wellbeing of Chinese ancestral spirits in the afterlife is precarious, requiring that their memory be celebrated by their descendants.[6] Among other things, the Chinese are asked to regularly pray and make offerings to their ancestors, such as during the aptly named Hungry Ghosts Festival.[7] The Chinese believe the next world is a shadow of this one and that the dead have everything in the world below which they had on earth, except that everything there exists as shadows instead of substance.[8] Since ancient times, the Chinese have conceived death as a journey requiring ritual prayers and sacrifices on the part of the living. Importantly, being the basis of Chinese civilization, the spirits in the afterlife do not follow distant and individual paths, but on the contrary remain connected to their descendants in a never-ending spiritual chain.

Hing hopes that his family will practice ancestor worship in his honor, as the further back his descendants honor their ancestors, the larger the Leung clan will be. A remnant of their pre-Columbian culture, Mexicans are also famous worldwide for celebrating the Day of the Dead, or Día de Muertos, which is very similar to the Chinese "Tomb-Sweeping Day."[9] Strangely, in both traditions, Chinese and Mexican, where cooking plays an essential cultural role, it is customary to share food with the dead, another similarity between the two countries which Hing notices.

Shortly after his death, the large Tlalpan house is sold, and, although El Dragon de Oro is bequeathed to Melchor, each son and daughter receives an equal share of the inheritance, showing Hing's wish to maintain the family's unity after his death. With their share, Concha and her brother Juan set up their own store in Mexico City, which they name Shanghai, but this venture is a fiasco, my grandmother losing what little money Yaiwai and Hing had left her. Her younger siblings, Lola and Pablo, open a pharmacy, which also ends up in failure. Doing business turns out to be more difficult than they expected, none of them making any money. Although equal partnerships, in all the stores' promotional leaflets the younger brother appears as the sole owner, with the elder sister as the sales representative, revealing the misogyny of the era.

On the other hand, under Melchor's wise leadership El Dragon de Oro recovers in post-war Mexico, regaining its clients lost during the war and enjoying a few more profitable years. The store remains a family business until the end, employing many of Hing's grandchildren and paying for their schooling, thus supporting the whole family, exactly as Hing would have wished. But over the years, the novelty of buying Chinese products as luxury items gradually goes out of fashion. Today, curio shops in Chinatowns around the world are better known for their cheap trinkets than for the beautiful and expensive art items that Hing used to sell at the turn of the century. The Leon children thus see the world their father built slowly vanish. If in recent centuries rich Westerners bought Chinese luxury goods in exchange for cheap Western manufactured products, today it is exactly the opposite, with the rich Chinese buying Western luxury goods in exchange for their cheap "made in China" articles, a world turned upside down, where Hing would no longer have a place. If Chairman Mao did not manage to get rid of the mercantile instinct of his people, decades of decrying the old ways sadly resulted in the death of thousands of Chinese artisanal traditions, the skills needed to make many old handicrafts falling into oblivion. Nor would Hing now recognize his village in Hoksaan, which is entirely buried under an industrial zone.

* * *

In the 1960s, after having survived fifteen changes of Mexican president over seven decades, El Dragon de Oro went into insolvency, unable to pay its many liabilities, closing its doors forever. Shortly afterwards, unwilling to face his creditors, to whom he had promised high rates of return, and who included family members, Melchor, like his father and sister before him, took his own life, believing this to be the only honorable path to take. None of his brothers was able or willing to repay the liabilities and resuscitate the business. The world that Hing had built was no more.

Decades later, Hing's legacy is not to be found in the inheritance he left, which was spent long ago, or in the few Chinese antiques he left behind, which are now scattered around the world. Instead, what remains are the strong family values he instilled in his children, as well as the memories of El Dragon de Oro and of the grand life he was once able to give his extended family. His three youngest sons worked for many years in the travel industry, a profession where they could use their English while keeping a connection with

Asia. In his eighties, sensing that I had an interest in the family's history, Pablo, Hing's second youngest son, drove me to Tlalpan, showing me with pride the large block which was once the grand family residence, now redeveloped into smaller properties. Reflecting the love they received, all his sons became respected and loving Mexican patriarchs themselves, with kind and good-humored character, and they cherished the memory of their father. If no one now remembers how to cook Chinese food or speak Cantonese, one habit which survives is playing the game of Mahjong, which is still practiced by Hing's grandchildren to this day at family reunions—but without betting money, since Hing would have disapproved.

Cruz ended her days in peace, surrounded by her children, who were all married in church, and her many grandchildren, who were all baptized. The day, sixty years earlier, when she had left Acaponeta in the state of Nayarit, holding the hand of a tall and enigmatic foreigner, now formed a hazy dream in her memory. This man had been her faithful and devoted husband for fifty years; he was not Christian by faith, but had been Christian in his rectitude, deeds and words. Her prayers had been answered, God having made of all her children true Mexicans, and she saw this as a sign from him that one day they would all meet in heaven, her beloved Hing and their entire family. With Hing and Cruz, two ancient traditions came together, Chinese and Mexican, each with different views about the afterlife, but both believing in spirits, life after death, and ancestor worship, and merging into one in the Leon family.

18

FORGOTTEN BY HISTORY

During his tenure as Mexico's president from 1934–40, Lázaro Cárdenas took control of the army and took power away from the generals, while implementing the largest program of social and agrarian reforms and privatizations in Mexico's history. These reforms were fairer than those of his predecessors, massively redistributing land to the poor and taking measures such as providing free books in schools. More than twenty million hectares were distributed to 800,000 farmers compared to only seven million hectares during the regime of the generals.[1] He also expropriated and nationalized foreign companies while ending the anti-Chinese campaigns. In 1936, former-President Calles was forced into exile in the United States, where, with a copy of *Mein Kampf* under his arm, he told journalists that he was "expelled from Mexico for fighting communism."[2]

In the 1930s, a victim of an international sugar crisis and poor management practices,[3] El Mante Sugar Company faced financial difficulties and was embroiled in conflicts with employees and sugar cane producers. For these reasons, stating that it was "founded with money from the nation and by people whose duty was to elevate the integrity of the revolutionary regime,"[4] President Cárdenas decided in 1939 to expropriate El Mante Sugar Company in order to turn it into a cooperative. A parcel of 1,276 hectares, part of the old Hacienda Canton, was also distributed among eighty-five local families. Under the leadership of Aarón Sáenz, the company, which was now owned by the generals, sued the government in the Supreme Court for fair compensation. They were still politically influential, and the court ruled in their favor; the new president Ávila Camacho, in power from 1940, was also more accommodating to the generals than his predecessor. In 1943, the government thus paid an indemnity of 22.5 million pesos, a shockingly large amount for a company in default of its financial obligations. After repayment of loans and expenses, this left eleven million pesos to be shared among the owners,[5] the equivalent of thirty million dollars today, of which Foon Chuck is likely to have received nothing or very little.

Making use of the indemnity received, over the following decades Aarón Sáenz became known as the "King of Mexican Sugar," and one of the country's most powerful businessmen. In 1992, President Salinas de Gortari even "returned" El Mante Sugar Company to the Sáenz family, demonstrating his industrial dynasty's influence and close links with politicians across regimes and generations, with the same political party founded by President Calles still firmly in power by then. The Sáenz family sold the El Mante Sugar Company in 2021 to a foreign sugar conglomerate.

In the late 1930s, with most Chinese in exile and the anti-Chinese groups gone, animosity toward those who remained disappeared. The Chinese Mexicans continued to operate their small retail stores and laundries, their customers slowly returning over time. In 1940, an inspection tour by the Chinese legation revealed that in ten cities where massacres had occurred, a good relationship now existed between the remaining Chinese and the Mexicans, including in Torreón and El Mante. This was the realization of something Foon Chuck had worked tirelessly all his life to promote, namely a friendly relationship between Chinese and Mexicans. In 1945, to celebrate the allies' victory in the Second World War, the small community of El Mante, where Foon Chuck still resided, raised both the Chinese and Mexican flags, singing both national anthems and bowing three times each to photographs of the Mexican and Chinese presidents,[6] demonstrating their shared allegiance.

After the Second World War, a survey conducted in Monterrey—a city where many descendants of Foon Chuck and Hing still live today—revealed that out of fifty-five male Chinese in the city, only two had oriental wives while more than half had Mexican partners, and they had together more than 210 mixed children.[7] After the war, a few schools for the Chinese opened in various cities, each enrolling more than a hundred students, but none survived the decade due to a lack of funding, their teachers not being paid enough.⁸ This only further accelerated the assimilation of second- and third-generation Chinese. Unlike in the United States, there were simply no Chinese communities left with enough critical mass to grow organically and preserve their Chinese identity, meaning that they were destined to completely assimilate in the end.

In 1939 Cárdenas's Expropriation Act came into force, which expropriated the assets of many foreign companies. Foon Chuck found himself with only forty hectares of land in El Limon, which he then sold to a general, fearing that this land would be confiscated from him again.⁹ The parcels of land held by his son Benjamín, his brother Yun Wu, and other Chinese, were also expropriated.¹⁰ In the 1980s, fearing that even their small remaining plot would be turned into a museum or confiscated, the family removed what was left of the ruins of Foon Chuck's home. This put an end to the history of the Chinese in El Mante, which had begun when Foon Chuck bought land there in 1897, the story of a dream come true and then lost.

Unlike with Hing, there is no record of Foon Chuck having returned to China after the Mexican Revolution. He was presumably too busy fighting for his agricultural project in Mexico. For many years, he remained a partner in the Hotel del Ferrocarril and several other businesses in Piedras Negras, many of them held under Mexican nominees to avoid confiscation, which were not returned to his family after his death. According to popular legend, the abandoned hotel is haunted today by the ghost of its last administrator, a Chinese man called Chong, who committed suicide in one of the rooms after having lost a fortune playing cards.

Oblivious to ghosts, Foon Chuck spent his retirement between Piedras Negras and his small farmhouse in El Limon of less than two hectares, alongside the Guayalejo River, where he grew fruit and vegetables until his death in 1950 at the age of eighty-eight, three years after Cristina. In China, gardens are designed to provide escape and consolation from the outside world. James Cahill, an expert on Chinese art and culture, said that "spending a day in a Chinese garden, a thousand years could pass outside,"¹¹ while Laozi recommended contemplation and retirement to purify one's nature. Tending his garden is hence an appropriate way for an educated

Chinese man to finish his life. According to Confucius, a gentleman must guard himself against female temptation when he is young and his qi or energy is unsettled, against contentiousness in his prime when his energy has become unyielding, and against acquisitiveness in old age when his energy is declining. Until his death, Foon Chuck continued receiving his weekly newspaper from San Francisco's Chinatown, devoting himself, as prescribed by Confucius, to his childhood passions, Chinese poetry and calligraphy.

Ten years before his death, he wrote two poems, lovingly kept to this day by the Chinese daughters of his son Angel in Hong Kong. A living tribute to his legacy, they emphasize the important features of Foon Chuck's existence.

Reflecting on myself and my soul, born in an old country,	相颜精灵生故国
After sixty years, I am young again, but now someone different in a foreign land,	甲子重少为异人
In my farm, I had a benevolent heart, everyone looked up to me,	农业慈心众群仰
People's welfare and charitable deeds bring blessings and prosperity to all forever.	民生善事永其祥

In new clothes, I was a young man with great ambitions and goals,	新衣少年壮志大
These sixty years made me a person quite rare in this world,	甲子造人世罕见
In a foreign land, I helped everyone daily and everyone was loveable,	番 济群众可爱
With my ancestors' blessings, I will have prosperity and peace forever.	祖宗福佑有恒泰

Around the same time, he also dictated a short autobiography in Spanish, listing the main events in his life, showing pride in his journey from China to Mexico and a desire to leave something to posterity. In 1946, Foon Chuck received a long tribute from the first Chinese newspaper in San Francisco, *Chung Sai Yat Po*, which details his life as a philanthropist and businessman. However, these two biographies only allude to the events in El Mante and completely omit those of Torreón, wanting to avoid trouble for his descendants. In these documents, and despite his ultimate defeat by greater and uncontrollable forces, Foon Chuck shows his philosophical side, glory and fulfillment existing in the aim and the journey itself rather than the results. Oblivion in the public eye does not mean that the heart has forgotten though. In 1946, a Torreón resident remembered that:

> around the municipal cemetery, there still existed some very extensive open areas where, on the Día de Muertos, a number of luxury automobiles used to park. Then Chinese families in deep mourning would leave a glass-framed photograph on the ground, light a small lamp or candle, add a plate of white rice, kneel, pray silently, and after a while, retrieve the portrait, leave the rest, and retire, all this before the curious eyes of those present.[12]

Despite having lost his fortune, Foon Chuck remained a respected leader of the Chinese community until the end of his life; a photograph from that time shows him surrounded by dozens of old Chinese gentlemen. Instead of becoming embittered by the abuses against his people, he stayed on good terms with some of his former partners, ending his days among them in El Mante. He left in his library various books in Chinese, some Christian and others about Chinese philosophy, showing his attachment to both his ancestors and his American family. Despite his journey as visionary and entrepreneur, Foon Chuck died a modest man. His son Rubén lived with him until the end, inheriting after his death the small property.[13] Foon Chuck is buried in El Mante municipal cemetery, but after the loss of the register in a fire in 1978, his exact burial place is no longer recorded. On his death certificate, under citizenship, the word "Mexican" is scribbled over the word "Chinese," which has become almost illegible, as if he, at eighty-eight years old, still had to demonstrate his nationality. This is ironic for someone who all his life was called "the most Mexican Chinese" by friends, politicians and journalists.[14]

Today, Foon Chuck is rightly and affectionately remembered by the locals of El Mante as one of the founding fathers of this thriving agricultural region and as a pioneer of mass irrigation agriculture. In an odd irony, a Chinese Mexican, José Chan Ramirez, a Mexican presidential appointee, became administrator of El Mante's sugar cooperative from 1947 to 1960, building various schools and public monuments in El Mante, maybe a posthumous nod to Foon Chuck. In 1986, the Chuck family received official recognition from the government of El Mante, and in 2018 a small commemorative plaque was unveiled in a primary school in El Limon in the presence of Rubén's widow and Foon Chuck's youngest granddaughter, his only two descendants in El Limon. A government official mentioned to me that the city did not accept a proposal to erect a statue, feeling that it would not yet be well received. In cadastral maps, a district of El Mante continues to be called Canton. In Chinese tradition, properties are shared equally among all sons, but Foon Chuck's will bequeathed his small farm to Santiago and Rubén—although Santiago died before Foon Chuck and so his descendants took up his inheritance. The younger siblings continued to live in their large home in Piedras Negras until 1954, the property being later sold and the proceeds shared equally amongst his descendants.

* * *

After Hing's death, Concha, now in her forties, is completely destitute. She is forced to move into a small rental apartment in a middle-to-lower-class neighborhood of Mexico City. It is quite an adjustment for the family after their mansions in Shanghai and Tlalpan, and her children feel ashamed of their home as they grow up. After almost ten years of service, Concha must also dismiss their beloved Mexican governess Felipa, leaving her three children heartbroken. To support them, she works hard as a saleswoman in a city center perfume store. She never remarries, remaining faithful to Yaiwai, her "Chinito" as she affectionately calls him. Concha lives in a Mexico that is different from two decades earlier, one that has put the revolution behind it and is more prosperous, just and welcoming.

She too has matured and is more confident after her experiences with Yaiwai and in China. Her poverty matters less to her now, since she knows her value and place in the world. True to her character, she never boasts to her children about their early years or Chinese civilization; they are in Mexico for a reason, and she accepts with humility the loss of her fortune and the tragedies and failings afflicting her husband's country, realizing that Mexico is now their only home.

Like her father before her, she wants her children to be fully Mexican, while teaching them not to be ashamed of their origins. Despite Yaiwai's absence, she manages to give them confidence, the same confidence that exists in many migrants, despite or perhaps because of all the vicissitudes that life places before them.

* * *

Although most of the acute animosity against the Chinese had disappeared by the 1940s, some of the racism continued for a few more decades, before Mexico became a more cosmopolitan society. Like their parents before them and many Eurasians of that generation, my two uncles remembered the bullying in their schools; they were always placed in a corner in annual school photographs, as if to show that they belonged, but not fully. In contrast, perhaps due to her cheerful disposition, or because she is among girls, my mother has fond memories of her girls' school, not remembering much discrimination.

In his 1947 painting *Dream of a Sunday Afternoon in Alameda Central Park*, Diego Rivera depicts an imaginary scene from before the revolution, featuring a policeman expelling a poor Indian from the park, a common scene at the time (see Chapter Six) other than the fact that the policeman in Rivera's painting has Chinese traits and is made to look evil. This mural is Mexico's most iconic and revered painting, supposed to show the racial and social injustice suffered by many Mexicans over the years. Yet in a strange and unexpected twist it also inadvertently illustrates the racial biases of the painter himself. As in the United States in the previous century, Chinese migrants are portrayed again as being on the side of the capitalist oppressors. This was from a painter with communist sympathies, but whose main clients and patrons throughout his life would be American capitalists.

* * *

My grandmother manages to make ends meet, offering a dignified life to her children, though they never have much money. She is careful, not wasting anything, keeping every old piece of clothing and paper. Her life in both the Wong and Leon families has taught her that fate can take one's fortune away, and she prefers to save for future rainy days. Unable to dress expensively, she still manages to be elegant in a simple way, showing her children that elegance is an attitude rather than a label. She has known wealth in the past, and she now lives from her memories of Yaiwai, which are more than enough for her. Being a Christian, she knows that they will meet again one day.

In 1950, a new tragedy strikes when her eldest son, then a bright nineteen-year-old student, is killed in an accident, so that within the space of only twelve years she has lost three men from her life. Years later she will move in with us, and I will never see her crying or displaying any sadness; on the contrary she will often smile at my mother and me. Perhaps this is because her eyes had by then run out of tears after so much crying; or, more probably, it is because her heart never really left her Shanghai home with her beloved Yaiwai. Like her father Hing, she is not one to complain.

Not having enough money, Concha asks my mother, aged only fourteen, to give up her studies and work as a secretary for a large company in Mexico City. Although a common occurrence for middle-class girls at the time, this is a major blow for my mother. Whereas Concha was bold in her marriage, she is not bold enough now to pay for her daughter's high school. My mother catches up two decades later, finishing high school by taking evening classes after work, followed by a master's degree in psychology of education at the Sorbonne University in Paris when she is in her forties. She studies purely out of interest, not being motivated by money or career; one day she admits that she wants me to have a university-educated mother, but maybe she does it in memory of her father, knowing that he would have wished this for her.

In her late teens, although she is deeply attached to Mexico and her family, being independent and curious to discover the world my mother decides to leave Mexico to work in the United States. She refuses the fate of her two aunts, realizing that opportunities for advancement for a poor, uneducated woman of color are limited in post-war Mexican society. Like her mother before her she chooses the path of exile, but unlike her, she takes it alone, the first among all the grandchildren of the Wong or Leon families to do so. After working in the United States for around five years, on a return trip to Mexico, she meets the young children of her cousin, the eldest daughter of Hing's son Melchor, recently married to a Swiss missionary in Mexico and now living in Geneva. She is impressed by how well educated her nephews are and soon she is on a cruise ship to Europe, where she settles permanently. After being born in the "Paris of the Orient" and growing up in the "Paris of the Americas," she finally settles in the City of Light itself in her thirties. It is as if her early exile as a young orphan had predestined her to a life of travel and rootlessness. Decades later, one of Foon Chuck's youngest granddaughters tells of how, when she was in her teens, being shown a photograph of my mother in Europe inspired her to pursue a career outside of Piedras Negras.

* * *

With the People's Republic of China closed to the world and most Chinese already out of Mexico, my mother has lived her adult life mostly alienated from Chinese culture. She has Asian features but never had a Chinese community to identify herself with, and never spoke the language. Cherishing the memories of her three missing relatives, she found China in books, which made her proud of its ancient civilization. Like her mother before her, she was not troubled by what she was, but by the ignorance and condescension of others towards her. She sought the friendship of intellectuals, whose curiosity towards China made them more sympathetic towards its plight, and she found in Europe an educated class more drawn towards and curious about oriental civilizations than in California and post-war Mexico. Also, the almost complete absence of Chinese migrants in Europe made her feel more special and authentically Chinese than in the United States.

My mother and my uncle never dwelled on their past: indeed, they were proud to be Mexicans. Young refugees, they had found a loving family and, despite the bigotry, a mostly welcoming society in Mexico. In the 1990s, my mother returned to Shanghai for the first time, finding that her Edinburgh Road house had been torn down decades ago.

Solidly settled in Mexico, her brother never expressed any interest in returning to China. He married a strong-willed young woman from northern Mexico and became a prosperous businessman. His wife is the proud granddaughter of a heroine and leader of the Mexican Revolution, Josefa Arjona (1875–1948), a founder of the Mexican socialist movement, an early feminist, and a liberal political activist all her life. She and her husband, a railroad worker, were forced to go into exile in the United States, where they too worked in a hotel in Eagle Pass. After the revolution, the couple returned to Mexico where their family settled in the north of the country, a story of exile which parallels that of Foon Chuck, but at the opposite end of the political spectrum. My Eurasian cousins inherited their business acumen from their Chinese grandparents and their fierce and indomitable spirit from their Mexican ones.

My uncle never left Mexico, except for occasional trips to the United States. Like Hing and other Chinese Mexicans of his generation, he grew up worried about his migrant status, preferring to never risk it by leaving the country. He was never ashamed of being Chinese—on the contrary—but searching for his roots was not something that concerned him, unlike my mother. I visited him with my young Chinese wife and our two children when he was in his seventies. His English being rudimentary, they could not easily talk to each other, but he was moved that his sister's son had married a Shanghai girl. Surprisingly, the two immediately got along well and were quickly joking and laughing together, having magically managed to understand each other, connected by common origins. This was the first time in seventy years that my uncle was speaking with a relative from China in his own home, and it was as if something had opened in his heart—perhaps long-forgotten images of a land forever lost to him.

The Chinese Mexicans who were expelled from the state of Sonora in the 1930s, many now stateless, resettled in their province of Kwangtung. They brought back their mixed families and their Mexican customs and ways of life. The popular Mexican Bun, or Pineapple Bun, dates from that period, ubiquitous today in most bakeries and on dim sum menus in Hong Kong and Macau. It is the Chinese equivalent of the concha, a fluffy brioche bread, created by French bakers in Mexico in the seventeenth century and to this day a favorite Mexican breakfast. This is the story of a French pastry becoming a Mexican sweet bread (aptly sharing my grandmother's nickname) and ending up as a Chinese dim sum. Fortunately, unlike people, good recipes do not need visas to travel.

These exiled mixed families went through difficult times in China, especially the stateless Mexican wives, who sometimes discovered that their husbands were already married to Chinese women. They struggled to assimilate into their husbands' rural and poor families, where women were relegated to secondary roles. After the war against Japan, they suffered from the Communist Revolution, when most overseas Chinese were treated suspiciously by the new regime. These families were discriminated against even further for being of mixed blood, some taking refuge in the Portuguese colony of Macau, which shared with Mexico a Catholic and Iberian culture. Rejected on racial ground by both Mexico and China, these families found a haven in Macau's Catholic Church.[15] In 1940, despite numerous petitions, the Mexican government showed its inhumanity by refusing to allow these families to return. It was not until 1960 that a small minority of the Chinese Mexicans from Sonora were finally allowed back, thirty years after their expulsion. This event closed the final chapter of the turbulent history of the Chinese in Mexico. In the 1990s, one of the returnees, now an old man, recounted how he never went out without his citizenship certificate, carefully folded in a plastic pouch, still traumatized and fearful of being deported all over again.[16]

In the 1960s, a Hong Kong primary school textbook in Chinese on famous overseas migrants featured a one-page biography of Foon Chuck. He is portrayed as sincere, honest and passionate about philanthropic work and helping the poor, having earned the trust of his fellow migrants and become their leader. Although naïve in style, this text shows the high prestige achieved by Foon Chuck, not only in Mexico but also in China, where he was still celebrated years after his death. Starting from the 1950s, overseas Chinese museums opened across China, including in Peking, Canton, Amoy and Kongmoon, recognizing the important role migrants have played in Chinese history for the betterment of their homeland.

Like the Galleon Trade two centuries earlier, the activities of the Chinese in Mexico left only scant memories in both countries. Now completely assimilated into Mexican society, most of the descendants of Chinese immigrants to Mexico preferred to forget these past tales of exclusion. They often find themselves to be the descendants of both victims and perpetrators of racial violence,[17] a heritage which attests to Mexico's mixed society and cultural melting pot but which does not necessarily encourage memories of the past. As of 2023, there are only 70,000 descendants of Chinese immigrants in Mexico, as well as 25,000 Chinese nationals recently immigrated to the country, together making up less than 0.1 per cent of Mexico's population. This figure contrasts with the more than one million Peruvians of Chinese origin (three per cent of its population), who call themselves Tusanos (meaning "born on the land"),[18] and the projected three million foreign-born Chinese in Canada by 2031 (six per cent of its population),[19] two countries that did not implement the kinds of extensive discriminatory policies against the Chinese that Mexico did, Canada even continuing to welcome them.

All my uncles, aunts and cousins, whether Chuck, Wong or Leon, feel entirely Mexican today. While having an eighth or a quarter Chinese blood, some of them also have Indian ancestry and hence have noticeable Asian features, contributing further to the complex Mexican melting pot. They are sometimes called "El Chino" or "La China" by their friends, but this is a sign of affection today, worn with pride. Strangely, few in my large family had heard of Torreón or had any knowledge of the family's history. Their fathers and forefathers preferred to forget and blend in, hoping that Mexico had now changed, and that the massacres of the past would never happen again, rendering those memories superfluous.

In the 1890s, a young Chinese man from Kwangtung province, surnamed Lok, arrived in the United States, settling just a few miles from Tacoma, Washington, from where the Chinese had been expelled a few years earlier (see Chapter Four). Almost a hundred years later, his grandson Gary Locke became the first Chinese American state governor in the continental United States and later secretary of commerce and ambassador to China. In the 1910s, during the Mexican Revolution, another young Chinese man from Kwangtung, named Chong, arrived in the Mexican state of Hidalgo just north of Mexico City, where he opened a café and married a Mexican woman. A hundred years later, their grandson Miguel

Ángel Osorio Chong also became a state governor and then Mexico's secretary of state. These two parallel lives across the US Mexico border illustrate the remarkable progress of some Chinese migrant families and the development of civil rights in both countries over the last century, something unimaginable in the time of Foon Chuck and Hing. On immigration, Congressman Gary Locke has written: "The constant influx of new cultures, new ideas and new ways of looking at old problems is a big part of the reason why America has been the most dynamic economy in the world for well over a century."[20]

In the 1990s, the Mexican ministry of education requested unsuccessfully that some dark passages of the state of Coahuila's history be removed from a third-grade textbook, including the Torreón massacre.[21] Around 2011, a remembrance plaque was placed on the former Chinese Bank's walls in Torreón to commemorate the centenary of the massacre, but it was then quickly removed, not being to everyone's taste.[22] At the request of the Chinese community, a street was officially named after Foon Chuck, again offending the residents' sensibilities and being quickly renamed.[23] In 2007, in a remembrance ceremony of the centenary of the city, attended by the Chinese community, the mayor, and the Chinese ambassador, a bronze statue of a Chinese horticultural worker was unveiled at the Venustiano Carranza Park in Torreón, on land which was once cultivated by the Chinese.[24] Days later, the statue was vandalized and had to be removed for safekeeping. On 17 May 2021, almost fifteen years later, after being restored, it was returned to the park in an official ceremony attended by the Chinese ambassador and this time Mexican President López Obrador himself, who made an official apology to the Chinese government for the events of Torreón.[25] A local activist told me that this apology was still opposed by many local politicians, who insisted that the past is better left forgotten.

A historian pointed out that in the background of this ceremony, meetings took place between Chinese investors and local politicians, ever eager to attract Chinese capital into Mexico, just like Porfirio Díaz before them. If more articles are now being written about Torreón, some of them paint the Chinese as merely powerless coolies, victims of racial violence, while purposely ignoring the fact that some Chinese were successful businessmen, with resentment being a key reason for the massacres. Today, China has become Mexico's second-largest trading partner, although far behind the United States, showing that the Mexico China relationship has come a long way since my ancestors' first trip to San Francisco 140 years ago. In recent years, to take advantage of Mexico's trade agreement with the United States, Chinese industrial investments in the country have been on the rise, reminiscent of Mexico's earlier role for Chinese migrants as a bridge to the United States.[26] Behind the façade of political messaging, there may now be a genuine desire to continue the rich history of trans-Pacific exchanges and friendships, which began centuries ago.

CONCLUSION

Writing this book has been a journey of discovery into my family's history and that of the Chinese, Americans, and Mexicans. I will always remember how I felt when I first heard about Foon Chuck, his Chinese school, his farm, and his association with Kang Youwei. Those stories had long been forgotten in my family, leading me on a long journey of research to bring them back to life. The many historical connections between facts, like lost puzzle pieces, have formed little by little a coherent image. While Foon Chuck and Hing spent their lives preserving or building roots in three countries, I fear they would have disliked a book where the history of these nations is judged. They would have probably reminded me of the famous Chinese saying: "family disgrace should never be aired in public."[1] Yet the history of China, the US and Mexico during the late nineteenth and early twentieth centuries is still rich in teachings for today, as a lot has changed since then—and not so much.

Like most educated Chinese of his generation, Foon Chuck was guided all his life by his Confucian education, to which he later added a solid Christian foundation. By contrast, the Chinese born after the Communist Revolution and until the reform era of the 1990s, which was mostly concerned with economic growth and modernization, grew up in a society which openly rejected Confucius' moral and political legacy, as well as any other spiritual faiths. Before that, the Nationalists blamed Confucius and religion in general for China's lack of development, while the Maoists criticized him as the father of feudalism. Since 2000, Chinese regimes have brought back Confucius' moral teachings, in both education and politics. In parallel, Chinese intellectuals and the educated class have made fashionable again the study of the country's ancient sages. This has happened only after China experienced a period of economic growth, which created a newly affluent class. Less concerned about daily subsistence than their forefathers, this class has now time to dwell on China's ancient culture and other contemplative and spiritual pursuits, which I hope reflects the future for Chinese society.

The attempt to establish a Chinese colony in Mexico differed in significant ways from the experiences of Chinese immigrants in Southeast Asia or more recently in Africa. The lives of my ancestors involved an attachment to two distinct cultures and a desire to get the best of both worlds, as Kang Youwei had dreamt. Returning to or even simply reconnecting with China was more difficult for my ancestors than for Chinese migrants in Southeast Asia or young Chinese emigrants today. Over a fifty-year period, China has modernized and enriched itself in exceptional ways, making travel between East and West much easier. The choices available to Chinese emigrants today therefore differ from those that presented themselves to my ancestors. The latter faced difficulties in their journeys that made their destinations seem more exotic than would be the case now, while old China was a dangerous place, to a degree that is almost unimaginable for contemporary migrants. In the future, as the Chinese population ages and becomes wealthier, there will likely be much less emigration from China. Thus, the experience of this Chinese colony in Mexico is almost impossible to replicate today, given the radical changes in the global political and social context: the magic of history is that it presents unique circumstances and exceptional phenomena. Foon Chuck and Hing suffered and struggled all their lives but at the same time were explorers and cultural pioneers, whose courage, journeys and unique experiences can only be admired.

The reception Foon Chuck and Hing received in the United States directly impacted their future relationship with that country. Foon Chuck was welcomed by Reverend Loomis, and he spoke English and made American friends throughout his life, thus contributing to the expansion of the United States' presence in Mexico. On the other hand, Hing failed to establish any human connection with the United States, and had no interest later in doing business with Americans. Although the generalization may not always apply, this illustrates the long-term economic benefits on a host country of an investment in migrants' education, both practical and spiritual.

CONCLUSION

It is obvious that Foon Chuck's exceptional life achievements can be explained in part by his formative years with Reverend Loomis, who set him on a path never trodden before by any Chinese.

Hing and Foon Chuck's stories thus display two types of Chinese migration. Hing's story exemplifies a purely mercantilist model of migration; this was the most widespread kind of Chinese migration. Foon Chuck's experience, involving agriculture, infrastructure and finance, along with a more complex relationship with local populations, exemplifies a rarer kind of migrant story. His path was more ambitious, but also more controversial, especially for Mexico as his host country, since it resembled the Western model of colonization. In his case, through his marriage, friends and projects, Foon Chuck displayed an attachment to his host country rather than a desire to exploit it for the sole benefit of his home country. He reinvested most of his money in Mexico and employed both Chinese and Mexicans (the latter also being his main clients), and had many local associates who helped him throughout his life.

Foon Chuck and Hing also diverged in terms of their approach to integration, although both of them formed mixed families. While Foon Chuck strove to preserve his language and culture for his children, recreating a Chinese world in America, Hing made a different choice by forbidding his children from learning Chinese or traveling to China. These were difficult choices and maybe they both regretted them, Foon Chuck during the revolution, seeing the dangers of not assimilating, and Hing when he got to Shanghai, seeing his daughter flourish by reconnecting with her roots. There is no right or wrong choice or ideal mix between two cultures; it remains a personal decision of second- or third-generation migrants to reconnect or not with their culture of origin. An interest in one's cultural background is not necessarily an obstacle to proper integration into a host culture, but on the contrary can be a source of mutual enrichment. Fortunately, migrants today are freer to choose as they please, whereas the choice was more difficult for migrants and their children in the last century, with circumstances often forcing them in one direction or another.

By today's standards, two aspects of Foon Chuck's life may be considered questionable: his role as a labor supervisor and organizer, especially in mining, and his involvement with politicians to achieve his goals. If he profited from the labor of his fellow Chinese, he also helped them find jobs while protecting them against abuse by their employers. His business must hence be viewed in the historical context of the time, when Chinese were forced to migrate to places without labor protection laws. His decision to discourage his people from working in mining and his many philanthropic activities prove that he cared for their wellbeing. Similarly, seeking political patronage was common, when rules and norms about what constituted corruption were different from today. Foreign investments in most emerging economies required political patronage; those were the rules of the game, as they continue to be today in some countries. Through his decisions, Foon Chuck only put himself on an equal footing with the other foreign investors in Mexico.

Like Foon Chuck, the Chinese diaspora today is mostly characterized by a desire not to get involved in local politics, for a number of reasons. First, like the early Chinese Americans, they may not feel fully comfortable about their citizenship compared to natives. Second, there is in China a clear differentiation between civil society and the world of politics, with the latter being strictly the business of the bureaucracy with its lifelong civil servants. If the state has always had the right to scrutinize and influence society, the reverse is not true. The Chinese in general tend therefore to be less involved in politics than in other countries, this phenomenon being replicated in the Chinese diaspora, both in the last century and today. Kang Youwei also considered his diasporic project to be essentially commercial and civilizational, much less political. Third, Chinese may sometimes be less direct and expressive than Westerners in the way they communicate, which may also impact their ability to become vocal politicians in the West.

The Torreón massacre raises the question of responsibility, including what could have been done differently to avoid it. Kang Youwei felt responsible for it but only because he misjudged the political situation, not because he felt that he acted wrongly. Perhaps if the Chinese had employed more locals, formed mixed couples, redistributed profits locally, or had not monopolized certain markets, things would have turned out differently. It is unfair to blame individuals, though, for wanting to succeed, especially since they complied with Mexican laws, not acting in more predatory ways than

CONCLUSION

investors from other countries. It is the responsibility of a country's legislative body to establish appropriate employment and tax laws to ensure that migrants contribute harmoniously to their host communities. But this must be done in the interests of fairness and justice for all, something that was lacking in Porfirio Díaz's Mexico; the Chinese were unfortunately among its first victims. In hindsight, while there was xenophobia from Mexicans, there might also have been some unwillingness and maybe fear to assimilate from some Chinese, who preferred to stay within their community rather than mingle with the natives. Past economic crises also shaped exclusionary policies against migrants in both the United States and Mexico. If Chinese migrants were at first welcomed to build those two countries, when crises occurred and unemployment rose they were then persecuted and driven out. This policy pattern continues to this day, often leaving migrants in difficult situations, especially when they have sacrificed their best years or founded families in their host country. These economic cycles continue to pose major challenges to migration policies in many countries and can hopefully be managed with more fairness and justice in mind for everyone.

At the time of writing, China's growing economic might and heightened global tensions mean that some Chinese migrants fear being seen as traitors by their host countries, as persons with shifting allegiances, agents of a fifth column, or communist spies trying to steal the latest Western technologies. Others are concerned about being used by China, like pawns in a geopolitical chess game, for economic or political purposes. Less dependent on foreign remittances than decades ago, in China itself some leaders view their foreign compatriots with irritation, as political exiles, traitors, corrupt officials on the run, or simply as a sign that their country continues to fail its people socially or economically. In contrast to the reform era two decades earlier, because of government policies and xenophobia, some foreigners in China today feel unwelcome too, like the Chinese migrants in the West. These growing fears and prejudices on both sides pose a great risk to dialogue, friendly immigration and exchange between East and West, which have been the pillars of world peace and growth over the last three decades.

There is an ongoing debate in China and the West on the nature and lack of Chinese "soft power," especially compared to the cultural influence that South Korea and Japan have been able to build. With its millions of restaurateurs, students, medical doctors, and traders of all sorts working abroad, I may venture to say that the Chinese diaspora has continued to be a large component of this soft power, and at times of political repression or trouble the only component. Instead of being looked down upon or used for political purposes, it is to be hoped that migrants on both sides can simply be valued for their hard work, their economic and cultural contributions, and for the bridges they build between East and West, a relationship which in my view has become too important to fail.

From Foon Chuck's time to the present day, it is worth noting that a constant factor in my family's story has been the desire to provide each generation with a US education. In China itself, the most coveted American export remains today not the iPhone but an Ivy League spot for one's heir. Ironically, even the most conservative Chinese dream of a US liberal education for their sons and daughters. This may not be surprising for a country with such a long tradition of erudition. Maybe one day Chinese universities will no longer have anything to envy with regard to American ones, but until then, I hope this exchange continues in the future and those returning students become strong advocates of a plural and free dialogue between East and West.

This story is the continuation of other authors' efforts and is not a static one, but remains entirely open: I invite all members of my family and more broadly all those whose ancestors were involved in these events to carry on this exercise by contributing to our collective memory. I hope that other books will follow, giving rise to further exchanges and reflections. Like Kang Youwei, I dream of a world where the migrants' children of tomorrow will not have to choose allegiance between countries, but will be proud citizens of various nations, a global village that embraces cultural differences, while preserving and protecting the diversity and richness of regional cultures in each host country, which remains of paramount importance. Cultural exchange and its promotion do not mean cultural fusion, degeneration or appropriation; it simply involves reaching out and admiring the diversity that the world has to offer, and looking at other cultures while learning to appreciate the beauty of our own. Like my ancestors, immigrants have a responsibility and

CONCLUSION

an important role to play in these exchanges and dialogues between continents. A society without exchanges is one condemned to extinction; it is by learning from each other that humanity has progressed towards higher civilizations.

APPENDIX

A MEMORIAL FROM REPRESENTATIVE CHINAMEN IN AMERICA (1876)

To His Excellency Ulysses S. Grant, President of the United States of America
Sir: In the absence of any consular representative, we, the undersigned, in the name and on behalf of the Chinese people now in America, would most respectfully present for your consideration the following statements regarding the subject of Chinese immigration to this country:

We understand that it has always been the settled policy of your honorable government to welcome immigration to your shores from all countries, without let or hindrance. The Chinese are not the only people who have crossed the ocean to seek residence in this land [...]

American steamers, subsidized by your honorable government, have visited the ports of China and invited our people to come to this country to find employment and improve their condition. Our people have been coming to this country for the last twenty-five years, but up to the present time there are only 150,000 Chinese in all these United States, 60,000 of whom are in California and 30,000 in the city of San Francisco.

Our people in this country, for the most part, have been peaceable, law-abiding and industrious. They performed the largest part of the unskilled labor in the construction of the Central Pacific Railroad, as also of all other railroads on this coast. They found useful and remunerative employment in all the manufacturing establishments on this coast, in agricultural activities and in family service. While benefiting themselves with the honest reward of their daily toil, they have given satisfaction to their employers, and left all the results of their industry to enrich the State. They have not displaced white laborers from their positions, but simply multiplied the industrial enterprises of the country.

The Chinese have neither attempted nor desired to interfere with the established order of things in this country, either of politics or religion. They have opened no whiskey saloons, for the purpose of dealing out poison and degrading their fellow men. They have promptly paid their duties, their taxes, their rents and their debts. [...]

It is charged against us that no virtuous China woman has been brought to this country, and that here we have no wives nor children. The fact is that already a few hundred Chinese families have been brought here. They are all chaste, pure, keepers-at-home, not known on the public street. There are also among us a few hundred, perhaps a thousand, Chinese children born in America. The reason why so few of our families are brought to this country is, because it is contrary to the custom and against the inclination of virtuous Chinese women to go so far from home, and because the frequent outbursts of popular indignation against our people have not encouraged us to bring our families with us against their will [...]

It is charged against us that we have purchased no real estate. The general tone of public sentiment has not been such as to encourage us to invest in real estate, and yet our people have bought and now own more than $800,000 of real estate in San Francisco alone.

It is charged against us that we eat rice, fish, and vegetables. It is true that our diet is slightly different from the people of this honorable country; our tastes in these matters are not exactly alike and cannot be forced. But is this a sin on our part of sufficient gravity to be brought before the President and Congress of the United States?

It is charged that the Chinese are no benefit to this country. Are the railroads built by Chinese labor no benefit to the country? Are the manufacturing establishments, largely worked by Chinese labor, no benefit to this country? Do not the results of the daily toil of a hundred thousand men increase the riches of this country? Is it no benefit to this country that the Chinese annually pay over $2,000,000 duties at the Custom House of San Francisco? Is not the $200,000 annual poll tax paid by the Chinese any benefit? [...]

It is charged that all Chinese laboring man are slaves. This is not true in a single instance. Chinamen labor for bread. They pursue all kinds of industries for a livelihood. Is it so then that every man laboring for his livelihood is a slave? If these men are slaves, then all men laboring for wages are slaves.

It is charged that the Chinese commerce brings no benefits to American bankers and importers. But the fact is that an immense trade is carried on between China and the United States by American merchants, and all the carrying business of both countries, whether by steamers, sailing vessels or

APPENDIX

railroad, is done by Americans. No China ships are engaged in the carrying traffic between the two countries. Is it a sin to be charged against us that the Chinese merchants are able to conduct their mercantile business on their own capital? And is not the exchange of millions of dollars annually by the Chinese with the banks of this city any benefit to the banks?

We respectfully ask a careful consideration of all the foregoing statements. The Chinese are not the only people, nor do they bring the only evils that now afflict this country.[1]

NOTES

FOREWORD

1. John K. Fairbank, as cited in Shah and Wasserstrom, 2012, p. ix.

INTRODUCTION

1. US Census 2019, American Community Survey 5-year estimates, the Immigrant Learning Centre.
2. International Organization for Migration, 2021. Statistics available online at https://www.iom.int/countries/china (last accessed 12/02/22).
3. China Labour Bulletin 2021. Statistics available online at https://clb.org.hk/content/migrant-workers-and-their-children (last accessed 12/02/22).
4. Confucius, *Analects*, chapter 19, book 4. Available online at https://china.usc.edu/confucius-analects-4 (last accessed 12/02/22).
5. Hung-Hui 1992, p. 26.
6. Liu 2005, p. 19.
7. Chao 2010, p. 15.
8. Chang 2003, p. 14.
9. Lu 2010, p. 35.
10. Lu 2010, p. 28.
11. As cited in Lu 1999, Loc. 1721.
12. Henderson 2013, p. 95.
13. Chao 2010, p. 17.
14. Chinese Exclusion Act files, as cited in Chao 2010, p. 14.
15. L. Ma and C. Cartier, *The Chinese Diaspora*, cited in Chao 2010, p. 14.
16. Walter F. Wilcox's figures, as cited in Chao 2010, p. 17.
17. Walter F. Wilcox, cited in Chao 2010, p. 16.

1. A BRAVE SON

1. 天高皇帝远, Tiān Gāo Huáng Dì Yuǎn.
2. Lin Yutang, cited in Lu 1999, Loc. 532.
3. 黄宽焯, Huáng Kuān Zhuō.

4. 齐塘, Qí Táng.
5. 潭江, Tán Jiāng.
6. 黄帝, Huáng Dì.
7. Mencius 3b9, as cited in Sterckx 2019, p. 357.
8. Bergen 1902, p. 37.
9. Lee 1887, p. 18.
10. 开平, Kāi Píng.
11. 碉楼, Diāo Lóu.
12. Liu 2005, p. 22.
13. 文帝, Wén Dì.
14. 千字文, Qiān Zì Wén.
15. Liu 2005, p. 131.
16. Bergen 1902, p. 43.
17. Liu as cited in Harrison 2005, p. 25.
18. Wong 1946.
19. 台风, Tái Fēng.
20. "A Terrible Typhoon in China," *Taranaki Herald*, 25 November 1874, p. 2.
21. 道德经, Dào Dé Jīng.
22. *Tao Te Ching* 78, as quoted in Sterckx 2019, p. 359.
23. 旧金山, Jiù Jīn Shān.
24. 番鬼, Fān Guǐ.
25. 光宗耀祖, Guāng Zōng Yào Zǔ.
26. 不孝, Bù Xiào.
27. Liu as cited in Harrison 2005, p. 53.
28. Kuhn 2008, p. 15.
29. Du Ruofu 1986.
30. Zhang 2017.
31. Liu 2005, p. 16.
32. Turner 1894, p. 91.
33. Bergen 1902, p. 17.
34. Nevius 1868, p. 63.
35. Bergen 1902, p. 14.
36. Liu as cited in Harrison 2005, p. 27.
37. 风水.
38. Bergen 1902, p. 29.
39. Turner 1894, p. 112.
40. 读万卷书不如行万里路, Dú Wàn Juǎn Shū Bù Rú Xín Wàn Lǐ Lù.

2. THE ONLY WAY OUT

1. 梁庆, Liáng Qìng.
2. 良庚, Liáng Gēng.

3. 鹤山, Hè Shān.
4. 哥哥, Gē Gē.
5. 江门, Jiāng Mén.
6. 四邑, Sì Yì.
7. 养儿防老, Yǎng Er Fáng Lǎo.
8. Pruitt 1945, p. 22.
9. Lu 2010, p. 148.
10. Pruitt 1945, p. 35.
11. Dong 2000, p. 45.
12. Lu 2010, p. 32.
13. 佛山, Fó Shān.
14. 城隍爷, Chéng Huáng Yé.
15. 衙门, Yá Men.
16. Pan 1994, p. 45.
17. Bergen 1902, p. 26.
18. Spence 1981, p. 44.
19. 衣锦还乡, Yī Jǐn Huán Xiāng.
20. Mei 1979, p. 486.
21. Mei 1979, p. 485.
22. Chen 1981, p. 122, and Mei 1979.
23. Kennedy 2019.
24. Mary Roberts Coolidge, *Chinese Immigration*, 1909, as cited in Chen 1981, p. 133.
25. Mark Twain, *Roughing It*, as cited in Leibovitz and Miller 2011, p. 97.
26. "Population, by Race, Sex, and Nativity," US Census Bureau, available online at: https://www2.census.gov/prod2/decennial/documents/1880a_v1–13.pdf (last accessed 12/02/23).
27. Treaty of Burlingame, clause V, 1868.
28. Liu 2005, p. 16.
28. As cited in Ou 2012, p. 52.
29. Chen 1981, p. 134.
30. Gibson 1877, p. 22.
31. Chang 2003, p. 22.

3. A WORLD UPSIDE DOWN

1. Lum 1988, p. 41.
2. Chua 2014, p. 121.
3. Chua 2014, p. 97.
4. Gibson 1877, pp. 163–4.
5. Liu, as cited in Harrison 2005, p. 27.
6. Ou 2012, p. 45.

7. Wong 1940.
8. Chen 1981, p. 59.
9. 背脊向天人所食, Beì Jí Xiàng Tiān Rén Sǔo Shí.
10. Eggs preserved for several months in barrels of clay and ash.
11. 换肠, Huàn Cháng.
12. Jan Duyvendak, as cited in Dikötter 2015, Loc 95.
13. Bergen 1902, p. 35.
14. Wong 1992, p. 16.
15. Nevius 1868, p. 219.
16. Pan 1994, p. 101.
17. Gibson 1877, p. 35.
18. As cited in Waley-Cohen 1999, p. 200.
19. As cited in Pomfret 2016, p. 95.
20. Gary Okihiro, as cited in Chong 2008, p. 90.
21. Henderson 2013, p. 89.
22. Newport, Frank, "In U.S., 87% Approve of Black-White Marriage, vs. 4% in 1958," Gallup, 2013, available online at: https://news.gallup.com/poll/163697/approve-marriage-blacks-whites.aspx (last accessed 12/02/23)
23. Wu 1926.
24. Gibson 1877, p. 17.
25. 假洋鬼子, Jiǎ Yáng Guǐ Zi. See Lu 2010, p. 137.
26. Pan 1994, p. 99.
27. Deyi Zhang, as cited in Qin 2016, p. 109.
28. McCarthy 1869.
29. 唐人街, Táng Rén Jiē.
30. Chen 1981, p. 63.
31. Pan 1994, p. 123.
32. See Lum 1981.
33. 好死不如鄂霍, Haǒ Sǐ Bù Rú E Huó.
34. Young 2014, p. 12.
35. Turner 1894, p. 106.
36. Chinese Repository, Vol. 4, p. 429 as cited in Welsh, 2010, p. 47.
37. Chen 1981, p. 58.
38. Karen J. Leong, as cited in Lee 2019, p. 76.
39. Spence 1981, p. 74.
40. Liang Qichao, as cited in Wong 1992, p. 12.
41. Pomfret 2016, p. 119.
42. Liang Qichao, as cited in Dikötter 2015, p. 51.
43. 六大公司, Liù Dà Gōng Sī.
44. Bergen 1902, p. 23.
45. Young 2014, p. 284.
46. Steevens 1898, p. 247.

NOTES

4. A VANISHED DREAM

1. Chen Ta, *Chinese Migrations*, 1923, as cited in Pan 1994, p. 94.
2. Chen 1981, p. 135.
3. Chen 1981, p. 135.
4. "The Chinese," *New York Times*, 3 September 1865, as cited by Qin 2016, p. 302.
5. Young 2014, p. 103.
6. As quoted by Huie Kin, *Reminiscences*, as cited in NPR, 26 August 2006.
7. Pomfret 2016, p. 89.
8. Zia 2000, p. 28.
9. As cited by Emma Teng, *Chinese Elites and U.S. Gatekeeping*, Cambridge University Press, 2021, p. 4.
10. Emma Lazarus, "The New Colossus," 1883.
11. Saum Song Bo, A Chinese View of the Statue of Liberty, as cited by Yung 2006, p. 56.
12. Wong 1940.
13. 三人行必有我师, Sān Rén Xíng Bì Yǒu Wǒ Shī.
14. Wong 1940.
15. Chua 2014, p. 120.
16. Wen Bing Chung, as cited by Yung 2006, p. 35.
17. Chong 2008, p. 95.
18. Chua 2014, p. 90.
19. Thomas Fraser as cited by Barry Waught, https://www.presbyteriansofthepast.com/2019/09/07/augustus-w-loomis-1816–1891/ (last accessed 12/02/23).
20. Wong 1946.
21. Tsai Shih-Shan, as cited in Pan 1994, p. 95.
22. Pomfret 2016, p. 78.
23. Huie Kin, *Reminiscences*, as cited in NPR, 26 August 2006.
24. Daniels 1990, pp. 61–3.
25. Lee 2019, p. 103.
26. James Wickersham, Washington State Historical Society, as cited in Lum 1988, p. 49.
27. Pan 1994, p. 93.
28. Mark Twain, *South Australian Register*, 1895, as cited in Ou 2012, p. 69.
29. 师父领进门修行在个人, Shī Fu Lǐng Jìn Mén Xiū Xíng Zài Gè Rén.
30. Wong 1940.
31. 白菜豆腐保平安, Bái Cài Dòu Fu Bǎo Píng An.
32. Lord Zhao, as cited in Sterckx 2019, p. 422.
33. 工头, Gōng Tóu.
34. Chang 2017, p. 112.
35. Suleski 2020, p. 61.

36. Wong 1940.
37. Wong 1940.
38. Zia 2000, p. 109.
39. 被爱给你力量, 爱人给你勇气, Bèi Ai Gěi Nǐ Lìliang, Aì Ren Gěi Nǐ Yǒngqì.
40. Helen Chien, *The European Diary of Hsieh Fucheng, Envoy Extraordinary of Imperial China*, Saint Martins, 1993, as cited in Waley-Cohen 1999, p. 178.
41. As cited in Arkush 1989, p. 71.
42. Levenson 1953, p. 27.
43. Arkush 1989, p. 71.
44. As cited in Spence 1981, p. 365.
45. Pomfret 2016, p. 117.
46. Ng Poon Chew, as cited in Yung 2006, p. 111.
47. Spence 1981, p. 106.
48. Dong 2000, p. 83.
49. Liu, as cited in Harrison 2005, p. 78.
50. Kang to Roosevelt, 30 January 1906, as cited in Worden 1972, p. 211.

5. SILVER, SILK, AND CHILIES

1. Jeronimo De Mendieta, *Historia Eclesiástica Indiana*, as cited in Kandell 1988, p. 156.
2. John Winthrop, as cited in Kandell 1988, p. 156.
3. Aguirre Beltran, *La Poblacion Negra de Mexico*, as cited in Kandell 1988, p. 213.
4. Carlos Fuentes at the University of Michigan, 1992, answering a question from the author.
5. 海禁, Hǎi Jìn.
6. William L. Schurz, *The Manila Galleon*, p. 15, as cited in Kandell 1988, p. 186.
7. Arturo Giraldez and Dennis Flynn, as cited by Tonio Andrade at https://www.youtube.com/watch?v=pztLtGlKRfM (last accessed 05/02/23).
8. Turner 1894, p. 84.
9. Cited by Dennis Flynn in his lecture, "Silk, Silver, and China, the Birth of Globalization," March 2002, available at: https://archive.org/search?query=Silk%2C+Silver%2C+and+China%2C+the+Birth+of+Globalization (last accessed 05/02/23).
10. 海椒, Hǎi Jiāo.
11. Dikötter 2015, p. 38.
12. Alexander von Humboldt, *Political Essay on the Kingdom of New Spain*, 1811, as cited in Gordon and Morales 2017, p. 28.

NOTES pp. [74–84]

13. Thomas Gage, *The English American*, 1648, as cited in Gordon and Morales 2017, p. 34.
14. Kandell 1988, p. 187.
15. Miguel de Cervantes, *Novelas Ejamplares*, as cited in Kandell 1988, p. 188.
16. Humboldt, as cited by Conder 1830, p. 260.
17. 大吕宋, Dà Lǚ Sòng.

6. A CHINESE ELDORADO

1. Kandell 1988, p. 397.
2. Carleton Beals, *Porfirio Díaz*, as cited in Krauze 1997, p. 220.
3. Daniel Cosío Villegas, *El Porfiriato*, as cited in Krauze 1997, p. 220.
4. Kandell 1988, p. 355.
5. James Creelman, *Pearson's Magazine*, 3 March 1908, as cited in Krauze 1997, p. 205.
6. Kandell 1988, p. 376.
7. Kandell 1988, p. 387.
8. Krauze 1997, p. 219.
9. Ortiz 1993.
10. Gonzalez-Garcia 2015, p. 71.
11. William D. Raat, *Los Intelectuales*, as cited in Kandell 1988, p. 374.
12. Kelly Lytle Hernández, Bad Mexicans: Race, Empire and Revolution in the Borderlands, talk in Stanford University, 2022, https://www.youtube.com/watch?v=JqKmkSagKps.
13. Secretario de Fomento, as cited in Cott 1987, p. 64.
14. Gonzalez Navarro, as cited in Cott 1987, p. 82.
15. Evelyne Sanchez Guillermo, as cited in Cinco 2017, p. 134.
16. Andres Molina Enriquez, *Los Grandes Problemas Nacionales*, as cited in Kandell 1988, p. 375.
17. Leibovitz and Miller 2011, p. 236.
18. Dong 2000, p. 5.
19. C. Luther Fry, *Illegal Entry of Orientals in the U.S.*, as cited in Chao 2010, p. 1.
20. Cott 1987, p. 70.
21. Gonzalez y Lara, *Chinos y Antichinos en México*, as cited in Chong 2008, p. 110.
22. Cott 1987, p. 70.
23. Chao 2010, p. 55.
24. Cott 1987, p. 72.
25. Bergen 1902, pp. 30–1.
26. 吃苦, Chī Kǔ.

283

27. Montesquieu, 1748, Chapter XX.
28. Dong 2000, p. 5.
29. Chao 2010, p. 99.
30. Camacho 2012, p. 25.
31. Cott 1987, p. 79.
32. Turner 1894, p. 136.
33. Ministerio de Fomento, as cited in Chao 2010, p. 67.
34. Dirección General de Estadísticas, Hermosillo and Chihuahua, as cited in Chao 2010, pp. 102–107.
35. *The Mexican Herald*, 29 July 1904.
36. *The Mexican Herald*, 29 July 1904.
37. Reaves 2015, pp. 24–7.
38. Bradley 2015, p. 62.
39. Pomfret 2016, p. 117.
40. The Letters of Theodore Roosevelt, 19 June 1905, as cited in Bradley 2015 p. 63.
41. Leibovitz and Miller 2011, p. 262.

7. BOURGEOIS AND MEXICAN

1. 聘金, Pìn Jīn.
2. Martínez Legorreta 1989.
3. Lee 1887, p. 66.
4. Chieng 2006, p. 60.
5. 美族, Měi Zú.
6. Lee 2019, p. 95.
7. "Los Chinos de México," *El Trafico*, February 1899, cited and translated by Gómez 2017, p. 4.
8. Erika Lee, *Washington Post*, 8 March 2022.
9. Marylin Chase, "The City's Secret Scourge," *Stanford Magazine*, May 2003.
10. Chang 2017, p. 154.
11. Cott 1987, p. 84.
12. Ortiz 1993.
13. *Revista de Revistas*, September 1910, as cited in Ortiz 1993.
14. Kandell 1988, p. 371.
15. Carranza Castellanos, as cited in Gonzalez-Garcia 2015.

8. THE LAND OF THE CANOES

1. Erika Lee, *At America's Gates*, as cited in Chao 2010, p. 4.
2. Pomfret 2016, p. 79.

NOTES

3. *The Day Book*, 29 October 1908, as cited in Gómez 2017, p. 3.
4. Dennis, *The Anti-Chinese Campaigns in Sonora*, as cited in Gómez 2017, p. 5.
5. Marcus Braun to Frank Sargent, commissioner general, as cited in Young 2014, p. 5.
6. Secretaría de Gobernación, El Servicio de Migración en México, 1926, as cited by Chao 2010, p. 63.
7. Wong 1940.
8. Wong 1940.
9. Wong 1946.
10. Kandell 1988, p. 369.
11. Hung-Hui 1992, p. 112.
12. Wong 1940.
13. Flores Morales, 2002.
14. Cott 1987, p. 72.
15. Young 2014, p. 118.
16. *New York Tribune*, "Arrest of Chinese Mexican," 17 May 1892, as cited in Young 2014, p. 119.
17. Consul in Eagle Pass to Secretaría de Relaciones Exteriores (SRE), May 1892, Archivo historico de la secretaria de relaciones exteriors, Mexico (AREM), as cited in Young 2014, p. 119.
18. "Los Estados Unidos contre Foon Chuck, Eagle Pass," AREM, as cited in Young 2014, p. 119.
19. *Washington Post*, "Mexico and the Chinese," 18 May 1892, AREM, as cited in Young 2014, p. 120.
20. Castañon 2021, p. 19.
21. Maciel 2016, Loc 808.
22. Wong 1940.
23. Ramos Salas 2019, p. 71.
24. Hu-DeHart, as cited in Leung 2012.
25. 菜园, Cài Yuán.
26. Chong 2008, p. 114.
27. Wong 1940.
28. 世外桃花源, Shì Wài Táo Huā Yuán.
29. "Perfil Histórico Cultural de Cd. Mante," at mante.com: https://www.mante.com.mx/historia.htm (last accessed 12/02/23).
30. Wong 1940.
31. Turner 1894, p. 114.
32. Chieng 2006, p. 206.
33. Liu, as cited in Harrison 2005, p. 143.
34. 士农工商, Shì Nóng Gōng Shāng.
35. Sterckx 2019, p. 388.

36. 好铁不打钉好汉不当兵, hǎo tiě bù dǎ ding hǎo hàn bù dāng bīng.
37. 重文轻武, Lei Duan, The Prism of Violence: Private Gun Ownership in Modern China, Syracuse University, 2017, p. 93.
38. 广东院.
39. Méndez 2012, p. 86.
40. Papeles de Miguel Cárdenas, 1911, as cited in Méndez 2012, p. 85.
41. Humboldt 1811, p. 115.
42. Humboldt 1811, p. 133.
43. Humboldt 1811, p. 145.
44. Wong 1940.
45. Méndez 2012, p. 94.
46. Mei 1979 p. 468.
47. Gladwell 2009, p 224.
48. Wong 1898.
49. Letter from Wong Foon Chuck to Tan Zhangxiao, 7 July 1907, Tom Leung Collection, UCLA Digital Library.
50. *The Baltimore Sun*, 17 April 1908.
51. Robert Taylor to Commissioner General, 5 October 1909, as cited in Young 2014, p. 181.
52. Letter from Wong Foon Chuck to Tan Zhangxiao, 31 March 1903, Tom Leung Collection, UCLA Digital Library.

9. A REFORMER IN EXILE

1. Chen, Campbell and Dong 2018, p. 930.
2. 国家, Guójiā.
3. 民族, Mín Zú.
4. 一盘散沙, Yī Pán Sǎn Shā.
5. Turner 1894, p. 111.
6. Lo 1967, p. 71.
7. 炎黄子孙, Yán Huáng Zǐ Sūn.
8. 康有为.
9. 孙中山.
10. Lee 1887, p. 68.
11. 天下, Tiān Xià.
12. As cited in Dikötter 2015, p. 11.
13. Sterckx 2019, p. 210.
14. Spence 1981, p. 242.
15. Spence 1981, p. 42.
16. Lo 1967, p. 183.
17. Worden, as cited in Leung 2012.
18. Liu, as cited in Harrison 2005, p. 102.

19. Spence 1981, p. 69.
20. John Fitzgerald, as cited in Leung 2012.
21. John Fitzgerald, as cited in Leung 2012.
22. 保皇会, Bǎo Huáng Huì.
23. 商务公司, Shāng Wù Gōng Sī.
24. Spence 1981, p. 62.
25. See Chang 2014, pp. 204–55.
26. Blitstein 2016, p. 234.
27. Blitstein 2016, p. 245.
28. Liang Qichao, *Travel Notes on America*, as cited in Dikötter 2015, p. 46.
29. Jane Leung Larson, personal correspondence with the author.
30. Lee 2015, p. 86.
31. 国民党, Guó Mín Dǎng.
32. Pomfret 2016, p. 129.
33. Spence 1981, p. 55.
34. 大同书, Dà Tóng Shū.
35. Spence 1981, p. 155.
36. Belinda Huang, *Creating Trans-Pacific Students*, as cited in Leung 2012.
37. Address to the Naval War College, 1897, as cited in Bradley 2015, p. 63.
38. 墨西哥日报, Mò Xī Gē Rì Bào.
39. Lo 1967, p. 201.
40. Blitstein 2016, p. 241.
41. Blitstein 2016, p. 241.
42. Kang Youwei, *The Mexican Herald*, 28 June 1907, as cited in Blitstein 2016, p. 250.

10. AN ERUDITE PHILANTHROPIST

1. Evelyn Hu-DeHart, *Kang and the Baohuanghui in Mexico*, as cited in Leung 2012.
2. Censo de Población, 1910, as cited in Chao 2010, p. 58.
3. Letter from Liang Qitian to Tan Zhangxiao, 10 June 1901, Tom Leung Collection, UCLA Digital Library.
4. Wong 1940.
5. *El Zocalo de Monclova*, 16 February 2014.
6. 育美学校, Yù Měi Xué Xiào.
7. Wong 1940.
8. Bergen 1902, p. 19.
9. 万般皆下品惟有读书高, Wàn Bān Jiē Xià Pǐn Wéi Yǒu Dú Shū Gāo.
10. 黄园活,.
11. 黄耀伟,.

12. Kang Youwei 1907, as cited in Wong 1946.
13. 新政, Xīn Zhèng.
14. Keith Schoppa, *Revolution and its Past*, p. 129, as cited in Lu 2010, p. 4.
15. Liu, as cited in Harrison 2005, p. 89.
16. 中为体,西为用, Zhōng Wéi Tǐ, Xī Wéi Yòng.
17. Lu 2010, p. 23.
18. Wong Foon Chuck private correspondence.
19. Pittsburgh-based newspaper, 1905 (further publication details are lost).
20. Sterckx 2019, p. 271.
21. Lo 1967, p. 202.
22. Lo 1967, p. 258.
23. 中墨银行, Zhōng Mò Yíng Háng.
24. Castañon 2021, p. 103.
25. Spence 1981, p. 107.
26. *The Baltimore Sun*, 17 April 1908.
27. Maciel 2017.
28. *The Mexican Herald*, 11 June 1907, as cited in Maciel 2016.
29. Letter from Wong Foon Chuck to Tan Zhangxiao, 7 July 1907, Tom Leung Collection, UCLA Digital Library.
30. *El País*, 20 September 1910.
31. *The Mexican Herald*, 29 July 1904.
32. Herbert 2019, p. 109.
33. Wong 1940.
34. Dambourgues 1974, p. 237.
35. Pittsburgh-based newspaper, 1905 (further publication details are lost).
36. 饮水思源, Yǐn Shuǐ Sī Yuán.
37. 开平碉楼与村落, Kāi Píng Diāo Lóu Yǔ Cūn Luò.
38. Chong 2008, p. 115.
39. Hu 1980, p. 288.
40. *The Mexican Herald*, 29 July 1904.
41. Evelyn Hu-DeHart, Cechimex Presentation (Centro de Estudios China-México), Universidad Nacional Autónoma de México, November 2022.
42. *The Los Angeles Herald*, 11 September 1904.
43. 人怕出名猪怕壮, Rén Pà Chū Míng Zhū Pà Zhuàng.
44. Opinion, *Los Angeles Times*, 29 March 2022.
45. Worden 1972, pp. 222–3.
46. Lo 1967, p. 217.
47. Lo 1967, p. 210.
48. Dambourgues 1974, p. 236.
49. Lo 1967, p. 274.
50. Cited in Herbert 2015, p. 106.
51. Nestor Jimenez, *Zocalo Monclova*, 25 September 2016.
52. Chao 2010, p. 91.

11. THE TORREÓN MASSACRE

1. Kandell 1988, p. 376.
2. Kandell 1988, p. 376.
3. José Maria Arana, as cited in Peña 2012, p. 110.
4. *The Agrarian Problem in Calles' Mexico*, 1928, Bancroft Library, as cited in Chang 2017, p. 107.
5. Chao 2010, p. 92.
6. Camacho 2012, p. 39.
7. Espinoza, 1931.
8. Chao 2010, p. 95.
9. Dambourgues 1974, pp. 234–6.
10. *El Tiempo*, May 1910, as cited in Chang 2017, p. 107.
11. Meyers, as cited in Maciel 2016, Loc 833.
12. Jesus Flores, as cited by Wilfley and Basset, 1911.
13. Perez Jimenez, *Raza Nación y Revolución*, as cited in Chang 2017, p. 102.
14. Chang 2017, p. 106.
15. Wilfley and Bassett, memorandum of the Law and the Facts, p. 6, as cited in Chao 2017, p. 152.
16. Carothers, *Report of Investigation*, as cited in Chang 2017, p. 102.
17. *El Tiempo*, 9 June 1911, as cited in Chang 2017, p. 102.
18. Hu 1980, p. 289.
19. Julián Herbert, *EFE News*, 16 May 2021.
20. Wilfley and Basset, 1911.
21. William H. Taft, as cited in Setzekorn 2018, p. 61.
22. 海圻, Haǐ Qí.
23. Qing diplomatic correspondence, as cited in Setzekorn 2018, p. 74.
24. "China Learning," *Pittsburgh Press*, September 1911, p. 10, as cited in Setzekorn 2018, p. 75.
25. Setzekorn 2018, p. 75.
26. Takai 2013, p. 168.
27. Chinese Legation in Washington, 27 June 1911, as cited in Takai 2013, p. 169.
28. Walker 2008, p. 35.
29. *El Paso Times*, 24 July and 9 August 1911.
30. Fidencio Rendon, *La Prensa de Coahuila* (publication date lost).
31. Castañon 2021, pp. 120–9.
32. Wong 1940.
33. Blitstein 2016, p. 252.
34. Lo Jun Pang, as cited in Spence 1981, p. 108.
35. Spence 1981, p. 134.
36. Kandell 1988, p. 404.
37. Krauze 1997, p. 367.

38. Hu 1980, p. 290.
39. Franco, as cited in Maciel 2016, Loc 860.
40. From Alger to secretary of state, as cited in Chang 2017, p 110.
41. Telegram received from consul at Piedras Negras, as cited in Chang 2017, p. 8.
42. Letter from Vice-Consul Blocker to secretary of state, as cited in Peña 2012, p. 130.
43. John Reed, "Con Villa en Mexico," *Metropolitan Magazine*, pp. 8–9, as cited in Krauze 1997, p. 316.
44. Peña 2012, p. 105.
45. As told by Cristina Chuck.
46. Chas Montague, acting consular agent, as cited in Chao 2010, p. 147.
47. Records of the Department of State, as cited in Chao 2010, p. 147.
48. Archivo General de la Nación, as cited in Gómez 2017, p. 10.
49. 三十年河东三十年河西, Sān Shí Nián Hé Dōng Sān Shí Nián Hé Xī.
50. *Washington Post*, 16 January 1912.
51. 守得云开见月明, Shǒu Dé Yún Kāi Jiàn Yuè Míng.
52. Méndez 2012, p. 106.
53. *Tampico Tribune*, as cited in Méndez 2012.
54. Méndez 2012, p. 92.
55. Wong 1940.
56. Crespo 1987, p. 95.
57. 三军可夺帅也，匹夫不可夺志也, Sān Jūn Kě Duó Shuài Yě Pǐ Fū Bù Kě Duó Zhì Yě.
58. Méndez 2012, p. 105.
59. Wong 1940.
60. Blasco Ibañez, *Militarismo*, as cited in Krauze 1997, p. 370.

12. UNDER THE PROTECTION OF THE GOLDEN DRAGON

1. Ramon Eduardo Ruiz, *The Great Rebellion*, as cited in Kandell 1988, p. 449.
2. Blasco Ibañez, as cited in Gómez 2016, p. 64.
3. Ricardo Perez Monfort, "Las Camisas Doradas," *Secuencia*, 1986.
4. Hamilton 1982, p. 41.
5. Madsen 1965.
6. Vasconcelos 1925.
7. Jayne Ifekwunigwe, as cited in Teng 2013, p. 11.
8. Renique, as cited in Chao 2010, p. 90.
9. Stoddard, *Rising Tide of Color against White World Supremacy*, as cited in Young 2014, p. 271.
10. 越挫越勇, Yuè Cuò Yuè Yǒng.

11. Boletin Oficial, as cited in Peña 2012, p. 163.
12. Kuhn 2008, p. 135.
13. Lee 2019, p. 110.
14. Lim, Lai and Yung, *Island*, as cited in Lee 2019, p. 110.
15. Robert Park, as cited in Young 2014, p. 8.
16. Cinco 2017, p. 264.

13. A BUTTERFLY OF THE AMERICAS

1. Brockmeier 2022.
2. Johnson 2005, p. 126.
3. Brockmeier 2022.
4. University of Pennsylvania archives, Wang Guixiang, available at www.paper.edu.cn (last accessed 12/02/23).
5. Pomfret 2016, p. 165.
6. Pomfret 2016, p. 166.
7. 四海为家, Sì Hǎi Wéi Jiā.
8. Zia 2000, p. 29.
9. Zia 2000, p. 29.
10. V.S. McClatchy as cited in Zia 2000, p. 31.
11. 一见钟情, Yí Jiàn Zhōng Qíng.
12. 有缘千里来相会, Yǒu Yuán Qiān Lǐ Lai Xiāng Huì.
13. Johnson 2017, p. 25.

14. THE GREAT PLUNDER

1. "Sonora, uno de los cinco estados más peligrosos de México en 2022," *El Sol de Hermosillo*, 7 February 2023.
2. Krauze 1997, p. 406.
3. Bergen 1902, p. 30.
4. The United Press, 8 November 1921.
5. Gonzalez 2017, p. 23.
6. US consul in Tampico to US secretary of state, as cited in Gonzalez 2017, p. 50.
7. Méndez 2012, p. 89.
8. Hamilton 1982, p. 41.
9. Wong private letter, 7 November 1925.
10. Wong 1940.
11. Gómez 2016, p. 61. Author's translation.
12. Wong 1940.
13. Wong 1940.
14. Méndez 2012, p. 138.

15. Méndez 2012, p. 165.
16. Méndez 2012, p. 171.
17. Crespo 1987, p. 96.
18. Wong 1940.
19. Martin Luiz Guzman, *El Excelsior*, 1961, as cited in Krauze 1997, p. 426.
20. Doralicia Carmona, "Memoria Política de México," available online at: https://www.memoriapoliticademexico.org/Biografias/OSA80.html (last accessed 12/02/23).
21. Report of the Chinese Legation in Mexico, 1930, as cited in Gonzalez 2017, p. 50.
22. Gonzalez 2017, p. 51.
23. Gonzalez 2017, p. 53.
24. Gonzalez 2017, p. 53.
25. Wong 1940.
26. Méndez in private correspondence 2022.
27. Méndez 2012, p. 150.
28. Dambourges, as cited in Chang 2017, p. 13.
29. 全墨国华侨总机关, Quán Mò Huá Qiáo Zǒng Jī Guān.
30. 邦有道, 贫且贱焉, 耻也, 邦无道, 富且贵焉. Confucius, *Analects*, 8:13.
31. Loomis 1869, p. 114.
32. Chang 2017, p. 186.
33. Camacho 2012, p. 71.
34. Plutarco Elías Calles, *Correspondencia*, 12 September 1931, p. 426. Author's translation.
35. Eugene Chen, Telegram to SRE, 5 September 1931, as cited in Young 2014, p. 238.
36. "Kwangtung Investigators Return from Mexico," Reuters Agency, Kwangtung, 15 June 1933, AREM, as cited in Young 2014, p. 242.
37. Instituto Nacional de Antropología e Historia 1991, as cited in Camacho 2012, p. 24.
38. John Calhoun, speech to US Congress, 4 January 1848, available in Chávez 2008, pp. 118–120.
39. Lee 2019, p. 150.
40. John Martinez, *Mexican Emigration to the U.S.*, 1971, as cited in Peña 2012.
41. George Clemens, as cited in Lee 2019, p. 150.
42. Hoffman 1972.
43. Lee 2019, p. 172.
44. Lee 2019, p. 179.
45. Instituto Nacional de Antropología e Historia 1991, as cited in Camacho 2012, p. 24.
46. Zia 2000, p. 182.

15. A CONFUCIAN AND AMERICAN LEGACY

1. 血浓于水, Xǔe Nóng Yú Shuì.
2. 仕而优则学，学而优则仕, Shì Ér Yōu Zé Xué, Xué Ér Yōu Zé Shì. Confucius, Analects, part 19.
3. *The Economist*, 13 May 2021.
4. 仁 rén, 义 yì, 礼 lǐ, 智 zhì, 信 xìn.
5. Confucius, *Analects*, 7:36.
6. Chieng 2006, p. 213.
7. 小康社会, Xiǎo Kāng Shè Huì.
8. 好彩, Hǎo Cǎi.
9. Chieng 2006, p. 214.
10. 君子怀德, 小人怀土, Jūn Zǐ Huái Dé, Xiǎo Rén Huái Tǔ.

16. THE ROARING THIRTIES IN SHANGHAI

1. Nicolas R. Clifford, *Retreat from China*, 1976, as cited in Wood 1998.
2. 人治, Rén Zhì / 法治, Fǎ Zhì.
3. Lu 1999, Loc. 147 and 927.
4. Lu 1999, Loc. 285.
5. Du Fu, as cited in Lu 2010, p. 34.
6. Huxley, as cited in Lu 1999, Loc. 382.
7. Lu 1999, Loc. 807.
8. Dong 2000, p. 209.
9. Dong 2000, p. 209.
10. Gibson 1877, p. 36.
11. Lu 1999, Loc. 255.
12. "Deportations of Chinese," *North China Daily News*, 10 May 1933, AREM, as cited in Young 2014, p. 242.
13. Wei 1987, p. 232.
14. Rebecca Karl, *Staging the World: Chinese Nationalism at the Turn of the Twentieth Century*, as cited in Teng 2013, p. 4.
15. Dong 2000, p. 101.
16. 会馆, Huì Guǎn.
17. Shenbao, as cited in Lu 1999, Loc. 193 and 4179.
18. 咸水妹, Xián Shuǐ Mèi.
19. Dong 2000, p. 45.
20. As cited by Lu 1999, Loc. 226.
21. Lu 1999, Loc. 826.
22. 旗袍, Qí Páo in Mandarin.
23. Dong 2000, p. 77.
24. 至今如图, Zhì Jīn Rú Tú. Lu 1999, Loc. 294.

25. 妇女能顶半边天, Fù Nǔ Néng Dǐng Bàn Biān Tiān.
26. Dong 2000, p. 215.
27. George Kates, *The Years That Were Fat*, 1933, as cited in Wood 1998, p. 275.
28. Hubei Xueshengjie, as cited in Dikötter 2015, p. 71.
29. International Military tribunal of the Far East, as cited in https://en.wikipedia.org/wiki/Japanese_war_crimes#cite_ref-71
30. 四面楚歌, Sì Miàn Chǔ Gē.
31. R.J. Rummel, *China's Bloody Century*, 1991, as cited in https://en.wikipedia.org/wiki/Japanese_war_crimes#cite_ref-68

17. BETWEEN EAST AND WEST

1. 华侨, Huá Qiáo.
2. 祝您福如东海, Zhù Nín Fú Rú Dōng Hǎi.
3. Sterckx 2019, p. 365.
4. Gonzalez 2017, p. 82.
5. 叶落归根, Yè Luò Guī Gēn.
6. Sterckx 2019, p. 272.
7. 鬼节, Guǐ Jié.
8. Lee 1887, p. 66.
9. 清明节, Qīng Míng Jié.

18. FORGOTTEN BY HISTORY

1. Lazcano Armienta, Secretaría de Desarrollo Agrario, as cited in Chang 2017, p. 208.
2. As cited in Kandell 1988, p. 478.
3. Méndez 2012, p. 177.
4. Méndez 2012, p. 189.
5. Wong 1940.
6. Gonzalez 2017, p. 95.
7. Chen Kwong Min, as cited in Gonzalez 2017, p. 73.
8. Gonzalez 2017, p. 73.
9. Wong 1940.
10. Marvin Huerta Marquez, *Expreso*, 16 May 2021.
11. Cited by Yang 2022.
12. Manuel Teran Lira, as cited in Herbert 2019, p. 20.
13. Mata Bravo, Juan José, in Wong 1940.
14. Jesus Gerardo Sotomayor Garza, *El Sol de la Laguna*, 1 November 2019.
15. Cinco 2017, p. 142.
16. Cinco 2017, p. 140.

17. Julián Herbert, *EFE News*, 16 May 2021.
18. 土生, Tǔ Shēng.
19. Statistics Canada, 5 July 2011, previously available on the Statistics Canada website at https://www.statcan.gc.ca/en/start. For more recent projections see: https://www150.statcan.gc.ca/n1/daily-quotidien/220908/g-a003-eng.htm (last accessed 12/02/23).
20. Quotation available at Quote Tab: https://www.quotetab.com/quotes/by-gary-locke (last accessed 12/02/23).
21. Herbert 2019, p. 21.
22. David Agren, "Mexico faces up to uneasy anniversary of Chinese massacre," *The Guardian*, 16 May 2021.
23. Jesus Morena Mejia, "El odio a los chinos en Torreón pervive aún de manera velada," *El Sol de la Laguna*, 15 May 2021.
24. Maciel 2017, Loc 3632.
25. "Regresan figura del Hortelano al Bosque Venustiano Carranza," *Milenio*, 17 June 2021.
26. "Chinese investment in manufacturing on the rise in Mexico," *Mexico News Daily*, 16 September 2022, available online at https://mexiconewsdaily.com/news/chinese-investment-manufacturing-mexico/ (last accessed 14/02/23).

CONCLUSION

1. 家丑不可外扬. Jiā Chǒu Bù Kě Wài Yáng.

APPENDIX: A MEMORIAL FROM REPRESENTATIVE CHINAMEN IN AMERICA (1876)

1. Chinese Six Companies, as cited by Yung 2006, pp. 18–23.

BIBLIOGRAPHY

Arkush, David and Leo Lee (eds), *Land Without Ghosts*, University of California Press, 1989.

Bergen, Robert Van, *The Story of China*, American Book Company, 1902.

Blitstein, Pablo Ariel, "A New China in Mexico, Kang Youwei and his Language of Cohesion," *Oriens Extremus*, Vol. 55, 2016.

Bradley, James, *The Chinese Mirage: The Hidden History of American Disaster in Asia*, Little Brown, 2015.

Brockmeier, Erica K., "How a Class of 'Brilliant Graduates' shaped Modern Chinese Architecture," *Penn Today*, 9 March 2022.

Castañon Cuadro, Carlos, *303. La Matanza de Chinos en Torreón*, Ayuntamiento de Torreón, 2021.

Chang, Iris, *The Chinese in America: A Narrative History*, Penguin Books, 2003.

Chang, Jason Oliver, *Chino: Anti-Chinese Racism in Mexico 1840–1940*, University of Illinois Press, 2017.

Chang, Jung, *Empress Dowager Cixi, The Concubine Who Launched Modern China*, Alfred A. Knopf, 2014.

Chao Romero, Robert, *The Chinese in Mexico 1882–1940*, University of Arizona Press, 2010.

Chávez, Ernesto (ed.), *The US War with Mexico: A Brief History with Documents*, Bedford/St. Martins, 2008.

Chen, Bijia, Cameron Campbell and Hao Dong, "Interethnic Marriage in Northeast China," *Demographic Research*, Vol. 38, No. 34, 2018.

Chen, Jack, *The Chinese of America*, Harper Collins, 1981.

Chieng, André, *La Pratique de la Chine*, Editions Grasset, 2006.

Chong, José Luis, *Hijo de un País Poderoso*, Palabra de Clio, 2008.

Chua, Christopher, *The Sacredness of Being There: Race, Religion, and Place-Making at San Francisco's Presbyterian Church in Chinatown*, UC Berkeley dissertation, 2014.

Cinco Basurto, Monica, *A mí no me pueden volver a sacar*, Casa Abierta al Tiempo, 2017.

BIBLIOGRAPHY

Collado Herrera, Maria, *El Espejo de la Elite Social (1920–1940)*, Historia de la Vida Cotidiana en México, siglo XX, Fondo de Cultura Económica, 2006.

Conder, Josiah, *The Modern Traveller. A Description, Geographical, Historical, and Topographical, of the Various Countries of the Globe*, James Duncan, 1830.

Cott, Kennett, "Mexican Diplomacy and the Chinese Issue, 1876–1910," *Hispanic Historical Review*, Vol. 67, No. 1, 1987.

Crespo, Horacio, *La Industria Azucarera Mexicana 1920–1940*, Secuencia, 1987.

Dambourgues, Jacques Leo, "The Chinese Massacre in Torreón of 1911," *Arizona and the West*, Vol. 16, No. 3, Autumn 1974.

Daniels, Roger, *Asian America: Chinese and Japanese in the United States since 1850*, University of Washington Press, 1990.

Dikötter, Frank, *The Discourse of Race in Modern China*, Oxford University Press, 2015.

Dong, Stella, *Shanghai: The Rise and Fall of a Decadent City*, Harper Collins, 2000.

Du, Ruofu, "Surnames in China," *Journal of Chinese Linguistics*, Vol. 14, No. 2, 1986.

Espinoza, José Angel, *El Problema Chino en México*, publisher unknown, 1931.

Flores Morales, Ramiro, *San Felipe y el Hondo: cuna de la región carbonífera de Coahuila*, Escuela de Bachilleres del Norte, 2002.

Gibson, Rev. O., *The Chinese in America*, Hitchcock & Walden, 1877.

Gladwell, Malcolm, *Outliers: The Story of Success*, Penguin, 2009.

Gómez Estrada, José Alfredo, *Elite de Estado y Prácticas Políticas: Una aproximación al estudio de la corrupción en México, 1920–1934*, Universidad de Baja California, 2016.

Gómez, Rocío, "Chinese Mexicans: Mexico's forgotten and Overlooked Mestizos," *History in the Making*, Vol. 10, California State University San Bernardino, 2017.

Gonzalez, Fredy, *Paisanos Chinos: Transpacific Politics Among Chinese Immigrants in Mexico*, University of California Press, 2017.

Gonzalez-Garcia, Jaime, *Desarrollo Urbano de la Ciudad, Mexico durante el Porfiriato*, Maria Lorena Lozoya, 2015.

Gordon, Peter and Juan Morales, *The Silver Way, China, Spanish America and the Birth of Globalisation 1565–1815*, Penguin Specials, 2017.

BIBLIOGRAPHY

Hamilton, Nora, "The State and the National Bourgeoisie in Post-Revolutionary Mexico: 1920–1940," *Latin American Perspectives*, Vol. 9, No. 4, Sage Publications, 1982.

Harrison, Henrietta, *The Man Awakened From Dreams: One Man's Life in a North China Village 1857–1942*, Stanford University Press, 2005.

Henderson Smith, Arthur, *Chinese Characteristics, 1894*, Ravenio Books, 2013.

Herbert, Julián, *The House of the Pain of Others: Chronicle of a Small Genocide*, Graywolf Press, 2019.

Hoffman, Abraham, "Mexican Repatriation Statistics: Some Suggested Alternatives to Carey McWilliams," *Western Historical Quarterly*, Vol. 3, No. 4, 1972.

Hu-DeHart, Evelyn, "Immigrants to a Developing Society," *Journal of Arizona History*, Vol. 21, Autumn 1980.

Hung-Hui, Juan, *Chinos en América*, Editorial Mapfre, 1992.

Johnson, Ian, *Wild Grass: Three Portraits of Change in Modern China*, Vintage, 2005.

Johnson, Ian, *The Souls of China: The Return of Religion after Mao*, Pantheon, 2017.

Jung, John, *Chinese Laundries: Tickets to Survival on Gold Mountain*, Yin & Yang Press, 2007.

Kandell, Jonathan, *La Capital: The Biography of Mexico City*, Random House, 1988.

Kennedy, Lesley, "Building the Transcontinental Railroad: How 20,000 Chinese Immigrants Made It Happen," History.com, 2019. Available at: https://www.history.com/news/transcontinental-railroad-chinese-immigrants (last accessed 05/02/23).

Krauze, Enrique, *Mexico, Biography of Power: A History of Modern Mexico 1810–1996*, Harper Collins, 1997.

Kuhn, Philip A., *Chinese Among Others: Emigration in Modern Times*, Rowman & Littlefield Publishers, 2008.

Lee, Erika, *The Making of Asian America: A History*, Simon & Schuster, 2015.

Lee, Erika, *America for Americans: A History of Xenophobia in the United States*, Basic Books, 2019.

Lee, Yan Phoo, *When I Was a Boy in China*, Lothrop, Lee & Shepard, 1887.

BIBLIOGRAPHY

Leibovitz, Liel and Matthew Miller, *Fortunate Sons: The 120 Chinese Boys Who Came to America, Went to School, and Revolutionized an Ancient Civilization*, W. W. Norton & Company, 2011.

Lethbridge, H. J., *All About Shanghai*, Oxford University Press, 1983.

Leung Larson, Jane (chair), "A Chinese Reformer in Exile," Association of Asian Studies Panel Report, 2012.

Leung, Tom, Archival Collection of the Chinese Royal Society in North America, UCLA Library Digital Collection, 1898–1928.

Levenson, Joseph, *Liang Qichao and the Mind of Modern China*, Literary Licensing LLC, 1953.

Liu, Haiming, *The Transnational History of a Chinese Family: Immigrant Letters, Family Business, and Reverse Migration*, Rutgers University Press, 2005.

Lo, Jung-Pang (ed.), *Kang Youwei: A Biography and a Symposium*, University of Arizona Press, 1967.

Loomis, Augustus W., *The Profits of Godliness*, Presbyterian Board of Publication, 1859.

Lu, Hanchao, *Beyond the Neon Lights, Everyday Shanghai in the Early Twentieth Century*, University of California Press, 1999.

Lu, Hanchao, *The Birth of a Republic*, University of Washington Press, 2010.

Lum McCunn, Ruthane, *Thousand Pieces of Gold*, Boston: Beacon Press, 1981.

Lum McCunn, Ruthane, *Chinese American Portraits*, Chronicle Books, 1988.

Maciel, Rico, *Mi Cuna El Ferrocarril: Efemérides de Torreón*, Kindle Edition, 2016.

Maciel, Rico, *El Tranvía de Lerdo a Torreón—Batallas en el Desierto*, Illhuicamina, 2017.

Madsen, William, "A Mexican Ulysses, an Autobiography," *Hispanic American Historical Review*, 45:131–2, 1965.

Martínez Legorreta, Omar, *Modernization and Revolution in Mexico: A Comparative Approach*, United Nations University Press, 1989.

McCarthy, Justin, "John Chinaman in San Francisco," *New York Independent*, 1869.

Mei, June, "Socioeconomic Origins of Emigration, Guangdong to California, 1850–1882," *Modern China*, Vol. 5, No. 4, 1979.

BIBLIOGRAPHY

Méndez Medina, Diana, *Proyecto de Irrigación en la Ribera del Rio Mante: Cambio Agrario y Corrupción en México (1900–1939)*, El Colegio de Sonora, 2012.

Montesquieu, C. L. de Secondat, *De l'Esprit des Lois*, Geneva, 1748.

Nevius, John L., *China and the Chinese*, Harper & Brothers, 1868.

Ortiz Gaitan, Julieta, *La Ciudad de Mexico durante el Porfiriato: El París de América*, openedition.org, 1993.

Ou, Hsin-yun, "Mark Twain, Anson Burlingame, Joseph Hopkins Twichell, and the Chinese," *Ariel*, 2012.

Pan, Lynn, *Sons of the Yellow Emperor: A History of the Chinese Diaspora*, Kodansha America, 1994.

Peña Delgado, Grace, *Making the Chinese Mexican: Global Migration, Localism, and Exclusion in the U.S.-Mexico Borderlands*, Stanford University Press, 2012.

Pomfret, John, *The Beautiful Country and the Middle Kingdom, America and China, 1976 to the Present*, Henry Holt & Co., 2016.

Pruitt, Ida, *A Daughter of Han: the Autobiography of a Working Woman*, Stanford University Press, 1945.

Qin, Yucheng, *The Cultural Clash, Chinese Traditional Native-Place Sentiment and the Anti-Chinese Movement*, University Press of America, 2016.

Ramos Salas, Javier, *Entre el Esplendor y el Ocaso Lagunero*, Archivo Municipal de Torreón, 2019.

Reaves, Joseph, *Taking in a Game: A History of Baseball in Asia*, University of Nebraska Press, 2015.

Schiavone Camacho, Julia Maria, *Chinese Mexicans: Transpacific Migration and the Search for a Homeland, 1910–1960*, University of North Carolina Press, 2012.

See, Lisa, *On Gold Mountain: The One-Hundred-Year Odyssey of My Chinese-American Family*, St Martins, 1995.

Setzekorn, Eric, "Military Engagement with a Responsible Stakeholder: The Taft Administration and Qing Imperial China," *Journal of American-East Asian Relations*, Vol. 25, 2018.

Shah, Angilee and Jeffrey N. Wasserstrom (eds), *Chinese Characters: Profiles of Fast-Changing Lives in a Fast-Changing Land*, University of California Press, 2012.

Spence, Jonathan, *The Gate of the Heavenly Peace: The Chinese and Their Revolution*, Penguin Books, 1981.

BIBLIOGRAPHY

Steevens, George Washington, *The Land of the Dollar*, Dodd, Mead, & Co, 1898.

Sterckx, Roel, *Chinese Thought, from Confucius to Cook Ding*, Penguin Books, 2019.

Suleski, Ronald, "A Confucian Classroom in Qing China," *Education about Asia*, Vol. 25, No. 3, 2020.

Takai, Yukari, *Revolution, War, Chinese Cooks and Labourers during the Mexican Revolution: First Refugees to the United States*, Auntlute Books, 2013.

Tang, Lin Yu, *The Importance of Living*, Reynal & Hitchcock, 1937.

Teng, Emma Jinhua, *Eurasian: Mixed Identities in the United States, China and Hong Kong, 1842–1943*, University of California Press, 2013.

Turner, John A., *Kwang Tung, or Five Years in South China*, S. W. Partridge & Co, 1894.

Valencia Islas, Arturo, *Los extranjeros en la conformación del sistema ferroviario mexicano, 1880–1914*, Mirada Ferroviaria, 2019.

Vasconcelos, José, *La Raza Cósmica*, Agencia Mundial de Librerías, 1925.

Von Humboldt, Alexander, *Ensayo Político sobre el Reino de la Nueva España, 1811*, Universidad Veracruzana, 2020.

Waley-Cohen, Joanna, *The Sextants of Beijing: Global Currents in Chinese History*, W. W. Norton & Co, 1999.

Walker, Joshua Charles, "Immigrants at Home: Revolution, Nationalism, and Anti-Chinese Sentiment in Mexico, 1910–1935," Senior Honors Thesis, Ohio State University, May 2008.

Wei, Betty Peh-T'i, *Shanghai: Crucible of Modern China*, Oxford University Press, 1987.

Welsh, Frank, *A History of Hong Kong*, HarperCollins, 2010.

Wong, Foon Chuck, *Outline of the Mexican State*, Tom Leung Collection, UCLA Library Digital Collection, 1898.

Wong, Foon Chuck, *Autobiography*, c. 1940 (unpublished).

Wong, Foon Chuck, *Seventy-three Year Commemoration of Emigration*, San Francisco, *Chung Sai Yat Po* (中西日報), 1946.

Wong, K. Scott, "Liang Qichao and the Chinese of America: A Re-Evaluation of His 'Selected Memoir of Travels in the New World'," *Journal of American Ethnic History*, Vol. 11, No. 4, 1992.

Wood, Frances, *No Dogs and Not Many Chinese: Treaty Port Life in China 1843–1943*, John Murray, 1998.

Worden, Robert L., *A Chinese Reformer in Exile: The North American Phase of the Travels of K'ang Yu-wei*, PhD dissertation, 1972.

BIBLIOGRAPHY

Wu, Jingchao, *Chinese Immigration in the Pacific Area*, University of Chicago dissertation, 1926.

Yang, Zhou, "J. R. R. Tolkien and the Magic of Chinese Gardens," Sixth Tone, 29 September 2022, available at https://www.sixthtone.com/news/1011298/j.r.r.-tolkien-and-the-magic-of-chinese-gardens (last accessed 10/02/23).

Young, Elliott, *Alien Nation: Chinese Migration in the Americas from the Coolie Era Through World War II*, University of North California Press, 2014.

Yung, Judy, Gordon H. Chang and Him Mark Lai, *Chinese American Voices: From the Gold Rush to the Present*, University of California Press, 2006.

Zhang, Chunping, "The Characteristics of the Chinese People Surnamed Huang," *Proceedings of 4th International Conference on Education, Language, Art and Intercultural Education*, 2017.

Zia, Helen, *Asian American Dreams: The Emergence of an American People*, Farrar, Straus & Giroux, 2000.

ACKNOWLEDGEMENTS

My gratitude goes first to my family for making this journey into history possible. Since I was a child, my mother has instilled in me curiosity towards all things Chinese, passing on her passion for books, history, and social sciences. My father made me an insatiable tourist, allowing our family to travel around the world. This book would not have seen the light of day without my wife, who supported me while contributing her knowledge of Chinese culture; she and our children were my first readers, all embracing this family project. Through their affection and care, my Mexican cousins Pepe and Moni remind me to this day of the true meaning of the word family and this book would not have been written without their love and support.

Before Alzheimer's took the best of her memories, my mother put on paper for me what she remembered about the house in Tlalpan and her grandfather Hing, and she kept a copy of Foon Chuck's short autobiography. Without those two documents, their stories would have been harder to trace. I must also thank my grandmother for keeping religiously all her documents and more than a thousand old photographs from Mexico, the United States and Shanghai, which detailed her life with Yaiwai. Tribute is due to my many relatives from the Chuck, Wong, Leon and Leung families in Mexico, China and elsewhere, especially those in El Limon, for opening their doors to me and contributing a multitude of anecdotes about our ancestors.

My interest in history has been cultivated through my student years in Paris by my secondary school teachers. History is an important academic subject in France today, and I am fortunate that those teachers inspired me to spend countless hours of my childhood devouring history books. They taught me early on to develop critical thinking, and also of the risks for democracies of ignoring, forgetting or distorting their past. Without them, the simple idea of this book would not even have come to my mind.

ACKNOWLEDGEMENTS

In the last thirty years, a new academic field has emerged with a growing number of researchers studying the Chinese diaspora, particularly in the United States, Asia, and more recently Mexico. They gave me the courage and inspiration to talk about my family's experience. Without them, this book would have been harder to research, their knowledge being the cement that glued together scattered family memories. Special credit is due to Evelyn Hu-DeHart for her pioneering work on the Chinese in Mexico, Fredy Gonzalez and Diana Méndez Medina for their remarkable studies on the events in El Mante, Elliott Young for his research on Foon Chuck's problems with US Immigration, Pablo Ariel Blitstein for his analysis of Kang Youwei in Mexico, Julián Herbert for his work on Torreón, and Jonathan Kandell and Enrique Krauze for their magistral opuses on Mexican politics. Separately, to describe Chinese society at the turn of the century, I have used the insightful works of John Turner and Robert Van Bergen on ordinary Chinese lives, Henrietta Harrison on Confucianism and reforms, Hanchao Lu and Stella Dong on Shanghai, and Roel Sterckx on Chinese culture.

Being a new author without much writing experience and introducing a somewhat arcane story have made my publishing journey a daunting task. I therefore feel grateful to my publisher Michael Dwyer, first personally for agreeing to engage with me directly, immediately telling me that my first manuscript was not for him, and six months later expressing interest in a revised version. Second, I feel indebted to Hurst Publishers for giving voices to stories from remote countries and cultures, like the ones in this book, which lie away from the mainstream. Finally, a big thanks to my editors Lara Weisweiller-Wu, Alasdair Craig and Mei Jayne Yew, for being passionate advocates of my book.

A special thanks to Evelyn Hu-DeHart and Jane Leung Larson for being so kind and sharing precious archival documents with me on Foon Chuck and the Chinese Reform Association. Gratitude is due as well to the other scholars and activists who have taken time off from their busy schedules to speak with or meet with me and answer my queries, including in alphabetical order: Carlos Castañon Cuadro, José Luis Chong, Monica Cinco Basurto, Fredy Gonzalez, Eric Guerassimov, Diana Méndez Medina, Ernesto Ramirez, and Elliott Young. Credit is due to Teacher Hu from Beijing for helping

ACKNOWLEDGEMENTS

me decipher old Chinese calligraphy. A loving thought as well to all my family's friends who have encouraged me by commenting on my manuscript, including Jean Benoit, Henrik, Veronique, Kan, Xurong, Emmanuel, Xi, François, Sylvie, and Nora. Finally, I am grateful to Jeanne Pham Tran for her precious publishing tips.

INDEX

Acapulco, 72, 74, 91, 219
African Americans, 133, 207
agriculture, 118–22
Ah Fong, 43, 44, 45, 46, 63
American Chemical Society, 191
American Dream, 28, 29–30
American silver, 72, 73, 75
Amerindians. *See* Native Americans
Analects of Confucius, 16
Angel Island, 179
anti-Chinese activists, 159, 198
anti-Chinese campaigns, 206–7, 251
anti-Chinese movements, 158–9
anti-Chinese riots, 47–8, 56
anti-Chinese sentiment, 65–6, 163
anti-miscegenation laws, 39
Arizona, 115, 123, 197
Arjona, Josefa, 260
Armstrong, Louis, 191
Atlantic trade, 76
Australia, 4, 39

Bank of China and Mexico. See Compañia Bancaria China y Mexico
Bank of Mexico, 202
Battle of Shanghai, 235

Beaumont Rice Company of Texas, 117, 118
Beijing Planning Commission, 190
Beijing's Forbidden City, 99
Bering Sea, 228
Berlin, 231
Black House (Mexico City), 75
Book of Great Unity (Kang Youwei), 135, 136
Boxer Rebellion, 65, 101
Brazil, 64, 77, 90
Burlingame, Anson, 29

Cahill, James, 253
Calhoun, John, 207
California Gold Rush, 28
California
    anti-miscegenation laws, 39
    Chinese in laundries, 43
    Chinese women in, 41
    criticisms against Chinese migrants, 49–50
    game ban, 84
    population, 29–30
    unemployment rate, 49
Calle Dolores, 184
Calle Madero, 105, 106
Camacho, Ávila, 251–2
Canada, 39, 132, 136, 139, 262

INDEX

Canton city, 3, 7, 19, 29, 36, 40, 42–43, 46, 90, 104, 189, 206, 218, 223, 261
Cantonese, 17, 83, 190–192, 229
  Diets, 35, 240
  as first migrants, 16, 28, 66
  merchants, 7, 38
Cárdenas, Miguel, 108–9, 113, 120, 141, 172–3, 201
Cárdenas, Lázaro, 171, 209, 251
Carnegie, Andrew, 66, 78
Carranza, Venustiano, 173, 175, 189, 202, 205
Central Pacific Railroad, 28–9, 59, 273
Centro Cultural Arocena, 150
Cervantes, Miguel, 75
Chaitong village (Kwangtung), 11, 16, 18, 19, 34, 43, 55, 115, 189, 220–1
  festivals, 9–10, 36
  games, 10
  natural disasters, 12–13, 31
  richness of the land, 8–9, 117, 118
  watchtowers, 149
Chamber of Commerce of Torreón, 152
Champs-Élysées, 226
Chapei district, 234
Chaplin, Charlie, 226
Chee Kung Tong, 199
Chen, Duxiu, 231
cheongsam, 232–3
Chew, Ng Poon, 66
Chiang, Kai-shek, 192, 195, 214, 229, 234, 244
Chicago, 39, 182, 231

Chihuahua, 140, 168
child trafficking, 3
chilies, 73, 79
China Sea, 26, 223
China, 164–5
  agriculture, 118, 121–2
  Chinese market, Westerners access to, 3–4
  Chinese way of showing affection, 103
  deception, 86
  diplomacy, 163, 220
  eating and agricultural habits, 35, 73
  education system, revolution in, 143–4
  longing for, 241, 244–5
  low value of human life, 38, 127, 128
  Mexico–China relationship, 69–70
  migrations within, 2
  military defeat against Japan, 130–1
  modernization and reforms, 143–4, 189, 195, 266
  organizing society, 15–16
  population (between 1650 and 1851), 2
  ports, opening of, 3–4
  poverty in south, 2–3
  rail infrastructure, building of, 81–2
  reforms in, 144
  republic under Sun Yat-sen, 135
  return to, 239–240
  role of migration, 1

INDEX

soldiers' class in, 119
taxation systems, 72
trading relationship with Mexico, 69–72
Treaty of Friendship and Commerce, 90–1
type of classes, 118–19
wave of emigration from, 1, 2, 4
war against Japan. *See* Sino-Japanese War
Western public opinion on, 101
Chinatown (San Francisco)
  adopted sons, 41
  Chinese grocery stores, 36
  Chinese women in, 40–1, 45
  de facto capital of the Chinese, 39
  devoid of US culture, 39–40
  during anti-Chinese riots (1877), 56
  family life, absence of, 40–2
  immigrants living conditions, 40, 45–6
  plague epidemic, 101
  return of the bones of Chinese immigrants' corpses, 46–7
  Sacramento Street, 40
  Six Chinese Companies governance, 46–7
Chinatown Presbyterian Church (San Francisco), 31–33, 54, 145
Chinese diet, 35
Chinese Empire Reform Association, 132, 134, 136, 139–140, 143, 146–150, 162, 165, 199, 306

Chinese Empire Reform Association in Canada, 139
Chinese Eurasians, 131, 216, 229–30, 257
Chinese Exclusion Act, 50, 55–6, 61, 63–6, 80, 82, 93, 107, 113, 124, 179, 191, 199, 209, 223
"Chinese Gardens", 116, 146, 161
Chinese immigrants, 150, 158, 175, 191, 208–9, 210, 220, 262
  alienation from US society, 30, 38, 41–2, 224
  Christian conversions, lack of, 54
  courage of, 84
  habits of gambling, 55, 84
  illegal, 124
  life expectancy, 30
  local trade and small businesses, 87–9
  meals preparation, 58–9
  migrants rate, 1, 49
  mixed marriages, 91–2
  naturalizations, 178
  negative stereotypes, 38–9, 177
  railroad workers, 59
  returnees rate, 28–29
  sales techniques, 88–9
Chinese merchants, 71
  Spaniards attitudes towards, 75
Chinese Mexicans, 91, 108, 153, 175, 193–4, 198–9, 208–210, 228, 252, 260–1
"Chinese nation", 127–8, 136, 189
Chinese Revolution (1911–12), 135, 167, 171, 180

311

INDEX

Chinese utilitarianism, 34, 120
Chinese World, The (newspaper), 134
Chinese
   Japanese views on, 235
   massacre of, 160–2
   mercantile mindset, 86–7
   struggles faced by, 209
   views on Western merchants, 86
Chuck, Arturo, 212–14
Chuck, Benjamín, 215–16, 217
Chuck, Elvira, 212–13
Chuck, Hortensia, 216
Chuck, Lily, 142, 153, 192–3, 195, 214, 218, 223, 228
Chuck, Margarita (later Margarita Lee), 192–3, 214, 218, 223, 228
Chuck, Rubén, 115, 117, 216–18, 255–6
Chuck, Santiago, 115, 142, 190, 215–18, 255
Chuck, Selina, 216
Chuck, Wong Foon. See Wong, Foon Chuck
Chung Sai Yat Po (newspaper), 66, 254
Churubusco Convent Museum, 182
Cixi (Empress Dowager), 82, 131–2, 143, 144
Classic of Filial Piety, 16
Coahuila Coal Company, 111
Coahuila (State of), 108, 114, 117, 120, 140–1, 166, 173
Coal Company of La Agujita, 148
Columbus, Christopher, 69

Comanches, 207
Commercial Corporation, 132–3, 146, 152, 166
Communist Revolution (1949), 3, 163, 261, 265
Compañia Bancaria China y Mexico, 146–147, 160–162, 167
Compañia de Tranvias Wah Yick, 146–147, 150, 166
Comte, Auguste, 77
Concha. *See* Leon, Concepción
Confucianism, 98–9, 118, 130, 306
Confucius, 1, 11, 98, 129–131, 134–135, 143, 144–5, 149, 205, 220–1, 254, 265
cooks, 35, 43, 58–60, 62, 168, 184
Coolidge, Mary, 29
"coolies" (indentured laborers), 25, 29, 82, 112, 223, 263
Cortés, Hernán, 70, 75
Cosmic Race, The (Vasconcelos), 176
Crosby, Alfred, 73
Cuba, 25, 91, 140, 159, 164

Day of the Dead, 103, 247, 255
demonetization, 76
Deng, Xiaoping, 127–8
Díaz regime, 105, 112, 141, 157
Díaz, Porfirio, 77, 78, 79–80, 89, 92, 104, 110, 116, 137, 149, 151, 153, 158, 167, 205, 263, 269
Do Sing Yuen (Chinese Garden), 116

INDEX

Dragon Boat Festival, 10
droughts, 3, 10
Du Fu, 225

Eagle Pass, 60–62, 107, 110, 113, 115, 124, 148, 166, 169, 176, 179, 214–5, 217, 260
East Asiatic Trading Company Ltd, 104–5
Eastern Hills, 240
Einstein, Albert, 226
Elías Calles, Plutarco, 175–6, 183, 197, 199–206, 251–2
Elías Calles, Rodolfo, 201–3, 205
El Dragon de Oro, 104–6, 181, 194, 232, 240–4, 247–8
El Mante, 117, 119, 122, 171–3, 200–5, 211, 213, 217, 219, 252–6, 306
El Mante Sugar Company, 205, 215, 251–2
El Nuevo Mundo (newspaper), 152
El Paso (Texas), 57–8, 60–1, 107, 115, 124
El Tráfico (newspaper), 100
Emerson, Ralph W., 38
emigration, 1–2, 11, 13, 28, 73, 226
    as organized international trade, 25
    policies, 64, 66
    prohibition of, 27, 71
    See also Chinese immigrants
Encyclopedia of Missions, 54–5
"Engagement Gold", 95
Eurasians. *See* Chinese Eurasians

famines, 9, 17–8, 20, 49, 157

Fan Tan (betting game), 84
Fatsaan (town), 24
female infanticide, 38
Fengshui, 18, 81, 190
filial piety, 14–15
Flint, Charles Ranlett, 132
floods, 3, 7, 9, 11, 13, 115, 170, 221, 225, 243
Florida, 39
foot-binding practice, 21–2, 38
Fuentes, Carlos, 70
Fukien (province), 2, 15, 73, 225

Geary Act (1892), 112–13
Genthe, Arnold, 39
George III, 82
ghosts. *See* spirits
Gladwell, Malcolm, 122
Globe Hotel (San Francisco), 32, 101
Golden Dragon. *See* El Dragon de Oro
Golden Shirts (anti-foreigner league), 176
Gonzalez, Fredy, 203–4
Gortari, Salinas de, 252
Grant, Ulysses, 50
Great Depression, 234
Great Wall (China), 118
Greater Shanghai Municipality, 229
Greeley, Horace, 38
Greely, A. W., 164
Guadalajara, 105, 177, 187
Guanyin (Chinese goddess), 111
Guayalejo River, 253

Hacienda Canton, 119, 121–2,

313

INDEX

148, 172, 200–204, 211, 213, 223, 251
Hacienda Limon, 120, 189, 190, 192–4, 217
Haiqi (vessels), 163–165
Han Chinese, 22, 39, 119, 127, 135
Havana, 164
He Zhizhang, 241
Hearst, William Randolph, 79–80
Herbert, Julián, 162
Hing. *See* Leung, Hing.
Hing and Cruz
  children, 99–100, 102, 105
  family life, 99
  marriage, 95–7
  settled in Mazatlán, 97–8
  wedding photo, absence of, 98
Historia (magazine), 153
Ho Tung, Sir Robert, 131
Hoiping (city), 11, 13, 19, 28
Hoksaan County, 19, 20, 43, 63, 85, 103–4, 239–40, 248
  laborers hiring to work in the United States, 24
  separation between the sexes, 22
  women in rice fields, 21
Hong Kong, 4, 7, 13, 31, 67, 104–6, 134, 190, 230, 232, 237, 241–2, 244, 260–1
  advertisement, Chinese colony for Mexico, 82
  Angel, 218–9, 254
  harbor, 18, 25–6
  Kang Youwei travel to, 129–31
  plague, 101
  steamships from, 91, 137, 146, 188, 223

upper-class white migrants in, 42
  wealth of, 28
The Hong Kong and Shanghai Bank, 227
Honolulu, 223
Hotel del Ferrocarril, 109, 110, 114, 141, 253
Hotel Internacional (Monclova), 141, 143
Hu-DeHart, Evelyn, 150, 199
Hundred Days Reform, 131
Hungry Ghosts Festival, 247
Huntington, Collis Potter, 111
Huxley, Aldous, 226

Iberian Union, 72
Immigration Act, 192, 198, 207
Immigration and Nationality Act, 66
Imperial College (Peking), 33
Imperial Examination, 11, 66, 129, 130, 142, 144, 189
Indian Ocean, 71, 72, 73, 76
industrial revolution, 76
International Settlements, 224, 229, 234
French Settlements 224
interracial marriages, 38, 39, 70, 188, 230
Ivy League, 270

J. C. Abbot company, 121
Japan, 93, 119, 133–6, 188–9, 192, 198–9, 214, 270
Japanese, 127, 161, 191–2, 230, 234
Japanese army, 235–7

314

INDEX

Jessfield Park, 227
Jews, 206

Kang, Tongbi, 136, 145
Kang, Youwei, 27, 38, 45, 65, 66, 109, 128–38, 139, 143–6, 150, 154, 160, 166–7, 171, 189, 191, 225, 236, 265–8
  background, 128, 129
  on Chinese diaspora, 133
  Commercial Corporation establishment, 132–3
  competition between Sun Yat-sen and, 134–5
  on education, 136
  exile, 131, 132
  first trip to Mexico, 137
  Hong Kong visit, 129–30
  hungry for modernity, 129, 130
  Imperial Examination, 129, 130
  as an internationalist and political opportunist, 135–6
  lived with Sir Robert's family, 131
  modern European culture, encountered, 131–2
  multiple talents, 133
  petitions to the Guangxu Emperor, 130–1
  his political theory, 135
  reforms proposal, 131
  relationship with Foon Chuck, 129, 137, 145–6, 152
  as visionary thinker/philosopher, 130, 133
  on "yellow peril" question, 138
  Yue Mae School visit (Monclova), 143
Karl, Rebecca, 228–9
Kearney, Denis, 49–50
Knives, 35–6, 219
Korea, 71, 93, 209, 270
Kuomintang, 134, 199, 214
Kwangtung province, 2, 15, 19, 21, 40, 42, 58, 63, 66, 101, 143, 189, 224–5, 240, 260, 262
  deaths, 3
  diplomats from, 65, 92, 128, 131, 137
  education, 11
  emigration rate, 4
  emigration, recognition of, 27
  ethnic violence, 20, 47
  festive dish, 8
  banning of gambling, 144
  land scarcity, 2–3
  geography, 7–8
  Mexican dollars in, 72
  population, 2–3, 85, 120
  richness of the land, 8–9, 121
  unemployment, 2–3, 4
  See also Chaitong village (Kwangtung)

La Chinesca, 92
La Rosita, 166
Lampacitos, 167
Land Colonization Act, 77, 120–1
Lavandería de Vapor Oriental (Oriental Steam Laundry), 148
League of Nations, 135
Lee, Ah Kian, 192–4, 214
Lee, Erika, 50
Legazpi, Miguel López de, 69

315

INDEX

Leon, Concepción, 177, 182, 246–7
  character, 187–190
  in Shanghai, 226–7, 229–230, 232–234
  meet Yaiwai, 193–6
  moved to Mexico City, 256–7
  moved to Monterrey, 243–4
  returned to Mexico, 237, 239, 242–4, 256, 258
  travelled to Shanghai, 223–4
Leon, Lola, 102, 177, 182, 247
Leon, Melchor, 100, 177, 179, 181, 195, 241, 243–4, 247–8, 259
Leon, Pablo, 103, 177, 179–80, 247, 249
Leon, Victoria, 177, 182, 188, 195–6
Leung, Antonio (brother of Hing), 104
Leung and Wong families' differences, 20
Leung, Hing (later Jorge Hing Leon)
  Acaponeta arrival, 95
  affection for family, 102–3
  back to China, 228, 239–241
  legacy, 248–9
  away from politics, 103
  background, 7
  birth of, 19
  boarding the United States-bound ship, 26
  brought his brothers to the Americas, 103–4
  children education, 178–181
  in Chapultepec Park, 153
  death of, 245–6
  difference with Foon Chuck, 266–7
  family's economic status, 20–1
  fond of Mexican traditions, 103
  his customers' views on, 86–7
  his father, 21
  his mother, 22
  immigration difficulties faced by, 178–9
  as an indentured laborer, 25
  insults during his deliveries, 62–3
  journey to Mexico, 63–4
  journey to United States, 24–5, 26–7
  laundry work, 43–5, 62
  local cantinas experience, 83–4
  meeting with Cruz Rivera Nava and marriage, 95–7
  meeting Yaiwai, 193
  as merchant, 85–7
  Mexican cuisine, 73
  Mexican name adaptation, 90
  moved his family to Mexico City, 105
  moved to Tampico, 101
  moved to the eastern United States, 63
  pigtail, cutting of, 86
  bought Quinta San Jorge, 183–4
  railroad extension work, 80–1
  relations with Mexicans, 69
  San Francisco arrival, 42–3
  Saturday nights (Mexico), 84–5

INDEX

sent more money to family, 104
sent to Fatsaan town, 24
Spanish learning, 84
surname, 19
Sze Yap Company membership, 43–4
transformation into a Mexican, 90
views on United States' women, 43
with daughter back in Mexico, 242–3
working in his early age, 23, 24
worship of his ancestors, 98–9
Leung, Tin Po, 103–5, 106
Leung, Tom, 139
Foon Chuck's letters to, 123, 124–5, 147, 149–50
Leung or Leon family
characteristics, 83
daily diet of, 23
economic status, 20–1
self-sacrifice, 21
Leunggang village (Hoksaan County), 19–20
Li Bai, 1–2
Liang, Cheng, 92–3, 148
Liang, Qichao, 45–6, 101, 127, 130–1, 133–4, 140, 189–90, 233
Liang, Qitian, 140
Liang, Sicheng, 190
Like Water for Chocolate (film), 110
Limantour, José Yves, 79
Lin, Yutang, 7–8, 226–7, 232, 246–7
Local Indians. *See* Native Americans

Locke, Gary, 262–3
Lombard, Richard, 60
Loomis, Augustus W., 31, 32–3, 52, 57, 122, 124, 172, 266
Foon Chuck's special bond with, 34–5, 52–4
Foon Chuck's views on, 33–4
proselytizing work, 54–5
shelter for Chinese prostitutes, 41
López Obrador, Andrés Manuel, 263
Los Angeles, 58, 60, 111, 139, 209–10
Los Angeles Record (magazine), 208
Lu, Xun, 232

Macau, 7, 13, 25, 73, 260–1
Madero, Emilio, 160, 161–2
Madero, Francisco, 79, 115, 152, 160, 197, 202
Madrid, 74, 75
Mahjong (game), 24, 249
Manchukuo, 234
Manchuria, 93, 234
Manchus, 22, 39, 71, 119, 127, 135, 137, 150
Mandarins, 82, 142, 170
Manila (Philippines), 71, 73
massacres of Chines (1603), 75, 209–10
Manila Galleon Trade, 71–2, 73–5, 76, 91, 261–2
Mante River, 121, 201
Mao, Dun, 232
Mao, Tse-tung, 136, 171, 199, 233, 248
May Fourth Movement, 189–90, 234

317

INDEX

Mazatlán, 97, 100–1
Mencius, 130
Mendieta, Jeronimo de, 70
Mestizo, 70, 77, 80, 91, 108, 110, 115, 157, 181–2
Metallurgical Company of Torreón, 160
Mexicali, 169
Mexican dollars, 72
Mexican Herald, 101
Mexican Mint, 75–6
Mexican Organization of Overseas Chinese, 204
Mexican peso, 151
Mexican Population Act (1936), 210
Mexican Railway Company, 110
Mexican Revolution, 79, 101–2, 109, 154, 157, 160, 166–7, 171, 175, 207, 217, 227, 260
Mexican Supreme Court, 198
Mexican-American War (1846–48), 28–30, 207
Mexico City, 74–6, 78–9, 104, 108, 137, 148, 169, 173, 187, 202, 208, 210, 246–7
  celebrations, 153
  infrastructures, 105
  railroad advertisement (1910), 105
  Travel to, 193–4, 214, 242–3, 256, 262
Mexico City Aviation Association, 244
"Mexico for the Mexicans", 157
Mexico Morning News (newspaper), 137
Mexico

Alienage and Naturalization Law (1886), 89–90
"A Chinese Eldorado" article, 92
Chinese immigrants' relationship with Amerindians, 82–3
Chinese immigrants' local trade and small businesses, 87–9
Chinese immigrated to, 39, 80, 82–3, 137
Chinese migrants in, 64, 69, 139–140, 149, 150, 262
Chinese population in, 82
Customs, 110, 233
coal mine in San Felipe, 111
coolies, abolition of, 25
Díaz's governance, 77, 78–9, 109
Díaz's modernization efforts, 79–80
deportations, 113
diplomatic relations with China, 90–1
economic crisis, 151–2
economy, 61, 71, 74–6, 121, 123
border with, 57, 60, 62, 92, 98, 107
exclusion from, 158–60, 162, 165–72, 175, 177, 180, 198–200, 203–4, 208–210, 214, 256–7
Filipinos and Chinese settled in, 76
first immigration law, 101–2
Hing move to, 63–64

INDEX

independence of, 77
land ownership, 77–8
local cantinas, fighting at, 83–4
mestizo population, 70
Mexican attitudes towards, 100
Mexican citizenship, 80
Mexican *haute bourgeoisie*, 104–5
mixed marriages, 91–2
mortality rates, 79
north-south cultural differences, 108
plague pandemic and blaming the Chinese, 100–1
political and economic power, 77
politics, 173
rail infrastructure, extension of, 80–1
recruitment of contracted Chinese laborers, 87
silver mining, 72
Treaty of Friendship and Commerce, 90–1
war of independence, 76
World War II entry, 244
Middle Kingdom, 7, 26, 36, 43, 50, 72
Mill, John Stuart, 38
Miller, John F., 49
Ming dynasty (1368–1644), 71, 73, 128, 199
"Sea Ban", 71
mixed marriages. *See* interracial marriages
Monclova, 141–2, 166, 173, 213
Monroe, Mr. (Los Angeles businessman), 60
Monterrey, 216, 243, 252–3
Montesquieu, C. L. de Secondat (philosopher), 86
Mount Olympus, 246–7
Mozi (philosopher), 145
music, 142–3, 153, 192, 214, 233

Nanking, 231, 235–6
National Commission of Irrigation, 201, 204
Nationalist Party. *See* Kuomintang
Native Americans, 69–70, 79, 82–3, 91, 108, 133, 137
Nayarit, 249
New York Stock Exchange, 151
New York Times (newspaper), 49, 164, 208
New York Tribune, 113
Ningbo, 224
nomadic civilizations, 240
non-white migrants, 177

Obregón, Álvaro, 175–6, 202
Old Summer Palace (Peking), 240
On Returning Home, 241
On Women's Education (Liang Qichao), 233
Opium War (1839–42), 3–4, 42, 224
Osuna, Gregorio, 172, 201
Outline of the Mexican State, 139

Pacific Central Railroad, 49
Pacific Mail Steamship Company, 42
Page Act (1875), 41
Paisanos Chinos (Gonzalez), 203–4

319

INDEX

Paramout and Ciro's Club, 233
"Paris of the Orient", 226
Paris Peace Conference, 189
Park Avenue, 226
Park, Robert, 182
Parral, 168
Pershing, John, P, 168
Peru, 25, 39, 72, 75
   massacre of Chinese, 162
Philadelphia, 190–1
Philippines, 71–2, 76, 163
Piedras Negras, 60, 107, 109–10, 112, 114–5, 117, 122, 141, 145, 147, 165–6, 169, 192–3, 211–2, 215, 219–20, 253, 256, 259
pigtail, 39, 45, 52, 60, 62–3, 86, 90, 134, 161, 168
Pittsburgh Press (newspaper), 164
plague pandemic, 100–1
political clientelism, 109
Portes Gil, Emilio, 202–3
Poverty Day, 191
Profits of Godliness, The (Loomis), 205
Prohibition Era, 233
prostitution, 3, 40–1, 45–6 57–8, 159, 180
Protestant Church, 54
Pyramide du Louvre, 190

Qianlong (Emperor), 82
Qing Dynasty, 2, 11, 47, 65, 91, 119, 128–9, 133–4, 179
   ban on emigration, 27–8
   banned maritime trade, 71
   beggary and peasantry, 23
   bureaucracy, 2
   child trafficking, 3

   diplomacy, 163–5
   fall of, 28, 131, 167
   loss of power, 135
   New Policies, 143
Quang Ki-Teng, 175

racism and xenophobia, 40, 58, 65, 70, 80, 83, 101, 103, 124, 133, 169, 177–8, 180, 182, 188, 204–5, 208, 210, 216, 236, 257, 269
Ramirez, José Chan, 255–6
Real de a Ocho (currency), 72, 91
Red Turban Rebellion, 3
rice, 8, 10, 13, 15, 21, 23, 35, 58, 82, 88, 99, 118, 120–2, 125, 200, 220–1, 240, 255, 274
Rio Grande, 107, 110
Rivera Nava, Cruz, 95–7, 103, 177–9, 187, 242–3
   Catholic conscience, 98
   last days, 249
   Spanish lineage and characteristics, 102
   views on Hing, 99
   See also Hing and Cruz
Rivera, Diego, 176, 257
Rock Springs riot (Wyoming), 56
Rockefeller, John D., 66
Romero, Matías, 91
Roosevelt, Theodore, 65, 66, 78, 93, 132, 137, 163
Root-Takahira agreement, 93
Rurales (rural police force), 78

Sáenz, Aarón, 176, 200, 202, 204, 251–2

INDEX

Sáenz, Juan, 172, 176
St George's Day, 245
San Felipe mine, 111, 112
San Francisco Board of
  Education, 32
San Francisco, 57–8, 61, 179
  anti-Chinese riot (1877),
    47–8, 56
  Chinese daily newspapers, 37
  Chinese population, 35, 39,
    116
  immigration to, 13, 42, 49, 55,
    83, 92
  laundries, 43, 44, 63
  law against Chinese migrants,
    63
  mafias, 64
  public schools, 31–2, 33
  See also Chinatown (San
    Francisco)
Setzekorn, Eric, 165
Shanghai Bund, 223
Shanghai Club, 228
Shanghai Settlements, 236
Shanghai, 4, 65, 73, 82, 129, 189,
  192
  architecture, 227–8
  clash of civilizations, 228–231
  growth of, 222–5
  Japanese invasion, 234–236
  people, 231–233
Shantung province, 189
Shaw, George Bernard, 226
Silk Road, 72
silk, 22, 28, 74, 76, 96, 106, 220,
  223, 229, 236, 239, 246
silver coins, 13, 72
silver, 35, 72–6, 125, 149, 233

Sinaloa, 206–7
Sino-Japanese war, 130–1, 163,
  244, 261
Six Chinese Companies, 46–8,
  49, 50, 64, 81, 87, 108, 112
Sonora, 82, 88, 122–3, 140, 151,
  158, 165, 173, 175–7, 197–8,
  200, 205–210, 228, 260–1
Southern Pacific Company, 58
Southern Pacific Railroad, 111
Spain, 69–73, 75–7, 153, 210
Spaniards, 70, 71, 75, 82, 158
Spanish Empire, 71–2
Special Economic Zone of
  Shenzhen, 28
spirits, 8, 9, 17–18, 20, 24, 26,
  36, 98, 128, 131, 145, 246–7,
  249, 253
Spring Festival, 9, 20, 21, 36
Statue of Liberty, 51
Stevenson, Robert Louis, 57
Stoddard, Lothrop, 177
Suez Canal, 228
Summer Palace, 240
Sun, Yat-sen, 128, 134, 135, 171,
  192, 199
Sun, The, 51
surnames, 15
Sze Yap, 19, 26, 32, 34, 45, 61,
  191, 193, 212
  Company 43–4, 46, 63, 85
Szechuan province, 73

Taam river, 8, 9
Tacoma (Washington), 56, 262
Taft, William Howard, 163
Taiping Rebellion (1850–64), 3,
  8, 224

321

INDEX

Tamaulipas, 114, 115, 117, 118, 121, 202–3, 205
Tampico, 91, 101, 115, 172, 203, 211–12, 220
Tang Dynasty, 40
Tao Te Ching, 13
Taoist, 98–9, 118
teachers, power of, 12
Tehuantepec railway, 112
Temple of Heaven, 240
Texas, 39, 57, 58, 61, 115, 117
"Thoughts on a Quiet Night" (Li Bai), 1–2
Thousand Character Classic (textbook), 11–12
Tlalpan, 183–4, 243–5, 247, 249, 256, 305
Tokyo, 231
"Tomb-Sweeping Day", 247
Tongzhi (Emperor), 17
Torreón Massacre, 160–168, 175, 204, 263, 268
Torreón, 114–17, 137, 139–141, 146–7, 148, 150–2, 254–5
Treaty of Burlingame, 29, 50–1, 90
Treaty of Friendship and Commerce (1899), 175
Treaty of Guadalupe Hidalgo (1848), 207
Treaty of Nanking (1842), 224
Treaty of Portsmouth, 93
triads (Chinese secret societies), 45, 47
Twain, Mark, 29, 34, 57
typhoons, 9, 12–13

"Unearthing of the Chinese, The" (poem), 154
unemployment, 2–4, 49, 208, 269
United Press, 198–9
United States, 15, 206, 207–8
  annexed from Mexico, 207
  anti-Chinese sentiments, 45, 65–6
  population, 29–30, 158
  Chinese immigration to, 1, 4, 7, 11, 13, 41, 46, 49, 92, 125, 169, 179
  Chinese population in, 40, 65, 82–3, 136
  Chinese restaurants growth in, 191
  coolies, abolition of, 25
  customs, 35–6, 42, 88, 191
  economic crisis (1875), 49
  exclusion from, 38–9, 51, 54, 56, 58, 60, 63, 66, 89, 101, 112–4, 124, 128, 133, 192, 207–9
  first corporation in, 75
  migrants smuggling into, 91, 107–8
  paramilitary schools, 136–7
  politics, 77, 137, 163
  success and failure of emigrants, 28
US Coinage Act (1857), 72
US Immigration Act (1924), 207

Vasconcelos, José, 110, 176
Vega Domínguez, Cristina, 115, 211–12, 215, 253
Venustiano Carranza Park, 263
Villa, Pancho, 168–9
Villistas, 169

INDEX

Virgen de Guadalupe, 110–11
Virgin Land Colonization Act (1883), 77–8
von Humboldt, Alexander, 74, 75–6, 121

Washington, 56, 163, 262
Washington Post (newspaper), 113, 171
Western Military Academy (Alton), 179
Whangpoo River, 223
Wilfley & Bassett, 163–4
Wing On, 213, 228
women
    Foon Chuck views on Mexican women, 110
    Foon Chuck views on United States' women, 36–7
    prostitution, 3, 40, 41, 45, 58, 180
    at rice fields, 21
    rural Chinese women's health conditions, 22–3
    separation between the sexes, 22
Wong, Angel Chuck, 218–19
Wong Dai (Yellow Emperor), 8, 128
Wong family
    education, 12
    natural disasters (1874), 12–13
    surname, 15
Wong, Foon Chuck, 158, 165–7, 170–2
    activist role, 147–8
    anti-Chinese riot (1877), 47–8, 56
    apprehended and deported from US, 113
    background, 7
    birth of, 8
    business discussion with his uncle, 37
    butler in Loomis' home, 34–5
    calligraphy practice, 37
    bought Central Hotel (Eagle Pass), 61
    certificate of naturalization, 114
    charitable work, 148–9
    Chinese products sales, 62
    as a cook and foreman, 58–60
    courted Mexican politicians, 108–9
    brought cousins and brothers to Mexico, 109
    Del Rio arrival, 60
    dinners in Reverend Loomis' house, 35–6
    Don Miguel and, 108–9
    Eagle Pass border as his base, 62
    expropriation, 200–205, 252–3
    his early childhood, 10–11
    early Confucian education, 11–12, 16–17, 265
    education in America, 16–17
    education in San Francisco, 31–2, 33
    El Mante region, pursuing agriculture in, 118, 119–20
    as an "erudite gentleman", 145
    established his family in Torreón, 115
    farming business, 114–15, 116, 119–23

323

INDEX

first Chinese multi-millionaires in the Americas, 148
First Presbyterian Church of Eagle Pass founding member, 60–1
focus on retail and hotel businesses, 111
friendship with Carranza, 173
friendship with Hing, 178–9
friendship with Tom Leung, 139
friendships and emotional connections in United States, 123–4
his uncle's business offer, 57
honorary distinction from the City's Founders' Committee, 151
Hotel del Ferrocarril, 109, 110, 114
Hotel Internacional (Monclova), 141, 143
invested in Torreón town, 114
investment opportunities, 60, 61–2
irrigation project, 121–2
journey to "Old Golden Mountain" (San Francisco), 13–14, 16
journey to El Paso (Texas), 57–8
legacy, 220, 254–5, 261
letters to Kang Youwei, 139
letters to Tom Leung, 123, 124–5, 147, 149–50
marriage and children, 55, 115, 142
Masonic lodge of Eagle Pass, joined, 148

Mexican cuisine, 73
Mexican naturalization, 89–90, 113
Mexican surname, 114
moved to Eagle Pass, 60, 107
natural disasters (1874), 12–13
new country's diet adaptation, 35
organizing mining workforces, 112
philanthropy, 149
politeness in the United States, 36
real estate business, 146, 147
restaurants and hotels (northern Mexico), 109
retirement life, 219, 253–4
return to his missionary school, 52
returned to China, 55, 89, 111
returned to San Francisco, 55
San Francisco arrival, 31
settled in Piedras Negras, 107
Spanish learning, 61
special bond with Reverend Loomis and his family, 34–5, 52–4
spiritual life, 145
street named after, 263
Torreón properties attack, 204
tram line project, 146–7
trans-Pacific trip, 17, 18
US residency permit application, 107
vegetable growing business, 116
views on Jesus and of Christianity, 53
views on Loomis, 33–4
views on Mexican women, 110

324

INDEX

views on politics, 183, 198–9
views on Sunday rest, 37
views on United States' women, 36–7
visiting San Francisco's Chinatown, 89
as a waiter, 51–2
Western way of life, likeness, 36–7
with Concha, 242
Wong, Kingfung, 109, 193
Wong, Yaiwai, 142, 188–95, 223, 226–230, 233–237, 242, 247, 256–8
Wong, Yun Wu, 142, 153, 189, 237, 253
Woo, Jovita (wife of Wong Yun Wu), 142
Woo, Lam Po, 162–3
World War I, 189, 192, 208
World War II, 175, 179, 183, 227, 241, 244, 252

Wu, Jingchao, 39

xenophobia. *See* racism
Xinhai Revolution. *See* Chinese Revolution
Xuan Wang (Emperor), 19
Xue, Fucheng, 64
Xunzi, 240

Yangtze River, 225
Yaqui, 78, 197
Yellow River, 170
Yokohama, 223
Yu the Great, 9
Yue Mae School (Monclova), 141–3, 153–4, 189, 212–13

Zhang, Yinhuan, 64–5
Zhang, Zhidong, 144
Zheng He (Admiral), 71
Zia, Helen, 50